WHY
DEMOCRACY
NEEDS
THE RICH

WHY
DEMOCRACY
NEEDS
THE RICH

JOHN O. McGINNIS

Encounter BOOKS

New York • London

First American edition published in 2026 by Encounter Books,
an activity of Encounter for Culture and Education, Inc.,
a nonprofit, tax-exempt corporation.
Encounter Books website address: www.encounterbooks.com

Manufactured in Canada and printed on
acid-free paper. The paper used in this publication meets
the minimum requirements of ANSI/NISO Z39.48-1992
(R 1997) (*Permanence of Paper*).

FIRST AMERICAN EDITION

LIBRARY OF CONGRESS CATALOGING-IN-PUBLICATION
DATA IS AVAILABLE

Library of Congress CIP data is available online under
ISBN 978-1-64177-4635.

To my girl and my little girl

CONTENTS

INTRODUCTION

The rich today are out of favor in many quarters. Bernie Sanders, the senator from Vermont and runner-up in the 2020 Democratic presidential primary, claimed that every billionaire represents a "policy failure."[1] The Democratic mayor of New York City, the city with the most billionaires in the world, stated baldly that we should not have any of them.[2] This distrust extends beyond billionaires, encompassing even much less wealthy individuals. One political theorist has even proposed a cap of $10 million on everyone's wealth, with the truly virtuous voluntarily limiting themselves to $1 million.[3]

But what exactly is wrong with the wealthy? Two-thirds of the Forbes 400, a list of the richest people in America, built their own businesses, a proportion that has been growing.[4] These entrepreneurs still greatly benefit the other 99 percent, contributing far more to the welfare of consumers, employees, and other shareholders than they retain in personal wealth. Highly paid chief executive officers also increase the wealth of others: For instance, the morning of August 13, 2024, Starbucks's stock jumped $19 billion because one man, Brian Niccol, accepted the CEO job.[5]

Inherited wealth often faces heightened skepticism because its beneficiaries did not perform the hard work necessary to earn it. Nevertheless, these resources typically fuel investments and propel innovation, benefiting society as a whole. Most fortunes do not simply exist as idle reserves for a privileged few. Instead, they provide the fuel powering the ambitions and dreams of many. And much of the money that the rich make continues to fund philanthropic ventures.

Many liberals think the rich could pay more taxes without harming the economy. Whether or not this is true, it is not a complaint about their presence in the polity. Peter Mandelson, one of the architects of New Labour in Britain, famously said he had no problem with people getting "filthy rich."[6] The extra funds that the rich would then provide through taxation would help fund social welfare schemes.

What is bringing the rich into new disrepute is the view that their very existence creates social costs (economists call this a "negative externality"). The most prominent externality offered is the disproportionate influence they wield in the political process, allegedly harming democracy. In his book *Why Does Inequality Matter*, Harvard philosopher T. M. Scanlon identifies the political consequences of wealth inequality as among the gravest harms inflicted by the rich on society.[7] The Yale political scientist Jacob Hacker and the venture capitalist Nathan Loewentheil assert more specifically that the sway of the wealthy obstructs policies that would help the middle class and the poor.[8] In his farewell address to the nation in January 2025, former president Joe Biden stated that the "ultra-wealthy" threaten the future of our constitutional order.[9]

The claim that the unfair social power of the rich undermines democracy underpins numerous policy proposals. They range from preventing people from spending their own money for the dissemination of their political views for reducing tax deductions even for philanthropy that supports public goods, such as charter schools and scientific research. The fear of unequal clout also bolsters the backing for taxes that are likely to harm economic growth and are difficult to administer, like some of those on wealth and unrealized capital gains. Even if they do not raise revenue efficiently and thus squander resources, such policy proposals could serve a higher political purpose—curbing the political power of the rich.

But the notion that everyone can wield anything approaching equal influence in our democracy is fundamentally unrealistic. American democracy, like most modern democracies, is almost entirely representative, not direct. In a representative system, citizens cannot be guaranteed equal leverage, because representatives vote for legislation according to what they deem is best, using the sources they find most compelling. Simply claiming that some people's greater influence is inherently unfair also misses a point of representative government: Sometimes greater influence results in better policy.

Nor are the rich even the group with the most outsized voice in our democracy. The intelligentsia, or chattering class, including journalists, intellectuals, and entertainers, wields more significant power by shaping the short-term agenda through the media, affecting the long-term agenda through universities, and directing the cultural currents that flow into politics through books, television, movies, and music. Bureaucrats also hold substantial sway over the day-to-day operation of government. Like an unseen current in a river, their influence is constant, even as often relatively inexperienced political appointees with different views struggle to control the flow. And these groups have homogeneous political viewpoints. Academics and civil servants, for instance, overwhelmingly favor Democrats; their standing thus drives politics systematically to the left.

Political scientists have also demonstrated that members of concentrated interest groups, such as unions or trade associations, hold sway over government on issues of concern to them.[10] The sheer coordination and access to information that these groups enjoy allow them to influence legislators and government agencies, even when their policies may not benefit the majority.

This book contends that the rich fortify American democracy in part because they counter the leverage of such groups. The intelligentsia broadly defined wields substantial power in a democracy because, unlike all other citizens, shaping public opinion either directly or indirectly is part of their jobs. That provides the intelligentsia an enormous advantage in shaping democratic outputs over other groups whose work focuses on material, not ideological, production. Influencing public debate is not part of the wealthy's vocation, but they have both the independence and the resources to pursue social influence as an avocation. As a result, they can make a difference in the political and policy fray and assure that it is not left to a group of professional influencers, such as the intelligentsia and bureaucrats.

The rich also serve as a vital counterweight to special interest groups, which often have a stranglehold on specific public policies using their organized clout against the interests of the unorganized majority. They ameliorate this inherent democratic deficit by funding broader, diffuse interests, like that in quality K-12 education or in environmental protection, that may resonate with the majority but are difficult for the majority to effectively advocate for on their own. In this way, the influence of the rich acts like a lever, amplifying the voice of the many against the concentrated power of the few. In serving as a counterweight to both the intelligentsia and special interests, the wealthy contribute to one of the virtues of democracy as a political system: its openness to contestation.

It is said that the wealthy are biased by their desire to retain their wealth, but every group has its own interests. Concentrated interest groups lobby to protect their own stakes, bureaucrats benefit from an expanded state, and academics thrive in a world where their status rises compared with those who create wealth. In fact, the wealthy can be focused on longer-term public interests because they have ample provision for themselves.

What also sets the rich apart from other influential groups is the diversity of their political views and more general perspectives. Ironically, intellectuals sometimes suggest that the ascendancy of the bourgeoisie leads to a bland consensus that stifles debate. But it turns out that the rich are far from conformist. Compare the partisan tilt at many college campuses to the political battles between billionaires who supported either Donald Trump or Kamala Harris in the 2024 presidential election. And this disagreement is as true among the rich in the tech sector as in others. While Elon Musk was once a prominent supporter of Trump, Bill Gates donated tens of millions to groups supporting Harris. Thus, the counterbalancing effect of the rich does not depend on their having a single viewpoint. Instead, they have enough different viewpoints to make sure that other groups with more uniform views do not hold uncontested sway.

The relative diversity in viewpoints of the rich should not be surprising, as the contemporary wealthy come from varied backgrounds, gaining their fortunes through different paths, including some in the media and entertainment. Their different paths to wealth give them unique perspectives and expertise, again reinforcing the openness of democracy by allowing issues to be addressed from multiple angles. Additionally, their financial independence frees them from the pressure to curry favor with colleagues or superiors, pressures that push others toward more uniform viewpoints. Finally, consumers rarely screen for ideology in choosing a good new product or service. The rich thus have far less power than professional gatekeepers of opinion, like academics and journalists, to exclude those with unorthodox ideas from joining their ranks.

The real issue is whether adding the power of the rich, on top of the power of other elites, improves outcomes. This book argues that it does. Beyond adding ideological diversity, the influence of the wealthy brings practical realism into politics, offering a grounded understanding of consequences that fosters economic growth. The rich naturally resist the bureaucratic inertia that can stifle new ventures. They also serve as a counterbalance not only to the ideology but also to the style of reasoning of the intelligentsia and their sometimes visionary excesses.

The wealthy also help correct some of democracy's well-known flaws, including its tendency toward intolerance, mediocrity, and soft despotism. With their resources, they can champion causes that are unpopular with the current majority, ensuring these ideas get a fair hearing and helping to correct serious democratic mistakes. By supporting excellence, they contribute to a national pride that strengthens our republic. Because they are not reliant on the state and fund more of government than the average citizen, they have incentives to challenge the paternalistic state. This pushback is essential for maintaining the values of self-reliance and fiscal responsibility, pillars of any democratic order.

In our technological era, the market ecosystem, where the wealthy play a significant role, also has increasingly egalitarian features. Advances in social media, driven by Silicon Valley and maintained by figures like Elon Musk, have democratized the spread of ideas. It is odd that Biden and some Democrats single out those in technology as threatening our politics by creating an oligarchy. Today, due to the rise of social media created by the companies of the very wealthy tech innovators, anyone with a popular voice can reach a global audience, unimpeded by the traditional gatekeepers, such as legacy newspapers and publishing houses. This unprecedented access levels the playing field in the distribution of information, allowing individuals without resources to sway public discourse as never before. Technological advancements generated by the few have expanded the capacity of the many to disseminate information.

While debates about the long-term impact of these innovations on equality will continue, there is a compelling argument that the dynamic actions of the wealthy, through their role in fostering technological progress, have made our experiences more similar to one another. The rich and middle class now have access to the same amount of information, whereas previously the rich had far more access with their own private or club libraries. Today the rich and the middle class alike can summon a car at the touch of a button—a luxury only the rich had before. The rich-led tech ecosystem is "dematerializing" consumption, letting people of all incomes share experiences once limited by scarce physical goods. In this sense, the contributions of the rich may be viewed as not only benefiting themselves but also helping to create a more level and connected world of consumption for all.

These are benefits that the rich would provide any representative democracy in our time. But the participation of the rich is even more important to America given the peculiar nature of our democracy. From the beginning, the United States has been a commercial republic. The rich provide its engine, and their efforts fuel economic growth, which in turn stabilizes the political order by expanding opportunities and creating more spaces where citizens can realize their potential without encroaching on others. Additionally, the constant churn of entrepreneurs at the highest echelons of society in a commercial republic prevents any one group from consolidating power, thus making sure that our republic remains fluid and dynamic rather than stagnant and controlled. Vibrant commerce also creates bridges among communities, as citizens become interconnected through shared advantages of trade.[11]

The wealthy have a stake in defending the commercial nature of our democracy, which itself benefits democracy beyond the wealth it creates. As Max Weber noted, capitalism brings a rationality to human affairs as people calculate what will work not only in business but in social matters as well.[12] Increased rationality is also important to a modern republic for evaluating policies and institutions that allow it to continue to thrive in changing circumstances.

While some critics argue that capitalism also makes greed central to society, Weber dismissed these complaints as "the illusions of modern romanticists."[13] Even in socialist countries, citizens maneuver to try to get ahead. Moreover, the motives behind commerce are not inherently greedy. Many pursue it to provide for their children and grandchildren or to acquire the means to support large-scale philanthropic endeavors. The rich's boosting of commerce is often about building a legacy that connects the living and even the unborn. It draws people from different walks of life into lasting enterprises—companies, schools, foundations—that survive their founders.

America historically has been a philanthropic polity as well as a commercial republic, where private action has produced public goods, like universities and hospitals, and where voluntary associations have helped constitute a civil society that both restrains and complements the power of government. They still do. During COVID, Jack Dorsey, the Twitter cofounder, moved $1 billion of Square stock—then 28 percent of his net worth—into StartSmall LLC to fund such charities as COVID relief, publishing every grant on a public spreadsheet.[14]

It remains important that the rich still energize civil society, which, given our constitutional limits on government, has an especially important role in the provision of public goods in the United States. The rich sometimes pioneer the discovery of novel public goods and more efficient ways of delivering them, as with education. Government, often hamstrung by inadequate information and fear of failure, cannot substitute for such efforts. The civic associations that the rich help fund serve as training grounds for democracy, teaching its citizens to deal civilly with people of different views in a shared endeavor.

Thus, today's attack on the rich is often not simply an attack on a particular class. They are merely visible scapegoats because they are prey to envy. The deeper aim of some critics is to change America's system of government from a commercial and civic republic to a more collectivist society, where the state—its bureaucrats and politicians advised by journalists and academics—hold greater and more unchecked authority. The effect will be not only to disempower the rich but also to shift power to others—journalists and academics as well as bureaucrats, and special interest groups, such as public sector unions and professional guilds. Like a magician's misdirection, the focus on the rich distracts from the real objective: to concentrate power in the hands of those who claim to speak for the people, while sidelining the diverse and decentralized forces that historically have kept American democracy vibrant and resilient.

Why Democracy Needs the Rich begins by exploring the nature of representative democracy, highlighting how it inevitably creates a contest for clout where some groups naturally wield more power than others. It also delves into the unique character of American democracy—one founded as both a commercial republic and a philanthropic polity. The book demonstrates how the influence of the rich plays a critical role in addressing the inherent flaws of democracy by bolstering the commercial republic and sustaining civil society.

What readers will not find here is a brief against the existence of the welfare state, although it does discuss how the rich may help assure its fiscal soundness. While the optimal size and structure of the welfare state are an important issue, it differs from the fundamental question addressed here: whether the rich harm or help society. That is a contentious issue that has been debated intermittently since the Renaissance,[15] and more of these perennial arguments will be reviewed in chapter 9. Importantly, this book does not argue against progressive taxation either, except when the goal is to eliminate the wealthy. Similarly, it is not a diatribe against non-confiscatory estate or inheritance taxes. But if the rich perform valuable functions in democracy, such benefits do offer a caution against exorbitant redistribution.

To avoid any misunderstanding, the argument here demonstrates the benefits of the wealthy in a society with both capitalism and democracy—particularly one like ours, in which technological change makes it difficult for one group of the rich to entrench itself for a long time. Being wealthy is a necessary condition for the benefits that the rich provide. It is their wealth that gives them independence, and resources are what allow them to be a counterbalancing, dynamic, and philanthropic force.

But wealth is not a sufficient condition for beneficial influence. The rich were likely not a net positive in a society where their wealth was obtained by getting grants from the government or by exploiting slaves, peasants, or others without full ownership of their labor. In such a social context, their wealth did not generally derive from innovation and risk-taking, and thus they did not develop the rational habits of mind that contribute to democracy. Additionally, in a more static society, in the absence of dynamism, the wealthy might well form an entrenched oligarchy—a rigid, enduring layer atop the social hierarchy that creates a barrier against all political ideas that might lead to progress. Ancient political philosophers were right to express this concern.

It is a thesis of this book, however, that the rich are likely more beneficial than ever. In a vibrant, capitalist republic, the rich are more likely to contribute positively, driving break-throughs and supporting the fluidity that keeps a democratic society dynamic and open to adaptation. The speed of tech-nological change accentuates this benefit as new technologies, often facilitated by their investments, rapidly create new groups of wealthy people with new ideas. One of the great errors made by critics of the rich is to reify them as a class rather than rec-ognizing the diversity of their paths to wealth and the different perspectives that arise from such diversity.

Nor is this book an argument for the rich governing alone. It does not advance the claim—sometimes attributed to John Jay, America's first chief justice and third author of *The Feder-alist Papers*—that those who own the capital and land of the nation should run it.[16] Just as the separation of powers advances good government by—in the words of James Madison, father of the U.S. Constitution—"pitting ambition against ambition," so does the dynamic tension between the wealthy and other influential groups, such as journalists and intellectuals.[17] Dif-ferent elites engage in debate, and the broader public plays a significant role in deciding whose ideas should guide society on any issue.

Throughout the history of modernity, different social theorists have argued that identifiable elites have a significant role in improving social governance. In the nineteenth century, such thinkers as Samuel Taylor Coleridge and Matthew Arnold believed that the "clerisy"—or intellectuals, broadly defined—needed to play a leading role because of their imagination and genius. Friedrich Hegel assigned this role to civil servants because he believed they reconcile the universal interests of the state with the particular interests of individuals and civil society. This book recognizes that the substantial influence of the clerisy and the bureaucracy offers benefits, but so does that of the wealthy. Social governance works better by recognizing that fact rather than railing against the influence of the latter while welcoming the influence of the former groups.

Of course, *Why Democracy Needs the Rich* does not claim that all rich individuals provide benefits. Like any group, "the wealthy" includes both misguided and malevolent actors. Even those who contribute to democracy through philanthropy or other ventures do not always exercise the independence that wealth ideally affords. In some cases, their fiduciary duties to the shareholders of the companies they continue to manage constrain their actions more than their personal wealth empowers them. Similarly, the foundations set up by the wealthy sometimes fund foolish causes. Nor does this book argue that the rich are inherently nobler or better than other people. Instead, its point is that by virtue of their wealth and talents they can play a sustaining role in our polity. Taken as a whole, the impact of the wealthy remains a net benefit to American democracy.

The nineteenth-century philosopher John Stuart Mill warned that commerce can overvalue material goals,[18] but it is wrong to think it promotes nothing else. By connecting people through markets, commerce reduces prejudice and elevates virtues like prudence and self-restraint. It also breathes life into the arts by providing more patrons. Nevertheless, this book does not argue that wealth builds the entire foundation of a good society. It remains crucial for our political order to have influential actors from other spheres, such as religion and the arts, that more directly emphasize the less material aspects of life. A democracy, like a tree, flourishes with many roots.

CHAPTER 1

◇◇◇◇◇◇◇◇◇◇◇◇◇◇

WHAT IS DEMOCRACY
AND WHO ARE THE RICH?

Although the thesis of this book has implications for all market democracies, my discussion centers on American democracy. First, the United States stands as the most powerful and wealthiest democracy in the world, making it a natural focal point. By per capita measures, our average income ranks eighth among nations, and our median income ranks sixth overall.[1] In both cases, it is the highest of any nation with more than twenty million people.

Second, it is not just its might and wealth that make America significant but also its magnetic pull—continuously drawing people from every corner of the globe. Immigrants, both lawful and unlawful, flock to America from less developed regions, but the United States also attracts a net influx of people from almost all developed nations.[2] This mass migration underscores the unique appeal of American society, a point that ideological disagreements among Americans cannot negate.

Moreover, once here, immigrants' median incomes exceed

those of compatriots who remain at home, often dramatically. Consider, for instance, American citizens of Indian origin. Their median annual income here is almost $150,000,[3] but in India it is the equivalent of only $5,500.[4] The substantial increase in human capital that immigrants gain in the United States provides more evidence of the value that American society affords. It is not merely idle boasting to speak of American exceptionalism: Our kind of commercial and civic republic has outperformed most rivals. Hence it is particularly worthy of preservation.

Third, since its founding revolution, America has served as a beacon of democracy, with its political developments closely watched by nations around the world. No other country garners such extraordinary attention outside its own borders. Of course, that does not mean that at all times American democracy is universally admired. Because of its importance, our political system can come in for justified and unjustified criticism abroad.

Fourth, historically, the United States has also defended other democracies, coming to their aid during times of crisis and continuing to protect other nations through alliances like the North Atlantic Treaty Organization (NATO) and the freedom of the seas through its powerful navy. The health of the American republic, and the role of wealth within it, ripple out far beyond its shores.

DESCRIBING DEMOCRACY

Alexis de Tocqueville famously described America as "the image of democracy," capturing its dual essence as both a legal system and a cultural phenomenon.[5] Understanding

American democracy requires not only a study of its political institutions but also an exploration of its social fabric. As John Stuart Mill noted, the latter analysis necessitates "a study of agencies lying deeper than the forms of government and that produce far greater change in the long run."[6] In this book, I examine the role of the wealthy within American democracy, considering both their place within the legal framework and their effect on the broader societal culture, which are inextricably linked.

Socially, democracy is above all an open-access system. Its pluralism allows experiments in government. It also promotes a circulation of governing elites that prevents tyranny. In this way, democracy as a whole operates in parallel with the structural features of its American version, such as the separation of powers, that are formally embedded in its constitutional design. The separation of powers makes it more difficult for any faction to control the entire government because it would have to control all the branches. Similarly, the fluidity of democracy's frequent elections prevents the long-term entrenchment of any one person or group in power.[7] The rich contribute to this fluidity. They promote pluralism by balancing the power of other influential groups, such as the intelligentsia and the bureaucracy. They help create economic dynamism that makes the entrenchment of any group of individuals difficult.

American democracy also promotes experimentation in policy by providing substantial power to the states. Citizens' ability to vote with their feet among American jurisdictions limits state and local coercive power and allows feedback from the successes and failures of policy experiments. Today, through funding think tanks that design and evaluate various policy ideas, the rich accelerate the process of policy discovery.

This design of limited government in our own Constitution in turn helps generate the democratic culture that Tocqueville saw in America. In contrast to the wide-ranging monarchical authority of France's ancien régime, and the French Revolution's democratic centralism, Tocqueville observed that the vibrancy, innovation, and beneficence of American society did not come from its rulers but bubbled up from below. The secular associations of public-spirited citizens and the churches and synagogues of spiritually oriented citizens were the underlying reasons for the self-regulating order of our society.

While political factions may try to use government coercion for their own ends, Tocqueville believed that civil associations organize to achieve the common goals of their members.[8] Civil associations cultivate reciprocity among their members and establish social norms that others may freely choose to follow in public life. In this way they generate what modern sociologists would call "social capital": the glue that binds society together through a group of interlocking networks.[9] They model democratic behavior by bringing together people of different views and backgrounds. Additionally, they provide public goods that limited government does not provide. This book considers how the rich facilitate the private provision of public goods and sustain civic associations, particularly in the modern world with its many distractions.

As Tocqueville observed, America at its best is a vibrant, commercial society. He contrasted the bustling energy of the entrepreneurial North with the relative torpor of the slave-owning

South, highlighting the American spirit of risk-taking and pioneering among businessmen in a market of free labor.[10] This dynamism in American commerce is not only a cultural trait but also a product of the nation's limited government structure. The growth spurred by this commercial vitality plays a crucial role in sustaining democracy by creating and expanding wealth, with the wealthy being key contributors to this process.

Tocqueville also identified the concept of "equality of condition" as a cornerstone of the American republic. However, by this he did not mean equality in income or wealth.[11] Rather, he contrasted America's fluid social structure with the rigid hierarchies of France, where law and tradition ensured permanent inequalities of condition. In France, aristocratic titles and occupations were inherited and restricted by guilds, creating a society where one's place was largely fixed at birth. Tocqueville saw the absence of such entrenched inequality as the very soul of democracy in America.

Yet, Tocqueville also expressed concern that the passion for equality could lead to a system where government becomes all-powerful, assuming the role of a benevolent parent that attends to every need.[12] He called this outcome "administrative despotism," a scenario in which the government, under the guise of serving the people, saps society of its energy and ambition. In modern America, the wealthy militate against this danger by funding centers for the promotion of greatness—in research, in training, and in the arts—and by embodying the importance of merit and achievement. Their prominence and support for excellence help preserve the dynamism that is essential to a thriving democracy.

IDENTIFYING THE RICH

Defining the rich is simpler than defining democracy, not because the concept is easy to pin down but because a rough definition is sufficient. While in some societies, wealth may be so scarce that the existence of a truly rich class is in question, the United States stands as the wealthiest large nation in human history. Most Americans have access to resources that would have been unimaginable in earlier eras. Thus, the wealth of the rich must be defined in terms that are relative to that of the rest of society. This relative definition aligns with common criticisms of the wealthy, which focus on the disproportionate power they wield due to their greater resources within a democracy.

The rich are best defined by their wealth, not by their income. Income can fluctuate significantly from year to year, and a temporary spike in earnings does not guarantee lasting wealth. Wealth, on the other hand, especially when wisely invested, provides a steady stream of income and the long-term security that allows for independence, influence, and freedom of action. For instance, it is this enduring wealth, rather than fleeting income, that enables the rich to make risky investments and engage in large-scale philanthropy, both of which can benefit society as a whole.

Some historians define the rich as those possessing ten times the median net wealth, a threshold today near $2 million in the United States.[13] But this sum is too low to capture the kind of wealth that critics believe translates into substantial political leverage or provides the kind of independence that can be argued to be a political benefit to society. Others, often critically, focus on the top 1 percent, where wealth begins at around $12 million for an individual, slightly more for a house-hold.[14] However, in the urban centers of the United States, people with this level of wealth might be better described as part of the upper-affluent class rather than truly rich, whether in relative or absolute terms. A more reserved definition of the rich might target the top 0.1 percent, where personal wealth starts at approximately $61 million. This threshold aligns with recent proposals to tax wealth or unrealized capital gains, which sometimes begin around $50 million.[15]

However, when evaluating the contributions of the wealthy, it is not essential to have a precise cutoff for what constitutes "rich." The influence and benefits provided by the wealthy—such as balancing the power of other influential groups, funding public goods, advancing civic society, and fostering a dynamic economy—tend to increase with their level of wealth. While the top 5 percent certainly make significant contributions, the top 1 percent do more, and the top 0.1 percent even more. Wealth, in this sense, acts like a lever: The more there is, the greater the impact.

A more substantive question is whether the source of wealth matters. One assumption here is that the rich have accumulated their wealth through legal means, which is why this book focuses on their role in a modern, rule-of-law country like the United States. Some may wish to distinguish between self-made wealth and inherited wealth, but this distinction is often blurry. Many individuals have used modest family resources to build much larger fortunes. In any event, both wealthy entrepreneurs and inheritors of wealth play important and sometimes distinct roles in American democracy, with entrepreneurs developing ideas and the already wealthy providing the money to turn those ideas into a business.

One might also ask who the wealthy are as defined by how they make their money. It is difficult to come by hard data on the top 1 percent in net worth by occupation. We have more accurate estimates of occupation by income. But while wealth and income are correlated, they are not the same. One proxy for wealth would be extremely high income. We can be more confident that those earning in the top 0.1 percent of income are also in the top 1 percent by wealth, more so than those earning only in the top 1 percent of income. A 2005 study suggested that about 40 percent of these top earners were involved in nonfinancial businesses, evenly split between executives of closely held small businesses and those working for large, publicly held corporations.[16] Another 18 percent were in the financial sector, again split between closely held businesses and large corporations. Doctors and lawyers made up about 10 percent, real estate professionals about 6 percent, and entrepreneurs about 4 percent. Interestingly, athletes and entertainers accounted for only 3 percent, likely better represented at high incomes than high wealth levels due to their highly variable earnings. Only about 6 percent reported no occupation at all, indicating that the "idle rich" are a small minority among America's wealthy. Even among the top 0.1 percent in earnings, 70 percent make more from their human capital—through salaries and business returns—than from financial investments.[17]

A more recent study of the Forbes 400, which lists the wealthiest individuals in the United States, reveals that financial entrepreneurs are significantly represented, comprising nearly

20 percent of the list.[18] They are still outnumbered by other kinds of entrepreneurs who together comprise almost 80 percent of the Forbes 400.[19] Particularly notable is the prominence of those in technology-related businesses, accounting for 27 percent of the list, illustrating how the ultra-wealthy are often at the forefront of new ventures.

The composition of this top echelon of the 1 percent mirrors the diversity found in the broader group of very high-income earners. It is a dynamic mix of individuals who have amassed their wealth in various ways, with a strong emphasis on entrepreneurship and the management of large companies, especially in the financial sector. This diversity reflects the human dynamism that drives the commercial engine of our republic.

One concern about the rich today may be that they seem wealthier than in the past. But the wealth of the richest has just grown alongside the wealth of the nation. Consider John D. Rockefeller, who in 1937 had a wealth equivalent to 1.5 percent of the U.S. GDP.[20] By comparison, the wealth of Elon Musk, America's richest individual, while more than that of Rockefeller in constant dollars, represents at current value approximately 1.6 percent of GDP.[21] Thus, the relative wealth of the wealthiest American today is not substantially greater than ever before, particularly taking account of today's higher taxes.

Moreover, as will be discussed throughout the book, the scale of operations required by the wealthy today has expanded significantly. Pioneering innovation, especially in critical fields such as artificial intelligence, demands immense resources, risk-taking, and investment. Similarly, the contemporary landscape of political communication has become more challenging as political messaging competes with ever more diverse entertainment options. Volunteering too has declined, requiring larger charitable contributions to fill the void.

Additionally, today's wealth is subject to great public scrutiny, which pressures the wealthy to visibly demonstrate their commitment to social responsibility. Today's wealthiest individuals routinely engage in ambitious philanthropic endeavors addressing worldwide issues, such as disease eradication and climate change mitigation. Global problems demand philanthropy on a grand scale.

Critics who emphasize only the sheer dollar amounts of wealth accumulation neglect these broader contemporary dynamics. They also ignore the historical context that suggests the wealthiest are not comparatively wealthier than in the past, when many more Americans faced grinding poverty in a far less prosperous nation.

CHAPTER 2

✧✧✧✧✧✧✧✧✧✧✧✧

AMERICAN REPRESENTATIVE
DEMOCRACY AND THE RICH

To understand the role of the wealthy in American democracy, we must first grasp the unique characteristics of American democracy itself. Unlike direct democracy, American democracy is representative, designed to prioritize deliberation, balance interests, and consider policy outcomes. Within this structure, the rich often serve as a vital counterbalance to other influential groups, contributing to the overall health and dynamism of the system.

Several features of the American republic highlight why the impact of the wealthy is not inherently harmful and can be beneficial. First, the representative nature of the U.S. political system means that influence is inherently unequal. Representatives are tasked with discerning which voices and ideas are most likely to produce effective policies. This process recognizes the value of staying in closer contact with the most informed sources, among whom are the wealthy.

Second, the centrality of free speech in American democracy naturally results in unequal sway due to differences in resources, talent, and access to the media. Notably, the wealthy are not the sole or even the most advantaged group in this regard. Journalists, academics, and entertainers wield more significant power by virtue of their platforms.

Third, organized interests often dominate democratic processes, leveraging coordination to achieve outsized influence. Wealthy citizens can act as a counterbalance, using their independence and resources to promote broader interests that may otherwise be overshadowed by narrower, more concentrated agendas.

Finally, the American political order's structural checks on legislative action, such as the difficulty of passing federal laws, create a unique need for private provision of public goods. The wealthy have historically played a crucial role in this domain, funding universities, advancing technical progress, and supporting civil society in ways that bolster the democratic fabric.

Thus, any evaluation of the wealthy's role in democracy must begin with a careful assessment of these foundational elements. Their influence is not merely a matter of power but also reflects how American democracy channels contributions of various groups toward shared governance and progress.

Aristotle defined democracy as a system where the many participated directly in governance, voting on significant issues themselves.[1] However, the Founders of our republic were deeply skeptical of this model. They believed that direct democracy often descended into the unreflective rule of the mob and the tyranny of majorities. Worse, its inherent flaws in decision-making frequently led to disastrous policy choices, paving the way for its own demise to be replaced by the very tyranny it sought to avoid.

In response, the American Constitution rejected direct democracy in favor of a representative democracy. This system requires that representatives be elected in regular, relatively frequent elections. Under the original Constitution, the people elected members of the House of Representatives every two years, while state legislatures chose senators every six years. It was not until the Seventeenth Amendment in 1913 that senators were directly elected by the people. Throughout American history, it has been these representatives—not the people themselves—who make decisions about policy.

The distinction between direct and representative democracy is profound. In a direct democracy, every citizen has an equal opportunity to vote on critical issues, exercising direct authority over every policy. By contrast, in a representative democracy, citizens elect representatives to make policy decisions on their behalf. While voters have a voice during elections, they do not have direct control of their representatives between elections. That period of legislative discretion elevates the importance of indirect influence in shaping policy.

As a result, citizens necessarily have unequal clout. While citizens are equal before the law, they are unequal in knowledge and ability and in their connections with other citizens, all of which make a difference to the amount of influence wielded. There is thus no reason to believe that in a representative democracy citizens will exert equal influence or that more equal influence would lead to a more flourishing polity in a world with natural inequalities relevant to delivering good policy.

Despite the inherent inequality of sway in a representative democracy, the Framers were adamant that citizens should not exercise direct control over decision-making, which could have led to more equal influence. They explicitly rejected the idea that citizens should be able to instruct their representatives on how to vote. At one point, a proposed amendment to the Bill of Rights would have allowed voters to impose such binding directions. However, James Madison successfully opposed this proposal, arguing that the nation's representatives "must be able to contradict the views of their district" and resist measures they believed would harm the "public good."[2] The Framers envisioned a republic where wisdom and deliberation, not mere numbers, guided American governance.

Representative government creates a politics wholly distinct from direct democracy, with important benefits. First, it allows representatives to consider the intensity of preferences. Unlike in direct democracy, where each issue is voted on separately, representatives can more easily negotiate and broker deals. This means that even minority groups with strong preferences on certain issues can prevail by trading support with other minorities on issues they care less about. After all, most people would be willing to support a policy that is crucial to them in exchange for tolerating another policy they dislike but consider less important. This system forces politics to become more about the art of compromise, balancing the voices of the passionate few with those of the broader majority. Sometimes the rich are among the passionate few.

Second, representative government is better structured than direct democracy for considering the long-term consequences of policy decisions. In a direct democracy, the people making decisions are only loosely accountable for their votes. Even if their votes were public, few would remember how others voted, and the repercussions of bad policies are shared broadly, diluting individual responsibility. In contrast, legislators' votes are recorded and remembered, and they face accountability at the next election. The prestige of their position acts as a prize they risk losing if their legislation has bad effects. Thus, this process tends to better tie the quality of governance to the long-term benefits of the laws passed, rewarding those who legislate wisely. This structure puts a premium on welcoming the influence of those who may have insights into how to create long-term benefits, such as economic growth.

To be sure, accountability in a representative democracy is imperfect. Citizens are often rationally ignorant of policy details, given that a single vote is extremely unlikely to sway the outcome of an election with an electorate as substantial as that for a federal office. Nevertheless, political parties provide an essential heuristic, linking policy outcomes to electoral choices. While voters may not follow every issue or representative closely, party affiliation helps bridge the gap, offering a clearer connection between a voter's preferences and the policies enacted.[3] Even with its flaws, representative democracy offers far more accountability than the extremely diffuse responsibility found in direct democracy, where individual voters bear little direct consequence for their decisions.

Because representatives of the people are more accountable for the outcomes of their decisions, they are more likely to consider the facts relevant to policy. Of course, representatives, like their constituents, have personal preferences, and they often emphasize how their views align with those of their voters in order to secure reelection. However, incumbent representatives also gain an edge by creating favorable social conditions, such as strong economic growth, high employment, low inflation, and low crime rates.[4] Successfully addressing high-profile crises, such as a widely debated crisis over immigration, further solidifies their position. As a result, representatives not only reflect their constituents' preferences but also work to find policies that create tangible, socially beneficial results. The more useful information they receive, the more likely they are to accomplish this goal. As will be discussed in chapter 4, there is every reason to believe that the rich will be particularly useful sources of information, especially in a commercial republic like ours.

Policies that sustain economic growth, reduce crime, or manage immigration effectively do not hinge solely on preferences or ideology. They depend instead on a rigorous, factual analysis of what actually works. While disagreements on these issues often stem from differing ideologies, real-world results serve as a check on these debates. Past outcomes provide feedback that can either reinforce or refute claims, helping to narrow the scope of disagreement. In this way, the republic performs better the more it draws on fuller streams of information and back-and-forth debate. The feedback also depends on those with more useful information having more influence.

Moreover, the consideration of consequences in representative democracy also provides some check on citizens' inconsistent desires—ones they have no incentives to rationalize. For instance, many, if not most, citizens would like to have low taxes yet high benefits from the government. The result would be ever-increasing deficits, which would have a variety of bad consequences from inflation to possible insolvency. Representatives must reconcile these different desires, advancing them with policies that are more coherent than those that would be created from raw popular desires. For instance, economic growth may help temper the contradictions by allowing government spending to increase while tax rates are kept constant. Thus, representatives would seek help to discover such policies, even if most of the electorate does not have much understanding of them. As discussed in chapter 4, both academic centers and think tanks supported by wealthy donors help articulate these coherent priorities, and in doing so the rich offset the intelligentsia's and entertainers' almost uniformly left-leaning views.

Besides the wealthy and the intelligentsia, another type of group with outsized clout in a representative democracy is what we commonly refer to as "special interests." Political scientists have long observed that in our system of representation, these concentrated interest groups—such as trade associations or labor unions—tend to have more sway with legislators than more diffuse groups, including taxpayers and consumers.[5] The reason is straightforward: Concentrated interest groups have a more intense and focused interest in specific issues. For instance, privileges granted to labor unions or car manufacturers are of immense importance to their members because they stand to gain substantial benefits.

In contrast, the general public may have only a mild interest in these issues, even if they come at a cost to taxpayers or consumers. That cost is often diffused across many products or services, making it relatively small to each individual and easier to overlook.

Moreover, concentrated interest groups possess mechanisms to ensure that their members contribute to lobbying efforts. Unions collect dues, corporations have access to shareholder funds, and trade associations can enforce long-term contracts requiring members to pool resources for lobbying and advocacy. In contrast, taxpayers and consumers lack such mechanisms and face a classic "free-rider problem": Why should an individual contribute to a collective cause when there is no guarantee that others who benefit will also chip in? This disparity in organizational capacity is one reason special interests can exert disproportionate power in the legislative process.

As with many influences in the political process, special-interest influence comes with both benefits and drawbacks. Concentrated groups, such as trade associations, provide legislators with essential information. The general public, largely disengaged from the nuances of politics, lacks both the incentives and the means to investigate policy trade-offs.[6] As a result, legislators often rely on these groups to navigate the complexities of how policies will impact society. The value of that reliance is well recognized in law, exemplified by the immunity that trade associations receive from antitrust liability when their members collaborate to shape legislation, although colluding among competitors is generally forbidden.[7]

However, these groups are self-interested, united by the common goal of advancing their own agendas. Political scientists express concern that this bond leads to legislation that bestows concentrated benefits on these groups while imposing diffuse costs on the broader public.[8] For instance, business associations might advocate for tax breaks that benefit their industries, while teachers' unions may push for policies that make their jobs easier, even if those policies do not serve students' best interests. The voices of taxpayers and students, despite their numerical strength, are often underrepresented in the legislative process. As I argue in chapter 5, the wealthy can give voice to the relatively voiceless in the political process, offsetting special interests.

Exerting political influence in America is also a long-term endeavor, akin to a marathon rather than a sprint. Legislation is the end result of a complex process that begins with the formulation of ideas, followed by the gradual building of support, and, finally, navigating the legislative maze. For instance, the structure of the American federal system emphasizes the need for gathering widespread backing. The House of Representatives, elected from individual districts within a state, and the Senate, elected statewide, create a bicameral system that effectively requires a supermajoritarian consensus. Moreover, the staggered election cycles of the Senate and the tradition of the filibuster, which allows for unlimited debate unless ended by a supermajority, add layers of complexity. Even after clearing these hurdles, a bill still faces the president's veto power, requiring a two-thirds majority to override. In this intricate system, fleeting majorities often fail to push through legislation, underscoring the necessity of sustained effort and broad support. Most states have similar bicameral systems with gubernatorial vetoes.

This consensus requirement has the advantage of creating more stable laws, which are necessary for the long-term planning of individuals and businesses. It also makes it somewhat harder for special interests to use their leverage to obtain benefits for themselves because they face more potential opposition that needs to be tamed.

Nevertheless, the substantial consensus requirement at times makes it more difficult for the federal government to fund public goods like education, medical research, or experimental policies. In our system, the rich play an important role in the private funding of such public goods, which might otherwise be undersupplied, as well as in the initiation of promising pilot projects that would not yet have the broad political support to elicit government action.

In American democracy, the right to influence politics is protected by the First Amendment, which guarantees free speech. This feature of American politics, like the nature of representation, underscores that our Constitution is comfortable with unequal sway in politics. Free speech provides equal protection against government restrictions on speech, but this equality in rights results in unequal impact due to differences in wealth, eloquence, position, and passion. Those who gain the most clout through the First Amendment are those whose jobs focus on molding public opinion, such as journalists, academics, and those in some of the arts. The wealthy also enjoy leverage because they can use their resources to broadcast their views even if such dissemination is not their profession. Other citizens gain influence through intense commitment to specific causes, joining groups that amplify their voices. However, many citizens are disengaged from the intricacies of policy and politics, choosing not to participate actively.

Thus, while our republic offers everyone an equal vote, the freedoms that the First Amendment protects inevitably result in widely unequal influence, reflecting the diverse strengths and interests of its citizens. Despite that inequality, free speech contributes to the flourishing of the polity by assuring that the views that are most useful to public policy have access to the public square.

Some people have argued that a proper interpretation of the First Amendment should curb the impact of the wealthy by preventing them from using their money to amplify their views—whether through purchasing advertisements during election seasons or funding media that promote their policy perspectives. However, this interpretation of the First Amendment is untenable. While it is true that buying ads to express political opinions requires money, the same is true of any effective form of speech. The *New York Times*, for instance, spends millions of dollars covering political campaigns and editorializing about them. Yet, no one would argue that laws limiting such spending by the press would be constitutional.

Such restrictions on spending impose unconstitutional conditions on a right explicitly protected by the Constitution. The limitation on spending money to publicize one's views is triggered by the exercise of free speech rights, making it fundamentally different from restrictions on spending for activities that are not constitutionally protected, like sending money abroad or buying cryptocurrency. The First Amendment does not protect the latter activities, but it safeguards the right to spend money in the service of speech.

Moreover, nothing in the language of the Free Press Clause of the First Amendment suggests that its protections are uniquely confined to those who own printing presses or their modern equivalents, such as radio, television, or social media platforms. The clause does not distinguish between different forms of property rights used to disseminate ideas through these channels. When citizens purchase space to broadcast their views, they are renting the press or its modern counterparts. Giving greater rights to those who own the press rather than those who want to rent it would make a fundamental freedom depend arbitrarily on the nature of the property right exercised.

Furthermore, a regime where the government decides who is entitled to press rights under the First Amendment and who is not would grant it dangerous discretion over who can engage in political speech. Such power is wholly inconsistent with the core purpose of the First Amendment, which aims to keep the government from regulating speech precisely because it cannot be trusted to wield that power impartially. The Founders understood that the government might be tempted to favor its allies and silence its critics, and the First Amendment was crafted as a bulwark against such abuses. Thus, the U.S. Supreme Court has rightly ruled that citizens as well as those in the institutional press have the right to make unlimited independent expenditures to disseminate messages about issues or candidates.[9]

Many people wrongly believe that the legal case popularly referred to as *Citizens United* was the Supreme Court's decision that permitted the wealthy to spend as much money as they wanted to publicize their support of candidates and causes.[10] *Citizens United*, however, concerned the ability to speak through the corporate form about candidates, not the rights of the wealthy. Specifically, it held that the government could not prevent a group of citizens from using a nonprofit corporation to disseminate an unfavorable movie about Hillary Clinton, a candidate for president, at election time.

Despite the numerous criticisms it has faced, *Citizens United* remains a sound decision. The First Amendment explicitly prohibits the government from enacting laws that abridge freedom of speech without making distinctions about who is speaking—whether it is an individual, partnership, or corporation. The media, almost universally incorporated, is a prime example. Would it be acceptable for the government to limit how much money the *New York Times* or the *Wall Street Journal* could spend covering elections or editorializing about them simply because they are corporations? If media corporations were exempt, who would have the power to decide which entities qualify as media corporations?

But even if *Citizens United* were overruled, the rich would be constitutionally entitled to spend as much money as they wanted to disseminate their views as long as they did so as individuals. In fact, a nonprofit corporation—like the one at issue in *Citizens United*—allows people of more modest means to more easily pool their resources and amplify their voices on issues or candidates of shared concern. Thus, *Citizens United* empowers groups of citizens to engage in public discourse, not just the rich.

Aristotle contrasted pure regimes—democracy (rule by the many), oligarchy (rule by the few), and monarchy (rule by the one)—with mixed regimes that blend elements of each.[11] The combination of liberties, including free speech, and representative democracy makes our system more closely resemble a mixed regime in the sense Aristotle described than a pure direct democracy of the ancient kind that tries to guarantee equal influence.[12]

A key difference between our modern mixed regime and the classical version is the identity of "the few." In classical regimes, the few were typically just the wealthy; in our system of differential influence, the few are a much more diverse group. Alongside the wealthy, the media, academics, and special interests play a significant role, setting much of the political agenda through their jobs in the media and in education. As the political theorist Harvey Mansfield has observed, this complexity is reflected in the composition of our two major political parties, each a coalition of the many and the few.[13] More of the wealthy have traditionally tended to support the Republican Party, while the intelligentsia, broadly defined, disproportionately back the Democratic Party. Yet, as we will explore further, the alignment is far stronger in the latter case than in the former.

A closer examination of the workings of our system of representation thus dispels simplistic criticisms of the impact of the rich. Representative democracy, particularly as fueled by free speech, does not offer equal influence for all; instead, it inherently favors a variety of groups, including those who can better foresee the consequences of policy. It does not mandate that majority preferences should always prevail; the intensity of those preferences also matters. While the wealthy may wield more influence than the average citizen, so do other groups, such as the intelligentsia and concentrated interest groups. Clout in representative democracy is not a straightforward function of wealth but of knowledge, interest, and the ability to mobilize resources.

Therefore, it makes little sense to argue that the influence of the rich should be curtailed simply because they possess more power than ordinary citizens. The real question is whether their impact yields negative outcomes in a system where many different groups exert differential influence. Suppressing such inequality is not only impossible but also counterproductive, as those most invested in a subject often provide valuable insights that the general public cannot. Just as Madison recognized that eliminating the causes of factions would be worse than the disease, so too would be attempts to ensure equality of influence. Instead, the premise of the American system of representation, with its strong free speech tradition, must be that the proliferation of many varied groups with substantial influence, as with factions, will ultimately lead to a more balanced republic.

The next three chapters demonstrate how the rich help countervail other influential groups, preventing a more skewed democracy, one that leans too heavily toward a single ideological pole or toward narrow special interests. In a world where the intelligentsia and bureaucracy gain additional sway owing to their roles, and where concentrated interests dominate because of their organizational structures, the wealthy play a vital compensatory role. Their diverse knowledge and interests serve as a counterweight, contributing to a more balanced and representative democratic process.

CHAPTER 3

<><><><><><><><><><>

THE POWER OF PROFESSIONAL INFLUENCERS: JOURNALISTS, ACADEMICS, ENTERTAINERS, AND BUREAUCRATS

In a representative democracy, the rich are not the only powerful group, nor are they the most ideologically uniform class with outsized clout. The intellectual class—comprising academics, journalists, and those in the arts and entertainment—wields significant power. Although scattered across campuses, newsrooms, and studios, their shared training and milieu yield a worldview far narrower than that of the nation as a whole. Through their platforms, they can set the agenda for the nation, influencing how citizens, particularly the young, perceive key issues. All of these groups share an advantage that most others do not: The work for which they are paid has significant influence on politics.

The effect of this group on the direction of society has been recognized since the early nineteenth century. As mentioned previously, Samuel Taylor Coleridge referred to them as the "clerisy," envisioning them as a class that would guide society's moral and political development.[1] He and other thinkers of his time hoped that this educated class would replace the hierarchical authority of the church and nobility, providing a stable foundation for national and political identity. However, as time has passed, the dangers of relying solely on the clerisy for shaping modern democracy have become evident.

Today, the intellectual class exhibits an ideological homogeneity comparable to that of the nobles and clergy they replaced. Like the nobles and clergy before them, they tend to form networks—now within academia, the media, and other professional sectors. This can lead to a reinforcement of specific ideologies or viewpoints that are often disconnected from the everyday experiences and values of the broader population.

As a result, their views tend to be dramatically more left-leaning than those of the general populace, with far less diversity of opinion than is found among the wealthy. Their work often focuses on abstract ideals of how society should function, with less consideration for the practical realities and constraints of change. This ideological uniformity and drift to abstraction expose the very flaws in arguments that target the rich as the sole group with disproportionate power in democracy. The clerisy's ideological asymmetry highlights the need for the ideological balance that the rich can provide in democratic discourse.

JOURNALISTS

Numerous studies confirm the long-standing leftward tilt of the media. For example, a 2004 Pew Survey found that self-identified liberals outnumbered conservatives in journalism by a ratio of five to one.[2] Even financial journalists, who one might expect to be more conservative than most, were "overwhelmingly liberal."[3] Their voting patterns tell the same long-standing story. In the 1972 election, despite Richard Nixon's landslide victory over George McGovern, more than three out of four journalists supported McGovern.[4] Indeed, in the period covered by one survey, no Republican would ever have been elected president had journalists constituted the electorate.[5] In 1992, 89 percent of the Washington press corps voted for Bill Clinton, with only 7 percent supporting George H. W. Bush—a staggering twelve-to-one ratio.[6] The constellation of views is similar today, with more than ten times as many journalists identifying as Democrats than as Republicans.[7]

Journalists' ideology shapes their perspectives on a wide range of issues. A study of the media elite revealed that these journalists tend to support the welfare state more vigorously than the average American and are more aligned with left-leaning cultural positions, such as abortion rights.[8] Additionally, according to the communication professor S. Robert Lichter and his colleagues, they are far less religious and more supportive of various sexual freedoms, including adultery.[9] This ideological slant influences not only their personal views but also the way they present information to the public.

Further studies have directly assessed how media outlets cover the news by analyzing the ideological bent of the experts they choose to quote. This research consistently shows that most print and television media lean more liberal than the average voter.[10] Only two outlets, Fox News and the *Washington Times*, were found to be less liberal, and yet even they were more liberal than the average Republican voter.[11] This pervasive ideological tilt in the media shapes public perception in subtle yet powerful ways.

The media exercises its influence through four principal levers. First, in daily reporting, journalists shape public discourse by deciding which stories to cover. Given that citizens have limited time to consume news, the stories selected by journalists effectively set the political agenda.[12] This selection bias further allows journalists to emphasize stories with a left-leaning orientation, such as giving more coverage to left-wing protests than to right-wing ones.[13] They can also frame stories in a way that skews them politically.

The mainstream media's impact on elections and governance often stems from its ability to shape the narrative through selective emphasis or omission, or, at times, through outright distortion. One glaring example occurred early in Trump's presidency, when the media devoted significant attention to the Steele dossier, a collection of unverified allegations paid for by the Clinton campaign. Despite the claims being unsubstantiated and many later proven false,[14] the dossier created a cloud over Trump's first administration, undermining his efforts to build political capital and legitimacy in its critical early days.

In Trump's 2020 reelection campaign, in contrast, the media largely downplayed reporting on the contents of Hunter Biden's laptop computer, which raised concerns about possible corruption involving the Biden family. Instead, the narrative pushed was that the story was the product of Russian disinformation—a claim later disproven when the contents of the laptop were confirmed as genuine.[15]

A third example of media distortion was its failure to address the cognitive fitness concerns about Joe Biden until it became unmistakable in the public eye following his June 27, 2024, debate with Trump. For instance, shortly before the debate, a story in the *New York Times* suggested that videos of Biden's mental lapses were partisan fabrications.[16] The driving force behind distorting the picture of the forty-sixth president's health and cognitive ability was the media's apprehension about the possibility of a second Trump presidency. Only when Biden's faltering performance in his debate with Trump likely made it impossible to win did the press make his potential senility a central subject of media reporting.

The bias of media frames is not limited to electoral politics. A striking example recently occurred with the *New York Times'* coverage of an artificial intelligence program called Gemini, which generated images with diverse ethnic and gender groups in historically inaccurate contexts, such as a depiction of a multicultural group of Vikings. The mistakes were driven by an institutional diversity, equity, and inclusion concern about the need for the presence of minorities to be constantly highlighted. But the *New York Times* used as its example a prompt for German SS stormtroopers that created a largely Black contingent.[17] The implication was that racism toward minorities was the driving factor of this egregious historical error rather than a desire to include minorities in every possible situation. The example of Gemini's inclusion of Black people among the Founding Fathers would have far better captured the reality of what was going on. While some citizens may apply their own critical frames to the news, many do not invest the time and energy required to challenge the narratives presented to them, allowing the media's framing to dominate.

Second, beyond daily reporting, journalists shape opinion through their gatekeeping role in determining the prominence of longer-form analyses of the political and social landscape. They decide which books, movies, and TV shows to review and how to review them. These decisions can profoundly shape the intellectual discourse by promoting the prevailing ideology of the journalistic class. Books, in particular, that go unreviewed are like trees falling in an empty forest—unheard and unnoticed. In contrast, books receiving extensive coverage become integral to the intellectual conversation. Journalists are more likely to publicize left-leaning books than those with conservative perspectives, thereby reinforcing their ideological influence on the broader public.[18] For instance, the *New York Times* appears to be reluctant to elevate conservative voices, particularly when it comes to best-selling books. A study by *The Economist* revealed that the *Times'* best-seller list appears to discriminate against conservative authors, making it more difficult for a conservative book to gain recognition, even when its sales match those of a liberal counterpart.[19] This subtle form of bias shapes the cultural conversation by selectively amplifying certain perspectives over others.

One of the most significant manifestations of this bias is the constant framing of discussions of the rich in terms of inequality.[20] The narrative of ever-growing inequality is treated as an unassailable fact even though its accuracy is open to serious doubt, as will be discussed in chapter 7. Yet, the conversation could just as easily focus on the benefits that rich entrepreneurs and investors bring to society through innovation, benefits that extend well beyond their own wealth. It is no coincidence that journalists choose to highlight inequality, as their own personal and professional backgrounds play a role. Professionally, the rich are a competing source of influence. Personally, the income disparity between journalists and the wealthy, despite often sharing similar educational backgrounds, urban lifestyles, and cultural interests, adds to the underlying tension.

The language that journalists use can further bias the reader. Conservatives are frequently labeled as "far right" or "hard-line," while liberals are described as "progressives" or "advocates for change." The term "progressive," now commonly used to describe those on the left, is particularly advantageous for that group—after all, who would oppose progress? The framing of issues also varies with word choice. For example, border policies might be described as "draconian" or "harsh," terms with negative connotations. Similarly, the allowance of abortion is often framed as "reproductive freedom." When the Supreme Court ruled on a case involving the federal Environmental Protection Agency's (EPA's) authority over wetlands, the press typically framed the decision as a reduction in the EPA's power rather than an expansion of individual rights and state authority.[21] This selective framing subtly guides public perception, shaping how issues are understood and discussed.

Third, the media's impact extends beyond simply reporting the news; it also shapes public opinion through editorials and opinion pages. Those who write editorials often share the left-leaning views of their colleagues in news reporting. While op-ed pages may feature a broader range of perspectives, the gatekeepers of these outlets determine what is considered mainstream. What they dismiss as outside the mainstream might still resonate with a significant portion of the public. A telling example is the *New York Times* editorial page editor resigning under pressure for allowing Republican senator Tom Cotton to publish an op-ed advocating for the military to restore order during the George Floyd protests against police brutality in May 2020.[22] Cotton, elected by a large margin, represents a substantial number of Americans, yet his views were deemed unacceptable by the nation's most influential print media outlet.

This incident highlights the narrow boundaries of mainstream media opinion, even within spaces supposedly dedicated to diverse viewpoints. The supposed principled stance of editorial writers is thrown into doubt by their inconsistency. For example, when a Democratic governor deployed the National Guard to patrol New York City subways, an editorial writer who had previously denounced Cotton's similar proposal as a "threat to Black people" praised the move, revealing the selective application of principles based on political convenience.[23]

While the sway of what is often called the mainstream media has waned somewhat, it remains substantial. Fox News CEO Roger Ailes once quipped that his company had found a "niche" business by representing "half the American people."[24] However, mainstream media overall still enjoys a more extensive reach. In 2023 the three major networks averaged about 20 million viewers for their nightly news broadcasts, whereas Fox, a cable-only station, attracted roughly 2.5 million viewers.[25] Moreover, liberal-leaning cable networks like MSNBC and CNN further dilute Fox's share of the media landscape, reinforcing the dominance of mainstream media in shaping public discourse. By most measures, legacy broadcast and their large digital outlets still reach a far larger share of news consumers than cable channels.[26] In addition, research suggests that exposure to Fox News has a less pronounced effect on voters compared with exposure to the *Washington Post*.[27] This imbalance highlights the disproportionate clout of mainstream media over the broader public discourse.

Talk-radio shows and podcasts where conservatives hold more sway enliven the public square, but they are second movers. They do not bankroll the reporting that unearths grand-jury subpoenas or pries loose FOIA caches. Instead, they often wait for important news media to publish and then riff in real time. In the economy of attention, facts are in this sense upstream of opinion. Because legacy newsrooms still own the costly infrastructure—bureaus, databases, and libel counsel—they decide which events receive the dignity of national notice. Their ideological priors seep into our world, including its textbooks and HR manuals. The dialectic provided by the new media ecosystem is useful, but the daily and weekly news agenda still leans left.

Despite the fragmentation of the media landscape, the mainstream media's ability to set agendas and frame issues remains powerful. Their decisions on what to cover and how to cover it can ripple through the entire news ecosystem, shaping the narratives that reach the public. This dynamic ensures that, while diverse voices exist, the mainstream media continues to play a leading role in shaping public opinion and political discourse. The narratives that the media chooses to amplify and the perspectives they marginalize contribute to the broader cultural and political environment. This effect underscores the importance of scrutinizing not just what stories are told but how they are framed and who gets to tell them, as these decisions ultimately shape the contours of public debate.

These three methods—framing, gatekeeping, and editorializing—significantly shape political and cultural opinion and, consequently, voting patterns. While the exact magnitude of this influence is challenging to quantify, there is no doubt that the media help mold public opinion. Experimental studies have shown that people are affected by the information they receive, even when they suspect it to be biased.[28] For example, one study found that individuals given the *Washington Post* to read in the lead-up to an election were 3.8 percentage points more likely to vote for the Democratic candidate than those who were given the *Washington Times*.[29] Electoral pundits consistently account for media impact. Political candidates believe in the media's power to sway votes, as shown by the significant effort they make to shape favorable coverage of themselves and negative coverage of their opponents.

Besides the media's influence through agenda setting, sorting and prioritizing information, and editorializing, a fourth, more direct, pathway connects media ideology to politics: its effect on policymakers themselves. Political actors are aware of the importance of favorable press coverage, and this recognition can shift their behavior leftward. In legal circles, this phenomenon has been dubbed the "Greenhouse effect." Laurence Silberman, a judge on the D.C. Circuit Court, suggested that liberal-leaning coverage by the *New York Times* reporter Linda Greenhouse might explain why some initially conservative Supreme Court justices moved sharply left during their tenure.[30] Similar dynamics have been observed in politicians, such as John McCain, who moved left during the 2000 Republican presidential primary, likely in response to more favorable media attention.[31] Thus, the ideological leanings of the press can incentivize political actors to pursue more liberal policies than they might otherwise choose.

One might have hoped that the rise of the internet and the disintermediation of information would eliminate ideological tilt, but evidence suggests that bias persists even on the mainstream internet. A 2024 analysis of sentiment on Wikipedia, based on the use of positively and negatively charged language, found that the platform depicted public figures on the right more negatively than those on the left, regardless of whether they were presidents, senators, representatives, governors, or Supreme Court justices.[32] This finding underscores that even on the modern internet, ideological framing continues to shape how information is presented and perceived.

ACADEMICS

Academia is even more ideologically homogeneous than the media. A study of top liberal arts colleges revealed that the ratio of registered Democrats to Republicans is ten to one, and when specialized military academies are excluded, the ratio climbs to thirteen to one.[33] Many prestigious liberal arts colleges have no Republican faculty members or just one. In my own field of law, this imbalance has grown more pronounced over time. Two decades ago, the ratio of active Democratic to Republican professors at the top twenty schools was estimated to be around six to one.[34] Today, it is even higher, likely coming close to twenty to one. Affirmative action for women and minority faculty members has exacerbated and entrenched this imbalance: While white male professors are generally liberal, women and minorities in academia tend to be even more so.[35]

Although the general tendencies of academia lean left, there are some pockets of greater intellectual diversity. Within universities, a small contingent of conservatives emphasizes the importance of markets and the unintended consequences of government intervention. Additionally, some social science departments have seen a rise in empiricism, where scholars focus on measuring the actual effects of social policies rather than merely theorizing about them. However, the empirical turn faces significant challenges in mitigating ideological slant. First, the choice of what to study often introduces selection bias, as researchers may gravitate toward studies that align with their ideological beliefs. Second, certain fields, like psychology, have faced a replication crisis, where many past studies cannot be reproduced, casting doubt on their validity.[36] Finally, the public impact of empirical studies is substantially determined by media coverage, which tends to highlight findings that reinforce its own ideological leanings. Thus, while in recent decades the empirical turn is arguably the most promising development in academia for aligning academic opinion with social reality, it remains insufficient to offset the entrenched ideological and structural biases that make academia a persistent force for left-wing influence into politics and culture.

Academics shape society through both their writing and teaching. Like journalists, academics in the social sciences and humanities have considerable discretion in choosing and framing their research topics, effectively setting the boundaries of academic discourse. Again turning to the field of law, radical left proposals, such as the abolition of prisons, now find space in top journals, while advocating for increased incarceration for certain crimes, even to save lives, particularly among minorities, would hardly advance a career.[37] On contentious issues like affirmative action or abortion, it would be substantially more difficult to secure a position at most schools today if one's scholarship challenges the prevailing academic orthodoxy.

This academic conversation profoundly influences journalists, as academics serve as primary sources of expertise in fields like law, economics, and psychology, which often shape the news. Ideas originating in academia frequently migrate into the broader political arena. Notable examples from the legal field include critical race theory and various strands of feminism. These ideas need not be fully embraced by the public to have an impact. Political scientists recognize the concept of the Overton window—the range of policies considered acceptable in mainstream discourse at a particular time.[38] Academics, functioning as idea entrepreneurs, often shift this window, making previously radical ideas seem more palatable. Given the dominance of left-leaning perspectives in universities, almost all of these shifts today open the window to the left.

Academia thus not only shapes the intellectual landscape within its own walls but also influences the broader cultural and political discourse. As academics introduce and normalize new ideas, they gradually expand the boundaries of what is considered mainstream, subtly steering public policy and societal values in a direction that reflects their own ideological leanings.

Ideas originating in academia need not be accepted in their pure form or under their original label to affect policy. For example, advocates of criminal justice reform have drawn on critical race theory to push for reducing sentences, ending stop-and-frisk policies, and rejecting the broken windows theory of crime control, which enforces strict penalties for minor infractions.[39] These practices are criticized as manifestations of systemic racism, which disproportionately harms communities of color. Similarly, critical race theory has shaped educational reforms, including anti-bias and anti-racist pedagogy and approaches that deemphasize grades and competition. Many of these reforms shift the ideological balance leftward, challenging conservative ideals of color blindness and meritocracy.

Academics also wield significant clout through their teaching. The American historian Henry Adams famously remarked, "A teacher affects eternity; he can never tell where his influence stops."[40] While Adams may have been somewhat hyperbolic, the impact of teaching undoubtedly reaches far into the future, shaping the generation of students in the classroom. For instance, modern historians often downplay the traditional view of the American founding as a step forward for Western civilization, instead emphasizing the era's flaws, such as slavery.[41] This shift in focus helps explain why a significant portion of Generation Z now views the Founders as villains—a stark contrast to the views held by liberals even a generation ago.[42] This oppositional narrative of American history may not directly drive policy, but it fosters pessimism about the nation, distrust in its institutions, and a readiness to consider radical change, as there seems little worth preserving. In essence, it cultivates a mood ripe for extreme politics.

Other humanities disciplines have similarly revised their curricula to emphasize race, gender, and colonialism in literature studies. While the choice of literature and its interpretation may not have direct policy implications, this focus fuels identity politics, producing students who view the world through the lens of what divides rather than unites the nation. Professors in these fields may not explicitly advocate for specific policy proposals, but they validate an approach to politics and society that prioritizes identity above all else.

This mindset has far-reaching consequences, extending beyond politics to reshape culture, including the culture of business. Today's elite graduates from such humanities programs are tomorrow's human resources managers. They enter the workforce already inclined to support and expand programs of diversity, equity, and inclusion (DEI) within corporations and nonprofits, thereby extending the identity politics of the campus into society at large. The intellectual currents that begin in academia wash outward, subtly but powerfully reshaping the landscape of American life.

Some subjects, like political science, have much more direct relevance to policy. Policy disagreement defines much of the difference between conservatives and liberals. Even with goodwill, very few people can present an argument with which they disagree as much as one with which they agree. Thus, it is hardly a surprise that political scientists tend to focus more on topics like the problems of inequality, racial discrimination, and global warming than the virtues of the free market or limited government.

Beyond the professoriate, today's universities have embedded their educational missions within a campus structure that carries significant ideological weight. Central to this structure are DEI offices, which affect many aspects of campus life. These offices often pressure admissions departments to prioritize diversity, defined primarily in terms of race, ethnicity, and, increasingly, sexuality and gender. They also push to ensure that curricula include "diverse" perspectives, which in practice means promoting ideologies like critical race theory and feminism. As I observe at my own school, DEI offices frequently organize their own programming, bringing in speakers who advocate for racial and ethnic preferences and the latest causes of the left, such as transgenderism. Thus, the leftward orientation of modern universities is not solely a product of their faculty but is also entrenched within their administration, supported by a growing bureaucratic infrastructure. It is true that President Donald Trump has demanded an end to DEI policies, but even if he were successful in the ongoing litigation about that order, it would likely not represent final termination of such programs, only an intermission until the next Democratic administration permits universities to return to their traditional ways.

Some argue that the impact of academics, unlike that of the rich, is not problematic. Their leftward leanings stem from superior knowledge and understanding, while self-interest drives the rich. This idea, that democracy should be shaped by an intellectual elite whose vision is untainted by the demands of productive labor, has a long pedigree. Aristotle, for example, believed that citizenship should be limited to those "unencumbered by the need to devote their energies to productive activity."[43]

Similarly, the nineteenth-century cultural critic Matthew Arnold envisioned society being guided by men of culture—intellectual elites who, while not alienated from society, would serve as its public-spirited and constructive critics.[44]

However, this argument overlooks several reasons why academics tend to lean left, incentives that have little to do with the truth of their claims. First, most academics are rewarded for creating grand systems of thought, often developed individually or in small groups. In contrast, economic and financial markets operate through the spontaneous order of many, where great achievements arise without centralized design. This fundamental difference predisposes many intellectuals to misunderstand and even disdain capitalism. Second, except for those engaged in empirical research, intellectuals' ideas are rarely subjected to rigorous testing, whether in the marketplace or elsewhere. Their theories are often evaluated on aesthetic rather than practical grounds, and even empirical studies are more likely to be celebrated if they support rather than challenge left-liberal policies. Third, as the philosopher Robert Nozick noted, academics often harbor resentment because, despite excelling in school, they do not receive the highest monetary rewards in life. Those go instead to entrepreneurs, inventors, and investors.[45]

Fourth, as the political scientist James Scott has observed, the high-modernism style of governance, with its emphasis on comprehensive planning—a position associated in America predominantly with the left—appeals to the interests of the intelligentsia who have the most to "gain from its worldview: the position accorded them is not just one of rule and privilege but also one of responsibility for the great works of nation building and social transformation."[46] This approach is characterized by a strong belief that through state intervention, experts can enhance life by applying both the natural and social sciences. Consequently, they often favor top-down strategies that involve sweeping, comprehensive schemes to reshape the social environment. However, these grand designs come with costs, often reflecting a hubristic confidence in human ability to engineer improvement. Consent becomes secondary, subordinated to the technocratic vision that overrides the preferences and values of the people.

Once a group tends to lean toward one political side, social pressures for conformity arise. Rational academics understand that a single individual's opinions are unlikely to sway the course of national politics. However, expressing heterodox views can disrupt collegial relations within the academic community, which often functions like a social club, where being "clubbable" is highly valued. The pressure to conform reinforces the ideological homogeneity within academia, making it difficult for dissenting voices to thrive.

ENTERTAINERS

The entertainment industry also leans sharply left and exerts a significant, though more diffuse, influence on the nation's social agenda. In a comprehensive study of Hollywood's political leanings, the economist Todd Kendall analyzed the political contributions of 996 top film actors, directors, producers, and writers, finding a staggering 115-to-1 ratio of Democrats to Republicans.[47] Of course, the entertainment industry extends beyond Hollywood. But the larger industry has relatively similar views; during the 2016 presidential campaign, a more informal report suggested the ratio in the entertainment industry was about 10-to-1 in favor of Democrats.[48] As Kendall argues, these contributions are likely more expressive than instrumental, because conservative politicians also impact the industry. If entertainment professionals were primarily motivated by securing favorable policies, contributions would be more evenly divided between the two major parties.

The entertainment industry influences the social and political landscape. In the United States, most people spend more time engaging with movies and TV shows than with news, making these stories a powerful force in shaping public values. When certain types of characters are more prominently represented, it can shift cultural norms, which in turn can affect political trends. For example, the decision to become a single mother rather than raising a child within a traditional family structure has deep cultural ramifications. The famous CBS sitcom *Murphy Brown* played a role in legitimizing this choice.[49] While the rise in single motherhood is driven by complex factors beyond the impact of a television show, the entertainment media's treatment of such issues—particularly those related to sexuality—tends to favor experimentation over traditional morality. This bias reflects the prevailing views within the entertainment community. Some of this slant is overtly partisan. Late-night comedians relentlessly skewer Republican presidents while going easy on Democratic presidents, even when the latter present a persona ripe for satirical jibes.[50]

More recently, television programs have targeted the wealthy. One of the most critically acclaimed cable series of the early

2020s, HBO's *Succession*, depicts the dynastic struggles of the children of a right-wing media mogul. The characters in this family drama are not only deeply flawed, but the series conveys a broader message: that the rich are a social problem. As a writer for the *New York Times* put it, "*Succession* argues that the problems of today's hyper-rich inevitably become ours because they wield enormous influence with little sense of responsibility. We are caught in the wake of their yachts, sliced by the propeller blades, while the billionaires, lounging on the top deck, barely notice a bump."[51] It is no surprise that the *New York Times* prominently seizes on this show to reinforce its editorial position on the dangers of inequality. *Succession* is by no means an outlier. Unfavorable treatments of the rich have become a common meme of popular entertainment.[52]

Though entertainment may not instruct viewers to support specific political parties or candidates, it shapes the social climate in which policy debates unfold, amplifying certain perspectives. Could it truly be argued that entertainment has no impact if it were to produce more dramas that celebrate traditional morality? Or if portrayals of the wealthy were more balanced, highlighting their innovations alongside the power struggles within their families? The stories told on screen have the power to shape public opinion; thus, the choices made by the entertainment industry are far from trivial.

The entertainment industry also sustains celebrities who, in turn, affect political and social discourse. These celebrities, often aligned with left-wing causes, leverage their public platforms to disseminate their views widely. For instance, more attention was paid to the musician Taylor Swift's endorsement of Kamala

Harris than to the endorsements of most politicians. Recent social science research has illuminated the mechanisms behind this leverage, highlighting the phenomenon of "parasocial relationships," where celebrities' opinions merit respect and attention across a wide range of issues, even those relating to medical advice.[53] These relationships have gained prominence in an era marked by declining social associations and increasing loneliness. As traditional human connections wane, citizens increasingly seek substitutes through media, forging emotional bonds with celebrities.[54] Consequently, celebrities have become potent catalysts for political engagement, directing public focus to their favorite causes.

Taken together, media, academia, and entertainment pull American politics leftward. Each sector operates through its unique channels, yet their impact is magnified by the synergistic relationships within a class whose members are employed to provide information in various forms. The term "chattering class" aptly captures this interconnected elite, whose members amplify one another's messages. The news media frequently reports on entertainment, often highlighting content with a left-leaning agenda. Similarly, it brings academic studies to public attention, disproportionately featuring the work of the predominantly left-leaning professoriate. Journalists, who themselves tend to lean left, are more inclined to favorably cover entertainment and academic outputs that align with their ideological perspectives. This interconnectedness creates a reinforcing loop: The leftward orientation of journalists incentivizes those in entertainment and academia to produce content that resonates with the media's preferences.

Nor is their power limited to ideological slanting. The choice of topics itself has profound implications. A study focused on the achievements of innovators or a film depicting the struggles and ultimate success of a tech entrepreneur will impart a different political message than one that emphasizes the inequalities resulting from such success. The selection of subjects, therefore, is a subtle yet powerful means by which the chattering class shapes public opinion and political discourse.

Even beyond their ideological leanings, journalists, academics, and the artistic class share a production function that is fundamentally detached from the practical realities of the world. While journalists describe the world, academics model it, and artists and entertainers imagine it, they rarely handle the concrete execution of plans in business or government. This detachment skews their perspectives and the products they create, as they may be disconnected from the everyday realities faced by those whose livelihoods depend on material outcomes. This disconnect is further intensified by their concentration in major cities and university towns. After Trump's first election, the editor of the *New York Times* issued a mea culpa, acknowledging a failure to understand the roots of his victory in regions like the so-called flyover country (as opposed to coastal areas), where journalists and intellectuals rarely reside.[55]

Academics, often criticized for living in an "ivory tower," naturally operate in abstraction from the real world. Their success is measured by the interest their models and ideas generate within academic circles. Artists, to an even greater degree, often gain acclaim for crafting imaginative realms beyond ordinary experience. As the historian Augustin Cochin observed,

"Whereas in the real world the arbiter of all thought is proof and its issue is the effect, in the [intellectuals'] world the arbiter is the opinion of others, and the aim their approbation."[56] In this intellectual house of mirrors, fashionable orthodoxies can thrive, irrespective of their long-term consequences.

These characteristics of the intellectual class undermine their evaluation of social problems. Being insulated from the practical world of the market, intellectuals are prone to over-look the viability of market solutions. More broadly, their overconfidence in their descriptions and models leads them to underestimate the unintended consequences of social policies, believing too readily in their ability to capture the entirety of reality. The intellectual class, therefore, often crafts policies that may resonate in theory but falter in the complex, unpredictable dynamics of the real world.

The combined influence of journalists, academics, and entertainers on public opinion is immense. Public opinion, in turn, shapes policy discussions, not only directly but also indirectly, by focusing attention on certain issues while sidelining others and by promoting certain ways of thinking at the expense of alternatives. As the British statesman and philosopher Edmund Burke observed of such publicists, "They make the manners—in fact, they make the laws: they make the legislator. . . . When, therefore, I am told that a war is a war of opinions, I am told that it is the most important of all wars."[57]

BUREAUCRATS

In the modern world, another formidable force is the bureau-cracy. Today's government is administrative government. The federal bureaucracy exerts substantial power, wielding delegated authority to issue thousands of rules each year, as documented in the tens of thousands of pages of the *Federal Register*. Indeed, agencies now produce more rules governing the public than does Congress itself.[58] The sheer volume and complexity of these regulations underscore the significant role that bureaucrats play in shaping public life, often with as much direct impact as elected legislators.

Some political theorists have praised bureaucrats as neutral stewards of the public interest, guided by expertise rather than partisan bias. Hegel famously referred to them as the "general estate," believing they represented the general interests of society.[59] Early twentieth-century American progressives, drawing inspiration from Hegel, similarly envisioned regulation as the product of apolitical experts.[60] However, this idealistic view has been decisively challenged by legal realists and cannot withstand the evidence that federal civil servants possess distinct political preferences.[61]

These bureaucrats, who populate federal agencies, lean significantly to the left of the average citizen. Their political contributions favor Democratic candidates. In 2016, for instance, Donald Trump received only 5 percent of donations from federal bureaucrats compared with Hillary Clinton's 95 percent, and in 2012 Mitt Romney received only 14 percent.[62] Political scientists consider the average bureaucrat to be generally to the left of political appointees of both major political parties.[63] Academics too confirm the left-leaning orientation of the American bureaucracy.[64] They also acknowledge the "policy activism" of bureaucrats in the United States.[65]

The issue extends beyond mere ideology. Like journalists, academics, and artists, bureaucrats often lack experience in the market economy, making them less attuned to the power and efficacy of market-based solutions. As a result, they have reason to favor government interventions, particularly when such interventions expand their own power and prestige. The larger and more significant their bureaucracy becomes, the more power they wield.

Career officials play an essential role at every stage of the regulatory process. They interpret the statutes that define an agency's authority, draft the regulations that implement these statutes, and then interpret the scope of the regulations themselves. They also shape decisions about granting waivers and variances from these regulations and manage the day-to-day operations of the agency, directing its focus and resources in enforcing its rules.

Career government officials do not determine most of the content of these regulations. Cabinet members and agency heads appointed by the president—politically accountable figures whose views shift with the party in power—ultimately run departments and agencies. Nevertheless, bureaucrats can delay policy and change it, at least at the margin. One mechanism that political scientists have identified as a source of independent power is their relative control over information. Agency heads rely on information to make their decisions. Bureaucrats are willing to use their superior policy knowledge to affect the political decision by framing it in a way that accords with their preferences.[66] Noting this power is not an indictment of civil servants. No doubt the extent to which they do this is constrained by professional norms. But their political and ideological worldview affects how they view information as it does for anyone.

Agency heads cannot simply disregard their civil service; they rely on their expertise and manpower to issue regulations and enforce them. Political scientists have described agency decision-making as a dialogue between "politicians and bureaucrats."[67] Consequently, political appointees often find themselves compromising with the bureaucracy to ensure smoother operations, thereby ceding some authority over the agency's activities to the permanent bureaucracy. The British sitcom *Yes Minister* humorously captures this dynamic, illustrating how the permanent bureaucracy can outmaneuver politically accountable ministers.[68] Given the left-liberal orientation of most bureaucrats, Republican administrations are particularly likely to face resistance.[69]

This bias is not an argument for eliminating the influence of bureaucracy. Modern government without expertise is dangerous, particularly because of its size and scope. Wholesale firing of civil servants is likely to lead to ineffective or chaotic governance. The ideological homogeneity of the bureaucracy may well be a cost that we need to bear, given the needs of modern administration and the political preferences of those who choose to work for the government rather than the private sector.

But the necessity of bureaucracy to modern governance again underscores a crucial truth: Democracy teems with powerful professionals whose vocation provides them political and cultural impact. Some, like journalists, academics, and entertainers, shape public opinion. Others, like civil servants, supervise the vast machinery of the state. All these groups lean in one political direction—toward the left.

CHAPTER 4

COUNTERBALANCING THE
PROFESSIONAL INFLUENCERS

The wealthy provide an essential check on professional influencers. Unlike these groups, the wealthy are not ideologically uniform; their views are far more diverse. This diversity allows the substantial share of conservatives and libertarians among the wealthy to offer alternative perspectives in the public sphere. Their wealth grants them the independence to make political choices unconstrained by convention and the resources to be heard. Unlike those of modest means, the rich can speak freely without the same fear of ostracism, because wealth ensures many will still seek their company.

Coming from the business world, the rich tend to bring a pragmatic perspective on social affairs, one grounded in results rather than theories. Where journalists and academics may be swayed by eloquence or presentation, the rich focus more on what actually works. As Joseph Schumpeter aptly noted, "Both business success and failure are ideally precise. Neither can be talked away."[1]

Compared with journalists, academics, entertainers, or bureaucrats, the wealthy are more ideologically balanced. The wealthiest 4 percent of Americans leaned a little to the Democrats in 2012 but favored the Republican presidential candidate in 2008.[2] Contrary to popular belief, the top 1 percent do not overwhelmingly support Republicans; studies and reporting reveal a more nuanced picture.[3] The wealthiest zip codes tilt slightly Democratic, and both political parties benefit from billionaires who contribute tens of millions of dollars during election cycles. Republican-aligned donors such as Charles Koch and the late Sheldon Adelson have been counterbalanced by Democratic-aligned donors such as Tom Steyer and George Soros. The vigorous activity of billionaire donors across the political spectrum underscores this diversity.

Several factors contribute to this ideological diversity among the wealthy. First, they earn their fortunes in a variety of ways, particularly in today's economy. While many accumulate wealth through finance, others succeed in a strikingly wide range of industries—from luxury goods to cosmetics, from coffee chains like Howard Schultz's Starbucks to innovative medical devices like those developed by the spinal surgeon Gary Michelson. Those connected to the entertainment and media industries often align their views with the prevailing attitudes of their sector, while others, prizing their image as mavericks, naturally gravitate toward eclectic political stances. Second, social clashes among the rich, such as the ostracism faced by the newly wealthy from old money, can lead to divergent political views, including strong support, like that of George Soros, for groups that live at the margins of society.

The heterogeneity of paths to great wealth benefits democracy by generating varied perspectives. Doctors who invent medical devices bring specialized expertise, and entrepreneurs who build worldwide consumer businesses see the world quite differently, reflecting varied paths to wealth. The distinctive knowledge they offer the polity likewise reflects the routes by which they prospered, since their ways of making money markedly differ. Those who became wealthy in finance tend to have a highly strategic view of the world, understanding broad trends that move markets. Entrepreneurs view the world as a set of challenges and opportunities that can be addressed through creativity and risk-taking. They focus on the importance of innovation in the economy, helping the economy break out of stifling habits.[4] Inventors see problems as opportunities for new ventures, believing that most matters can be solved by the right idea. Even investors of inherited wealth have a useful perspective when they prioritize tradition, stability, and long-term planning.

It has often been noted that society does best through the competition of ideas. But it is a mistake to think of the diversity of ideas as being confined only to ideological differences. The diversity in expertise and perspective that the rich bring because of the different ways they create their fortunes also make America's public discourse stronger and more productive, particularly in comparison to groups like journalists and bureaucrats who earn their money in more uniform ways.

The wealthy serve as a counterbalance through various mechanisms. In response to the ideological uniformity of university social science departments, they have funded alternative research centers outside academia. A prime example is the American Enterprise Institute (AEI), a Washington-based think tank that organizes serious public policy conferences and publishes influential intellectual periodicals such as *National Affairs*. AEI is largely supported by conservative individuals, such as billionaire Bruce Kovner and Carlyle Group cofounder Daniel D'Aniello, as well as foundations like the Searle Freedom Trust, established by Daniel Searle, the former CEO of his family's pharmaceutical company.[5] Donors like the hedge fund manager Paul Singer also support more specialized think tanks, such as the Manhattan Institute for Policy Research, which advocates for conservative urban reform and publishes *City Journal*, a quarterly magazine on urban policy, law, and culture.[6] This tradition of private funding for intellectual diversity is not new: In the 1920s, when German universities were dominated by illiberal forces, the Rockefeller Foundation funded the Institute for Business Cycle Research. There, a young Friedrich Hayek worked long before he became a leading advocate for limiting governmental power and won the Nobel Prize for economics.[7]

These think tanks play a vital mediating role in politics. Even without such donors, a conservative political party would still exist, but it would face a steeper uphill battle against the intellectual class because it would lack richness and depth in its formulation of ideas. When such a party occasionally gained power, it would struggle to present coherent and plausible policy ideas. Politicians, skilled in electoral campaigning, are not necessarily adept at crafting policies that lead to social improvement. Intellectuals are needed to translate electoral victories into meaningful policy changes. On the left, these ideas primarily come from universities and, to a lesser extent, from journalists. However, the right receives far fewer ideas and policy frameworks from these traditional intellectual sources. As a result, even those who do not align with conservative views benefit from the initiatives, such as think tanks, funded by the wealthy. Without this support, right-leaning policies would likely be cruder, shaped more by the chaotic interplay of electoral interests than by thoughtful policy design.

The wealthy also temper the ideological orthodoxy of campus life by funding alternative centers of discussion on campus and by supporting visiting speakers. For instance, at Princeton University, the James Madison Program in American Ideals and Institutions, run by the legal and political theorist Robert George, and funded in large measure by foundations established by the wealthy, invites fellows of conservative disposition every year, some of whom go on to teach at the university.[8] The Madison Program also provides opportunities for counterpoints to the generally left-liberal offerings on campus. I have seen how the program has been an enormous success in injecting a measure of ideological diversity at a university often ranked first in the nation for undergraduate education. The diversity is not just ideological. The program also offers courses in education about civics and statesmanship, like "Abraham Lincoln Politics" and "Topics in American Statesmanship." These are the kinds of courses that universities once offered but rarely do so today. Yet they are important to educating the next generation of leaders for a democratic society.

Moreover, fostering debate at the undergraduate level cultivates virtues essential to democracy. Respectful disagreement nurtures the capacity for compromise, a cornerstone of policy advancement and social stability. Yet, universities dominated by a single ideology struggle to model such constructive debate. Institutions like the Madison Program offer a necessary platform where these vital exchanges can occur, enriching both the academic environment and the broader democratic society.

The success of the James Madison Program has spawned other, similar enterprises throughout the country, such as the William F. Buckley Jr. Program at Yale and the Benson Center for the Study of Western Civilization at the University of Colorado. States have also been inspired to create alternative colleges and centers within their flagship universities, such as the School of Civic and Economic Thought and Leadership at Arizona State; the Salmon P. Chase Center for Civics, Culture, and Society at Ohio State University; and the School of Civic Life and Leadership at the University of North Carolina. Like the James Madison Program, these schools and centers offer not only ideological diversity but also course programming that fosters a civic education and fills a gap in the current university curriculum. Without the demonstrated value of the Madison Program and other similar programs, legislators would not have been as likely to commit funds to the model. Donors can provide the philanthropic seed capital for movements that then gain funding elsewhere.

But the wealthy have not been content simply to establish programs that promote intellectual diversity on campus. They have provided large gifts to fund a new university, the University of Austin (UATX), which was founded on the principle of open inquiry and a commitment to free speech, aiming to provide a forum where diverse perspectives can be examined. In doing so, it challenges the prevailing orthodoxy, offering a model that could catalyze the revitalization of academic life across the country.

UATX also seeks to reinvent the curriculum to focus on what the modern university too often neglects: the cultivation of independent, critical thinking. Eschewing the narrow preoccupations of identity politics and bureaucratic credentialing, UATX places entrepreneurship, leadership, and civic engagement at its core. In the spirit of the new campus centers, it pairs intellectual breadth with the practical competencies needed to contribute to contemporary civil society.

The Walton family is currently creating another kind of university in Bentonville, Arkansas—an entrepreneurial institution that will place computation at the core of an intensive STEM curriculum while treating laboratories as launchpads for commerce.[9] The design borrows directly from Sam Walton's great logistical insight: velocity is value. Just as Walmart collapsed the distance between factory and checkout aisle,[10] this new school means to collapse it between discovery and deployment, more quickly driving ideas from whiteboard to marketplace. The Walton heirs want to shake up higher education through philanthropy, as their forebearers did retail through enterprise.

These initiatives do not seek to prevent traditional universities from offering their current courses or to eliminate tenure for their faculty, as some legislatures have done. They seek to correct the problem of partisan imbalance by addition, not subtraction, through competition, not government fiat. This approach typifies the way wealthy donors exert influence. Because they do not need to work through government, their independent resources allow them to set up parallel corrective institutions rather than tearing down current ones. The impact of such new institutions will be felt gradually, not through radical change that invites upheaval and social backlash. Democracy and the institutions that support its culture need self-correcting mechanisms. Among the benefits the rich provide are the resources and initiative to establish such institutions.

The wealthy can also significantly diversify thought on campus without establishing permanent institutions by funding guest speakers and fostering debate. One prominent example is the Federalist Society, which receives substantial funds from foundations set up by wealthy individuals.[11] It supports student chapters nationwide that host hundreds of debates on legal issues at law schools. The ideological uniformity prevalent in many law schools often stifles such debates. For instance, after the Supreme Court's 2022 decision in *Dobbs v. Jackson Women's Health Organization* ended the constitutional right to abortion, many schools, including my own, held panels featuring only opponents of the decision, with no supporters present.[12] Even the American Association of Law Schools, the leading professional organization in the legal academy, hosted a wholly one-sided panel. When an audience member questioned why

Dobbs supporters were absent, a panelist replied, "Because we are right!"[13] At my own law school, the law review put on a symposium about *Students for Fair Admissions v. Harvard College*, the 2023 case that held that racial preferences in college admissions are illegal. All invited speakers criticized the decision. Without the Federalist Society, the stranglehold of orthodoxy in legal education would be even tighter.

Introducing greater ideological diversity into law schools in particular strengthens the fabric of a democratic society, benefiting not just conservatives but the entire nation. Law schools that expose students to a wide array of ideas do more than educate. They fortify the rule of law itself. Unlike arbitrary governance, which bends to the whims of individuals, a government of laws benefits from stable, well-reasoned rules, enabling citizens to make informed, consistent decisions. The integrity of the legal system must remain shielded from political caprice.

Laws, however, often possess inherent ambiguities, and reasonable minds may justifiably debate their meaning. The legal system exists to resolve these ambiguities through the adversarial process, where competing arguments are presented before neutral tribunals. Just as the adversarial system in the courts sustains the rule of law, a culture of free speech and inquiry bolsters this process by fostering debate long before issues reach the courtroom. The best arguments are often hidden and require rigorous exploration to be unearthed. A society that encourages such exploration, free from fear of retaliation, ultimately enhances its governance.

An example of a perspective that shed new light on law was the law and economics movement that began to take hold at law schools in the 1970s. Scholars working within that perspective interpreted laws, where possible, to promote economic efficiency. They applied price theory throughout law, including in antitrust, contract law, and torts. This movement was initially funded in large part by the Olin Foundation, a legacy of the industrialist John Olin.[14]

The rule of law, the adversarial system, and a culture of free speech form the bedrock of a free democratic society, a truth particularly evident in the United States. Alexis de Tocqueville's observation, nearly two centuries ago, that almost all political issues in America eventually become legal issues remains as relevant as ever.[15] The law serves as the guardian of the Constitution's balance of powers, a bulwark against tyranny. It functions at its best when courts rigorously evaluate arguments from every perspective. The wealthy have helped broaden the range of views available at law schools, which remain the incubators of legal theory and analysis.

The wealthy not only temper the influence of the knowledge class by injecting their own views into public discourse, but they have also created platforms that amplify the voices of those with far more modest means. By driving the disintermediation of the media, wealthy innovators and their early investors have unleashed a torrent of diverse perspectives now available to citizens. Social media sites like Facebook, YouTube, and Twitter (now X) have become the new town squares, opening up ever more decentralized avenues for expression. In doing so, the wealthy have bolstered the cause of speech equality, allowing those who do not speak for a living to contribute to public debates.

Contrarian ideas now cascade onto the internet by the hour through podcasts and blogs, with social media companies serving as vital conduits for these ideas to reach the public debate. Twitter/X, Facebook, and YouTube play the crucial role of clearinghouses, distilling longer content into digestible summaries. These platforms facilitate swift exchanges between people of differing views, creating a dynamic arena for discussion.

Facebook accomplishes this through its posts, while Twitter/X's shorter posts, or "tweets," offer quick bursts of information. But Twitter/X also allows for the expansion of content through its thread feature, creating a tool for more in-depth exploration. Both Facebook and Twitter/X enable users to link to longer discussions, fostering interactions among citizens with diverse perspectives. These mechanisms have generated a vibrant new method of information exchange. For instance, a scholar of Chinese politics has used Twitter/X threads to illuminate the opaque machinations of that totalitarian regime, often getting ahead of legacy media in breaking news. Similarly, Twitter/X threads have been abuzz with insights on the latest advancements in AI, like ChatGPT, well before major newspapers catch on.

These platforms are the products of Silicon Valley's fertile ecosystem, where the wealthy, both individually and through venture capital firms, fund promising enterprises, even though most of them will not survive long enough to provide a return. Thanks to these efforts, one no longer needs access to a newspaper or a television station to broadcast one's views. Nor does one need deep pockets to gain an audience. Individuals of modest means can now reach millions should their messages resonate. In many ways, these innovations have democratized speech, making it more broadly egalitarian.

The potential of these new platforms to serve as true clearinghouses of diverse information ultimately hinges on their policies. Yet, even here the wealthy have played a pivotal role in keeping these channels of distribution open. Over time, Twitter began to falter in its role as a distributor of stories that mainstream media often sidestepped. It restricted the sharing of stories about the contents of Hunter Biden's laptop during the 2020 election and even banned the *New York Post*'s Twitter account for seventeen days for attempting to share its own reporting on the matter.[16] The *Babylon Bee*, a right-leaning satirical magazine, saw its account suspended after it refused to delete a tweet that satirically misgendered a government official.[17] And Twitter even banned President Trump for years from the platform following the riots of January 6, 2021, silencing a former president from remarking upon the state of the nation on its site.

Twitter's ability to function as an open forum for information was compromised by both its corporate structure and its internal culture. As a publicly traded company, its primary fiduciary duty was to its shareholders, which often meant avoiding controversies that might deter advertisers. Given the ideological tilt of the mainstream media, which still holds significant sway in our culture, such controversies were more likely to arise from right-leaning posts than left-leaning ones. Like any corporation, Twitter's culture was also shaped by its employees, 99 percent of whose political donations went to Democrats, reflecting significant ideological homogeneity.[18]

The only individual who could alter this culture to one that aligns with the broadest possible dissemination of information and ideas was someone wealthy enough to take the company private. Thus, Elon Musk, currently the wealthiest person in the world, stepped into this role. To be sure, Musk's acquisition of Twitter, which he renamed "X," was met with a renewed call to curb "disinformation" from some of the knowledge class. Although this sentiment has not been codified into American law, it still poses a threat to X's mission in disseminating information and viewpoints, as Musk is aware. Companies often feel pressured to comply with government demands to remove content. Mark Zuckerberg has admitted that Facebook removed information about COVID-19, including humor and satire about government policies, due to pressure from authorities.[19] Perhaps inspired by Musk or worried about the competition a more freewheeling X can create, Zuckerberg is also moving away from top-down removal of content.

In the debate over disinformation, wealthy actors keep the media and academia from dominating. Some of the legacy media, threatened by disintermediation caused by the rise of the internet, have sought to preserve their gatekeeping role by advocating for restrictions on social media information. Similarly, the intelligentsia, driven by a historical preoccupation with shaping public opinion to achieve their vision of human perfection, align with these restrictive tendencies. Yet, as in other arenas of public life, the wealthy emerged as a countervailing force, championing disruption and greater freedom through their advocacy of laissez-faire principles. The wealthy thus block the professional opinion shapers from dominating discussion of speech rules for our information age, assuring a genuinely plural debate about debate itself.

Legacy media's reaction to new forms of communication has often been one of resistance, mirroring historical patterns of hostility to technological innovation. After the French Revolution, for instance, there was a surge in pamphlets on current events, which disrupted traditional publishing. In response, the Paris Book Guild petitioned the government to require that any book published in France receive the imprimatur of an official guild publisher. Their petition warned, "From these abuses of freedom, countless persons who can barely read have established shops in every quarter of the capital, hanging over their door their name and the title of Bookseller, which they have no scruple about usurping. France will soon be infected by the sale of bad books if everyone is free to do business as a bookseller."[20] The fear was clear: A flood of uncontrolled, potentially dangerous ideas or false statements, spread by unqualified individuals, threatened the established order.

Similarly, today's mainstream media, with its left-leaning slant, generally views competitive social media platforms with suspicion, as they empower voices across the ideological spectrum. Just as the media have historically supported restrictions on political spending—efforts that could dilute its own influence—it now harbors a natural aversion to forums that challenge its role in shaping the national conversation.

The professional influencers also have deeper philosophical reasons for their concern about disinformation. Those favoring government suppression of disinformation view individuals as shaped by their environment and believe that society can be perfected through controlled information flows. This vision demands intellectual elites, or the clerisy, to curate and direct these inputs, creating a rational environment that molds citizens' thoughts and moral character.

As the historian Richard Pipes has shown, this perspective traces back to John Locke's epistemology, which saw human understanding as molded by sensory experience.[21] The French philosopher Claude Helvétius extended Locke's ideas, arguing that controlling these inputs could remake society.[22] For the clerisy, this meant controlling not only education but every influence shaping thought. Yet, the internet has disrupted the clerisy's control, democratizing media through blogs, social media, and podcasts, breaking the intelligentsia's dominance in shaping public opinion. Losing its gatekeeping role, the clerisy has turned to government as an ally to restore order. Sharing their worldview, bureaucracies have moved to regulate disinformation, pushing platforms to remove "misleading" content. This effort reveals their instrumental view of the First Amendment: Free speech is valuable not as a fundamental right but only if it furthers collective progress approved by the clerisy.

In contrast, another strand of Enlightenment thought emphasizes autonomy and distrusts government control of speech. Locke's political philosophy, which underpins Madison's First Amendment, framed free speech as an individual right.[23] It is a view that fears harm from systematic government overreach more than that from particular individuals. This tradition warns against granting government authority to suppress "digital misinformation," recalling the greater danger of state power silencing dissent. The wealthy will naturally include many who espouse that philosophy since it also underlies laissez-faire in economics and limited government.

This philosophical divide between different elites is evident in Twitter's evolution. Under prior management, Twitter aligned with the clerisy, banning news that was thought to be disinformation and speakers thought too divisive. These actions reflected the clerisy's confidence that they could determine which narratives served society's progress. With Musk, however, X has embraced a different model. His expansion of the platform's "Community Notes" exemplifies greater confidence in the spontaneous order created by the decisions of its multitudes of users.[24] By allowing users in Community Notes to collaboratively provide context to posts, X taps collective wisdom to address disinformation—not through mandates but by voluntary cooperation. Community Notes, shaped by diverse perspectives, reflect a model rooted in individual liberty and free interaction that competes with the model in which a designated group of censors suppress "disinformation."

To be sure, there is always the theoretical danger that a single group of the ideologically like-minded will capture their generation, but the system relies on diverse contributors with different viewpoints, and its algorithm prioritizes broad consensus across ideological lines, reducing the risk of capture. And Community Notes take time to appear, but the delay helps ensure deliberation and accuracy. The notes are dynamic and change, thus improving accuracy over time. Although they do not blot out inaccurate posts, their placement next to the relevant post provides incentives to pay attention. Community Notes is not a perfect system, but on the whole it is better than one that allows a small group within the company to make decisions about censorship on their own.

The diversity of views fostered by decentralized platforms like Musk's X is a testament to the rich's indispensable role in challenging the dominance of any single worldview. Wealth empowers individuals to support new ventures and ideas that resist the homogenizing instincts of the professional influencers. Musk's leadership has not only broken the clerisy's hold on what is permissible to say but also challenged their belief in who should decide what can be said. By funding decentralized processes that harness the wisdom of a broad and diverse public, Musk demonstrates how the rich can create spaces for a freer exchange of ideas, ensuring that society benefits from competition not just in markets but in the realm of thought itself.

Elon Musk's acquisition of Twitter may result in financial losses, but it exemplifies the unique capacity of the wealthy to take significant risks in the service of their political and social ideals. For Musk, this venture transcends mere investment. It is a bold experiment aimed at what he claims is a freer and more interconnected digital forum for public discourse.

To be sure, critics have accused Musk himself of improperly excluding certain users from X. Yet the gravity of these exclusions pales in comparison to more sweeping ones of his predecessors, such as banning President Trump and conservative satirists. Musk, for instance, prohibited accounts on X from broadcasting the real-time whereabouts of his private jet, but this action plausibly represents an effort to curb an especially invasive variant of doxing (revealing identifying information about someone's home or whereabouts) rather than arbitrary suppression of substantive speech.[25] He has also allegedly blocked some personal detractors, though these removals were brief and sporadic. Little evidence suggests sustained or widespread exclusions.[26] Certainly Musk has done nothing resembling Twitter's previous suppression of a story relevant to the 2020 presidential campaign or its permanent exclusion of Trump and the *Babylon Bee*.

Finally, claims that Musk has increasingly complied with governmental demands to censor posts overlook a crucial distinction: Such requests typically emanate from foreign jurisdictions lacking America's robust First Amendment protections, thereby placing X at genuine legal risk.[27] Significantly, no credible evidence indicates Musk's compliance with censorship directives from the U.S. government—the category of suppression that most seriously threatens American democracy.

In any event, Musk's actions are not an endpoint but part of a broader pattern of wealthy individuals reshaping the social media landscape. Jack Dorsey, Twitter's co-founder and himself a billionaire, provided early funding for Bluesky, an alternative platform with stricter content moderation.[28] After the 2024 election, in which Musk publicly supported Donald Trump, left-leaning intellectuals gravitated toward Bluesky as their preferred medium, made possible by Dorsey's initial contribution. This shift highlights how the diversity of thought among the wealthy translates into a diversity of institutions, each reflecting distinct ideals and priorities. If Musk uses X to unduly promote his ideas or prevent others from presenting theirs, another similar medium is available to publicize contrary views—one that itself got an essential boost from a very wealthy man. Such pluralism in social media infrastructure strengthens democracy by offering varied forums for expression, ensuring that no single ideology or platform monopolizes the marketplace of ideas.

Some might argue that the wealthy nevertheless pose a threat to other parts of the media ecosystem, pointing to Jeff Bezos, the billionaire founder of Amazon, who as the *Washington Post*'s new owner ended the newspaper's long-standing tradition of endorsing presidential candidates. Critics claim this decision reveals that his business interests overshadow any commitment to journalism's public role, speculating that he feared retaliation from Donald Trump. But such conjectures face counterevidence. Bezos bought the *Post* when it was hemorrhaging money, and he has continued to sustain it through financial losses for years.[29] His actions can be understood as revealing not a retreat from public interest but a dedication to preserving a vital journalistic institution despite financial pressures and political threats.

Bezos has argued that ending presidential endorsements would bolster the *Post*'s credibility in a polarized environment. He recognized a prevailing view that major newspapers, including the *Post*, suffer from perceived partisan bias—a perception that our previous discussion has shown is not unjustified. By refraining from an endorsement, he sought to cultivate a perception of editorial partisan neutrality, a move he articulated as follows: "We must be accurate, and we must be believed to be accurate. It's a bitter pill to swallow, but we are failing on the second requirement. Most people believe the media is biased. Anyone who doesn't see this is paying scant attention to reality, and those who fight reality lose. Reality is an undefeated champion."[30] Here, Bezos underscored the stakes of public perception, advocating for credibility as the foundation of journalism's impact. His statement reveals a strategic choice rooted in long-term credibility over short-term editorial power.

Indeed, it is Bezos's extraordinary wealth that grants him the independence to make decisions that are unpopular with some journalists, risking unfavorable publicity. Unlike most media owners, he is not dependent on the goodwill of the press or their favorable coverage to succeed. Wealth, in this instance, has given him the freedom to prioritize his view of what will contribute to the reality and perception of journalistic independence.

Recently, Bezos has faced additional criticism for altering the editorial stance of the *Washington Post* to emphasize freedom, including both free markets and personal liberties. Some critics claim this editorial shift is merely an attempt to curry favor with President Trump, but this charge is not backed by the evidence. Before Trump became president, Bezos consistently demonstrated libertarian leanings,[31] and a sincere commitment to liberty is likely to place him at odds with aspects of the Trump administration's agenda. The *Post* in fact hired Adam O'Neal as its news op-ed editor.[32] O'Neal had previously been executive editor of *The Dispatch*, an outlet very critical of Donald Trump.

More broadly, newspaper owners have long reflected their personal ideologies through editorial policy. The *New York Times*, for example, consistently mirrors the left-liberal perspectives of its publisher and CEO, A. G. Sulzberger, and his extended family.[33] In fact, numerous wealthy individuals have recently acquired or established media organizations and influenced their direction toward left-liberal causes. ProPublica, a nonprofit investigative journalism outlet primarily funded by wealthy foundations, consistently adopts a left-liberal investigative agenda.[34] Its muckraking was exemplified by its publication of illegally obtained tax information of prominent figures, including Bezos himself.[35] Likewise, the Omidyar Foundation, which calls itself a "philanthropic investment firm," financially supports Associated Press investigative reporting aimed at uncovering secret support by tech companies for the Israeli government.[36] Laurene Powell Jobs employs her Emerson Collective to fund digital media and publications like *The Atlantic*, promoting progressive causes. Indeed, immediately following the 2024 election, Powell Jobs convened a meeting to analyze why digital networks, including her own, failed to effectively support Kamala Harris's campaign.[37]

Consequently, there exists a clear double standard in condemning Bezos for steering the *Washington Post* toward liberty-promoting yet nonpartisan editorial positions while simultaneously ignoring the numerous wealthy individuals who openly advance left-wing or partisan media agendas. Such selective criticism underscores journalists' ideological biases rather than genuine principled concerns about the wealthy's control of media. Those committed to a well-informed democratic society should welcome the financial support provided to legacy media institutions by wealthy individuals across the ideological spectrum.

Another way that the wealthy serve as a counterweight to the intellectual elite is through their actions in the political arena.

Today their influence is not primarily through direct contributions to politicians—now capped at thirty-five hundred dollars per year. Instead, as permitted by Supreme Court jurisprudence described in chapter 2, they are allowed to make unlimited independent expenditures.[38] These expenditures fund advertisements supporting candidates, albeit without coordination or control by the candidates themselves. In 2011, the wealthiest individuals in America (roughly the top 0.01 percent) accounted for about 25 percent of all political donations and independent expenditures from individuals.[39] More recently, billionaires like Elon Musk and Miriam Adelson provided independent support for Donald Trump, while Bill Gates and Michael Bloomberg boosted Kamala Harris.

Since the political contributions of the wealthy on the left and right are relatively balanced, one might naively question how they can counteract the dominance of the overwhelmingly left-liberal intellectual class. The answer lies in the power of large, *relatively equal* expenditures: The equality of these efforts at least guarantees that the right can voice its message. These expenditures are particularly valuable for the right because the left's message already enjoys widespread dissemination through academia and the media. This reality is reflected in the differing positions of Republicans and Democrats on private campaign expenditures. Democrats generally seek to limit these expenditures, while Republicans oppose such restrictions. The intellectual class naturally supports measures that curb the influence of the wealthy, who are not uniformly aligned with their views. When newspapers editorialize in favor of restricting campaign expenditures by the wealthy, they also face a clear conflict of interest. The less competition from outside the media, the greater its own power.

The value of political spending by the wealthy for democracy is not limited to counterbalancing the sway of the clerisy. It is generally difficult to take on incumbents because many people fear retaliation from political leaders. For instance, Minnesota politician Eugene McCarthy had enough funds to run a campaign that focused on the Vietnam War and forced the incumbent president, Lyndon Johnson, out of the race over the issue. That intervention was made possible in part because Stewart Mott, heir to the General Motors fortune, bankrolled McCarthy at a time when large direct donations were still permitted.[40] Mott reveled in his image as a maverick and, not needing to work for a living, was happy to provide the equivalent of millions of dollars in today's money to finance a candidate who would make the case that President Johnson was wrong on the most important foreign policy issue of the day. Citizens without such resources and independence would have been unlikely to spend money in what would have seemed initially an unpopular and losing cause.

Nor is it only diversity in ideology that the rich promote but diversity in perspectives as well. For instance, it is the wealthy who facilitate the political empowerment of religious groups in the political sphere.[41]

The fear that the rich can "buy" elections by contributing heavily to one candidate or financing independent expenditure ads is misguided. The true value of campaign spending lies in allowing a candidate to introduce themself and establish credibility as a serious contender.[42] Beyond this initial phase, however, spending faces diminishing returns.[43] Voters become saturated with information and are unlikely to react to more.

Donald Trump offers the clearest recent proof that money is not the sovereign of American politics. While he wrote a sizable personal check to launch his 2016 bid, that sum was soon dwarfed by the torrent of free airtime his larger-than-life persona commanded. Television producers chased ratings and Trump pocketed the exposure. [44] His reality-show catchphrase—"You're *fired*!"—already etched in the public mind, became a ready-made brand for an outsider crusade that promised to sack a complacent political class. In short, celebrity, not self-funding, vaulted Trump past better-bankrolled rivals and illustrates that once a candidate has bought a microphone loud enough to introduce himself, the next decisive currency becomes political resonance, not cash.

The wealthy provide a necessary counterweight in public life not only by challenging left-wing ideology but also by bringing a greater focus on economic consequences. Public choice theory, which applies economic principles to politics, sheds light on why the affluent are well-positioned to advance good ideas on economic policy. Most voters have little incentive to form responsible views because their individual votes are unlikely to make a difference in an election's outcome.[45] Consequently, people remain rationally ignorant of most policies. Instead, citizens often vote to affirm their self-image as virtuous individuals rather than based on the practical consequences of their choices.[46] People must live with themselves regardless of who is elected.

For the wealthy, predicting consequences is central to their identity. Successful business people, whether forecasting market trends or anticipating regulatory impacts, spend their lives sharpening their predictive abilities. For them, accurate prediction marks the line between success and failure. Additionally, those in business possess a deeper understanding of the intersection between policy and reality. They witness firsthand how a minimum wage increase affects their operations or how a tariff hike raises costs. By using their wealth and prominence to inject this practical economic knowledge into the political sphere, the wealthy help ensure that the realities of the marketplace are not overlooked.

The concern that democracies might falter due to widespread economic ignorance is long-standing. Edmund Burke, in his time, feared that when food prices rose, those unfamiliar with market dynamics might mistakenly believe that the government could simply mandate lower prices or higher wages to resolve the issue.[47] Perhaps naively, given his own skepticism about some groups of intellectuals like the French *philosophes*, Burke expected intellectuals to educate the populace about market realities, thereby preventing democratic impulses from undermining prosperity.[48]

The concern over mass economic ignorance remains relevant today. The electorate is broader than in Burke's era, now encompassing many voters with limited education and little understanding of economics. Meanwhile, government policies have become more interventionist in social and economic life.[49] Social scientists have documented that many in the contemporary electorate hold false economic beliefs. For instance, Bryan Caplan has identified four biases that people have: (1) an antimarket bias, the tendency to underestimate the benefits of the market mechanism and to overestimate the role of government intervention in improving economic outcomes; (2) an antiforeign bias, the tendency to distrust foreign trade and immigration despite the economic benefits they bring; (3) a make-work bias, the tendency to value jobs for their own sake rather than understanding that the purpose of an economy is to produce goods and services efficiently, not just to create employment; and (4) a pessimistic bias, the tendency to believe that economic conditions are worse than they actually are, leading voters to favor protectionist or interventionist policies.[50]

The wealthy, in contrast, have knowledge and the interest to put the virtues of the market system before the public. For instance, the wealthy tend to understand the virtues of markets because they make their money from those markets. They also have incentives to promote economic growth for economic, psychological, and sociological reasons. Economically, growth is likely to raise the value of their assets; psychologically, it is likely to confirm the social utility of their work; and sociologically, it will make them feel more secure as a growing economy leads to a more socially stable society. As a result, they are less likely to share the public's biases identified by Caplan against economically beneficial policies. Their voices will thus likely improve economic policy, particularly reforms that spur growth.

Entrepreneurs, like military generals, also understand that most plans fail upon first contact with reality. Their enterprises thrive through constant experimentation and feedback loops. Investors, too, are keenly aware of the risks of committing to a single, overarching idea and instead recognize the value of diversity and flexibility. In this way, the wealthy tend to bring a discipline of concrete, economically realistic reasoning.

Contrast their focus with that of intellectuals. As described earlier, intellectuals who are insulated from the actual consequences of their theories and dependent for status on the approval of their peers are more inclined to construct abstract theories and envision social plans that reflect their ideals of justice. This perspective naturally leads them to favor broad societal engineering. As Richard Pipes demonstrated, the catastrophic outcomes of the Russian Revolution were the result of intellectuals gaining dominance over social movements.[51] In modern society, the wealthy serve as a crucial check to such dangerous abstractions and the class that promotes them. However, they do not suppress intellectual ideas; these remain prevalent on campuses and in the arts. Instead, the wealthy help maintain a greater pluralism in public discourse.

Corporate executives are not up to the task of counteracting the influence of the chattering and bureaucratic classes. Lacking the independence that substantial wealth confers, corporate managers are often more susceptible to cultural pressures shaped by the intellectual and political currents of the day. The incentives of corporate executives align them with these trends, not out of conviction but because doing so benefits their companies in the short term, the period that makes the most difference for most executives. For instance, embracing campus-born ideologies, such as DEI, may help corporations attract new talent and burnish their image with younger, more ideologically attuned employees.[52] Similarly, aligning with the values of the entertainment industry can help sell more products to a culture increasingly shaped by that world. Company officials have fiduciary obligations to advance corporate interests, not to act independently.

Indeed, the political theorist James Burnham observed that the corporate managerial class shares a symbiotic relationship with the bureaucratic class.[53] Both operate in large, hierarchical structures where command and control are the preferred methods of governance. Additionally, corporate managers often benefit from government regulations that, while burdensome, entrench their companies by raising barriers to entry for smaller competitors. The regulatory landscape can shield established corporations from the pressures of innovation and market disruption, allowing managers to be more secure in their positions.

Affluent corporate managers, unlike the truly wealthy, rarely have the independent resources to act alone.[54] A billionaire, for instance, can invest a portion of their fortune into large-scale advocacy or political campaigns to advance issues that may not yet have mainstream traction. By comparison, a corporate executive earning millions is still constrained by the same free-rider problem that affects the broader public. Unless they are sure that others will contribute to a cause, their individual efforts are unlikely to move the needle. Unlike the truly wealthy, they cannot, on their own or with a small group of peers, create large-scale change.

Thus, because of their independence, resources, and diverse perspectives, the wealthy provide an essential counterweight to the ideological conformity and insular viewpoints of the clerisy and bureaucracy. Elite influence in democracy is not only inevitable but often beneficial, channeling expertise and coherence into public debate. Yet democracy flourishes not merely through elite guidance but through competition among elites. The rich are not just another elite faction. Instead, they are uniquely positioned to inject ideological and strategic diversity into governance. More than any other elite group, they encompass a pluralism of worldviews within themselves, ensuring that democracy remains a contest of ideas rather than a monologue.

CHAPTER 5

◇◇◇◇◇◇◇◇◇◇◇◇◇◇◇

COUNTERBALANCING
SPECIAL INTERESTS

The wealthy also play a vital role in addressing a fundamental problem well-known to political scientists: Legislators tend to be more responsive to concentrated special interests, leading to legislation that favors them over the broader public. As discussed in chapter 2, special interests enjoy leverage in democratic politics because they are well organized with strong incentives to steer policy.

By contrast, energizing broad public interests, such as consumers, conservationists, or parents, faces the free-rider problem, which dulls incentives to organize. For these groups, the benefits of successful political efforts (e.g., consumer or environmental protection) are shared widely, even among those who do not contribute to the cause.[1] This fact reduces citizens' incentives to participate, as they can enjoy the benefits without personally bearing the costs.

In addition, citizens of modest means are unlikely to contribute to political campaigns and causes. First, their individual contributions are unlikely to make a difference. Second, while their interests are real, they are often limited compared with more pressing personal needs. Third, many political projects require long-term commitment, but it is difficult for those without the resources to pre-commit to sustained efforts.

Wealthy individuals can mitigate these challenges. Their contributions, whether alone or in coordination with a few others, can have a significant impact. Because of their financial resources, they can afford to sustain these efforts over time. Moreover, they can establish mechanisms, such as foundations, specifically designed to support long-term projects and causes.

It is therefore unsurprising that funding from the wealthy has been pivotal in advancing some of the most significant public interest causes in our time. Environmentalism, for instance, is a classic example of a diffuse benefit: Clean air and water are vital to everyone, yet their very universality creates a free-rider problem. The challenge for environmental advocates is not only their structural weakness but also the entrenched interests of their opponents. Manufacturers, for instance, can boost profits by neglecting safeguards against pollution, while unions may secure better wages and more jobs from companies that pollute or produce harmful products. This congruence of interests explains why auto companies and their unions have often combined to resist regulations aimed at protecting clean air.[2]

In the face of these obstacles, the wealthy have played a crucial role in initiating and sustaining the environmental movement. To be sure, writers such as Rachel Carson, with her powerful blend of lyrical prose and scientific insight, ignited public awareness of ecological issues. But writers alone cannot sustain a political movement.[3] Their words may light the spark, but it takes the resources of the wealthy to keep the flames burning.

Wealthy benefactors and their foundations played this sustaining role. The Rockefeller Foundation, for example, was a trailblazer in environmental philanthropy.[4] The organization's Special Projects Fund, specifically targeting environmental issues, was instrumental in establishing the Environmental Defense Fund and the Natural Resources Defense Council. These national organizations began shaping public policy and litigation strategies to protect the environment. Some may call this leadership ironic, given that Rockefeller wealth was largely derived from oil, a major pollutant. At the time that these companies were founded, the environmental impact was not fully understood. Through the social metamorphosis of transforming profits into philanthropic foundations, the Rockefellers were positioned to help address the unintended consequences of the innovations they had championed—innovations that, in the meantime, had provided warmth to billions and enabled millions to embark on journeys and careers unimaginable to their ancestors.

The Ford Foundation, established by a car manufacturer, soon made its own significant contribution to the environmental cause. In 1970 it launched its environmental program, dedicating millions of dollars to scientific research, policy development, and grassroots organizing.[5] By providing the initial capital needed to establish organizations, the foundation spurred citizens of even modest means to believe that their contributions could make a difference, thereby energizing broader public engagement in environmental causes.

The efforts of the Ford and Rockefeller foundations were soon followed by many others, amplifying the impact on environmental causes. The David and Lucile Packard Foundation lent its support to the Environmental Defense Fund, Conservation International, and the World Wildlife Fund.[6] The W. Alton Jones Foundation funded a broad range of advocacy campaigns against water and air pollution,[7] while the Pew Charitable Trusts focused on maritime and land conservation.[8] All of these foundations, established by extraordinarily wealthy individuals, play a crucial role in addressing environmental challenges. They show how the rich not only help society through their entrepreneurship but also deploy the fruits of that entrepreneurship to address social problems that stymie representative democracy. David Packard, for example, not only contributed to economic growth through his innovations in computing but also promoted environmental causes by donating the rewards of his labor to his foundation. Thus, many of the wealthy contribute to the nation twice over—first, through their work in commerce, and second, to counterbalancing special interests and thereby improving the political order.

The wealthy also played a significant role in revitalizing and repurposing existing organizations to address environmental issues. The Nature Conservancy, originally an exclusively scientific organization, transformed into a powerful advocacy group for conservation with the help of wealthy donors like Gordon Moore, a founder of Intel, who gave over $100 million.[9] Its focus on reforestation inspired other philanthropists, including

Marc Benioff, founder of the software company Salesforce, to launch their own initiatives.[10] These networks of wealthy donors created a cascade of grassroots organizing and funding for environmental infrastructure, transforming a diffuse but essential interest like environmental protection into a potent political and social force. Just as entrepreneurs compete to provide the best products, the same competitive spirit leads them to try to outdo one another in significant philanthropy.

Another area where the wealthy have been instrumental in protecting diffuse interests against special interests is the reform of K-12 education. Americans broadly share a vested interest in a strong K-12 system. It lays the groundwork for further education, which in turn fosters the high skills necessary for sustaining innovation and economic growth. It also supplies the literacy and civic knowledge required for responsible participation in democracy. More generally, education is a cornerstone of human flourishing.

However, American K-12 education has faced significant challenges. As with environmental concerns, the publication of critical assessments sounded the alarm over K-12 education. The most important was the government's 1983 report *A Nation at Risk*, which revealed that the United States was performing poorly in education compared with other nations across a wide array of measures.[11] For instance, among nineteen subject-matter tests, the United States ranked last among industrial nations in seven of them, including mathematics. This stark revelation highlighted the urgent need for educational reform and underscored the importance of the wealthy in driving efforts to improve the system.

Debates have raged over how to improve educational performance, but one factor is clear: Entrenched special interests have been significant barriers to reform. Among these are teachers' unions.[12] While most individual teachers are genuinely committed to helping students succeed, the unions often prioritize protecting teachers from discipline and resist rewarding the excellence of some at the expense of others. Educational bureaucracies, too, have a vested interest in maintaining the status quo, as change threatens to disrupt the established power and status within government structures.[13]

The wealthy and their foundations stepped in to offer diverse strategies for improving education and circumventing these special interests. Some focused on promoting school vouchers. For example, a group led by the investment banker Ted Forstmann and the Walmart heir John Walton provided $200 million in scholarships for poor children to attend private schools.[14] Others, like the DeVos Foundation, funded grassroots campaigns advocating for government-provided vouchers to expand school choice.[15] The rationale was twofold: First, many private schools offer a superior education compared with public schools, and, second, introducing more competition into K-12 education would drive long-term improvements by forcing public schools to raise their standards.

Another approach to improving education by spurring competition was the promotion of charter schools within the current system. These schools, though public, operate independently of the central education bureaucracy and are often nonunion. The list of wealthy charter school supporters is extensive. Donald and Doris Fisher, founders of The Gap clothing stores, established the Charter School Growth Fund to support charter schools nationwide.[16] The Broad Foundation, created by the real estate and insurance entrepreneur Eli Broad, has funded programs for charter school leaders and principals.[17] The Bill and Melinda Gates Foundation has also invested in charter school networks and provided funds for research and evaluation to drive further improvements.[18] Other foundations, such as the Walton Family Foundation and the Laura and John Arnold Foundation, started by the hedge fund manager John Arnold, have played a significant role in advancing charter schools as well.[19]

Some wealthy individuals and foundations have focused on improving education within traditional public schools. The Ford Foundation, for example, has funded initiatives aimed at addressing disparate outcomes among marginalized students.[20] Laurene Powell Jobs, widow of Steve Jobs, has worked through her organization, the Emerson Collective, to explore new forms of collaborative learning at the public high school level.[21] Each of these efforts represents a different approach, but all share the common goal of enhancing educational opportunities and outcomes for students across the nation.

Not all initiatives have turned out well in every respect. Beginning in 2010, Mark Zuckerberg gave $100 million to Newark, New Jersey, schools to be matched dollar for dollar by other philanthropists.[22] A study showed that compared with other, similarly situated schools, the gift helped students achieve higher scores in reading largely by closing poorly performing schools and opening new ones. Math scores were stable but likely would have declined without Zuckerberg's intervention. However, critics pointed out that some of the money was largely wasted, merely fulfilling a previous teachers' contract.[23] Studies of the effects of vouchers have been mixed. While they improve the likelihood of high school graduation, the satisfaction of families with schools, and the performance of competing public schools, they do not generally appear to raise test scores.[24] Nevertheless, they appear to improve a key predictor of important life outcomes—enrollment and graduation from college.[25] Charter schools have a stronger record on test scores with improved performance for students in both reading and math.[26]

We have more evaluations of such programs because wealthy donors have also funded research into their outcomes.[27] This focus on results is unsurprising, as successful entrepreneurs are results-driven. In this effort, academics are often enlisted to provide the necessary evaluations, illustrating how the intellectual class and the wealthy can unite to combat special interests that might otherwise stifle reform in a democratic society. That some initiatives do not work does not mean they are not valuable in the larger scheme of things. As John Dewey said, democracy is government by experiment.[28] And the philanthropic efforts of the rich intensify the necessary trial and error that helps move democratic society forward.

Environmentalism is typically associated with the left, while education reform is often linked to the right. Yet, the wealthy, with their diverse political views, have supported both causes. Within each movement, the variety of beliefs among the wealthy has led to a wide array of approaches, including more right-leaning strategies in environmentalism and more left-leaning ones in educational improvement. For example, the Environmental Defense Fund pioneered the market-friendly cap-and-trade solution to reducing environmentally harmful emissions.[29] This system sets a cap on the total amount of pollution that can be emitted and divides this cap into allowances, which are then distributed to companies. These allowances can be traded on an open market, ensuring an efficient mechanism for reducing pollution.

Mark Zuckerberg's donations were to public education, a cause enthusiastically supported by liberals. His primary ally in this endeavor was Cory Booker, a Democrat who was the mayor of Newark at the time and in 2013 became a United States senator.[30] Booker even highlighted this educational reform as a key achievement during his campaign for the Democratic nomination for president. These examples demonstrate that the wealthy's efforts to counteract special interests through social initiatives are ideologically diverse, defying simple political categorization.

While environmental and educational reform are among the most significant causes funded by the wealthy against entrenched interests, they are by no means the only ones. Another crucial area is licensing reform, which seeks to dismantle unjustified occupational requirements that create barriers to entry in various professions and trades. These requirements are particularly detrimental to the poor, who may lack the capital or be unwilling to incur debt to meet licensing criteria. By limiting competition, these requirements also drive up the costs of licensed services, disproportionately affecting those of modest means. Although libertarians have long opposed these restrictions, criticism is not confined to the right. President Barack Obama's Council of Economic Advisers, for instance, issued a report highlighting the harms caused by unjustified licensing regimes.[31] According to the report from the Obama administration, "The percentage of the workforce covered by State licensing laws grew from less than 5 percent in the early 1950s to 25 percent by 2008, meaning that the State licensing rate grew roughly fivefold during this period."[32] This consensus between the right and left underscores the broad recognition of the need for reform in this area.

Special interests thrive on the licensing barriers they help create, particularly in professions and trades. Incumbents in these fields fiercely defend these barriers, as they effectively suppress competition. With both a greater stake in maintaining these obstacles and a superior capacity to organize around their shared interests, incumbents present a formidable challenge to reform. Their power explains why so many professions, such as law, and trades, such as plumbing, taxi services, and cosmetology, face criticism for licensing regimes that create costly hurdles for new entrants.

Wealthy individuals, through their foundations, have played a crucial role in countering these special interests and challenging unjustified restrictions. The Mercatus Center at George Mason University, for example, has produced reports highlighting specific unjustified licensing regimes and recommending reforms, such as state laws that would require licensing requirements be the "least restrictive" necessary to protect public safety.[33] The Mercatus Center receives substantial funding from the Koch Foundation, the Walton Family Foundation, and the John

Templeton Foundation, all established by wealthy pioneers in their respective fields.[34] The Institute for Justice (IJ), founded with seed funding by the Koch Foundation,[35] has taken up the fight against unjustified licensing regimes, often through litigation. IJ has achieved notable successes, such as rolling back regulations in hair braiding—a profession that attracts many minority entrepreneurs—which previously required practitioners to obtain a cosmetology license demanding hundreds, if not thousands, of hours of training.[36] IJ has also successfully forced Florida to eliminate licensing for interior decorating altogether.[37] Even if some of the litigation against these rules proves unsuccessful, it spotlights a problem that requires legislative correction.

The environment, education, and employment opportunities are hardly obscure issues but are among the most pressing concerns that Americans believe are facing the nation.[38] The wealthy play an essential role in advancing policies that might otherwise remain buried under special interest opposition. Their involvement ensures that crucial issues receive the attention and action they deserve, even though they may experience resistance from entrenched interests.

Yet for all these benefits, critics respond that wealth brings its own price tag. In their view, rich donors do not merely offset special interests—they are a special interest. One cost is that they will use their power to prevent competition and hinder economic growth. Another is that they will use it to prevent policies that help others more generally at their expense, such as tax and regulatory policy that will harm people of modest means but benefit the rich. Still another is that they will more generally form an oligarchy, exercising dominion over society.

In short, some critics argue that, like other interest groups, the wealthy may use their power to secure unearned benefits from the government and entrench themselves against ambitious newcomers. However, given our history of entrepreneurial churn, as discussed below, such suppression of competition is unlikely in the context of a dynamic commercial republic that thrives on pioneering ventures. As James Madison foresaw, a commercial republic naturally generates diverse interests—different factions—that do not align on policy. This diversity of interests helps prevent any single group, including the wealthy, from monopolizing power and stifling competition.

In international trade, for instance, those wealthy individuals who profit from exports are natural advocates for free trade, while others may find protectionist policies more beneficial. Each group of individuals has the resources to promote its members' views with compelling information and argument, aiding both voters and representatives in making informed decisions. Similarly, tech entrepreneurs, who profit from innovation rather than directly from fossil fuels, often support environmental causes, contrasting sharply with those who gain from extraction industries. Inherited wealth can also detach the rich from commitment to the positions of the industry in which it was earned. For example, many members of the Rockefeller family, whose wealth was originally built on fossil fuels, have turned to radical environmentalism, demonstrating how inherited wealth can provide the independence to challenge even one's ancestral foundations.[39]

Nevertheless, a concern may well remain that billionaires will bankroll policies—laxer antitrust rules or hypertechnical regulations—calibrated to shield incumbents from fresh competition. That fear misconceives the architecture of political influence. A trade association, financed by every firm in a sector, exists precisely to press rules that raise collective profits; a lone donor's campaign, by contrast, often stems from personal conviction. The venture capitalist Nick Hanauer, for instance, has poured millions into $15-minimum-wage initiatives even though higher labor costs would squeeze his family-owned pillow firm.[40] Industry lobbies defend their shared turf, whereas wealthy donors can act as free agents whose money can land on either flank of a policy fight.

Large corporations and unions still petition legislators for protective favors, because fiduciary duty all but demands it. Agency capture thus flows more from tightly organized blocs than from scattered individuals with deep pockets.[41] The affluent lack the machinery, such as dues, closed-shop contracts, and collective bargaining, to bind one another to a common agenda. In diversifying their fortunes, many of the wealthy migrate toward venture capital and startups that flourish only in an open, competitive economy. Others channel resources into foundations whose charters require public-interest missions. Unencumbered by guild obligations, they can oppose the very privileges that trade groups and unions demand. Precisely because their wealth leaves them untethered to any formal coalition, the rich are likelier allies of an economy without barriers to entry and a polity less distorted by concentrated interests.

Nevertheless, critics argue that, despite some differences in perspective, the wealthy predominantly support policies that oppose regulation and redistribution and allow them to retain their wealth. The critics claim that the rich, rather than acting in the public interest, use their clout to protect their financial interests. For instance, a study that surveyed the wealthy—generally the top 1 percent in the Chicago area—suggests that the rich do hold views that differ from those of the general public.[42] According to this study, the contrast is particularly stark in economic policy. For instance, the public tends to be more supportive of raising the minimum wage and more enthusiastic about regulation than the wealthy are.[43] Politicians, it is argued, tend to align with the views of the rich on issues like taxation, fiscal spending, and the minimum wage rather than the views of the broader population. The implication is that the wealthy, with their substantial sway, skew political debate to favor their own class interests, posing a problem for democracy.[44]

However, the study has significant omissions that undermine the force of its conclusions. It fails to compare the magnitude of the difference between the views of journalists or academics and those of the average citizen with the difference it finds between the rich and ordinary citizens on the same issues. By not considering how the influence of the wealthy contributes to the balance of discourse in a democracy, the study implicitly assumes that the outsized influence of the rich is uniquely problematic, without examining its full context. For instance, if the wealthy have more impact on policy, they may contribute to sound governance by balancing other influential groups with opposing interests.

Moreover, the study does not establish whether the views of the wealthy are driven by their wealth or merely correlated with it. The rich differ from the public in many ways beyond their financial status, and these differences should be considered in a representative democracy. As discussed earlier, government policy benefits from informed perspectives. The study does not compare the levels of knowledge about the nature and effects of regulations between the wealthy and the average citizen. Wealthy citizens likely possess more knowledge about regulations for several reasons: They are better educated on average,[45] have higher IQs on average,[46] and, importantly, are more likely to be involved in businesses where they directly observe the impact of regulations. On one of the few issues where the study does provide a knowledge comparison, the wealthy have a better understanding of what various income levels pay in taxes—a foundational prerequisite for setting sensible tax policy.[47]

The study of the views of the rich would predict that because of their contemporary impact, taxes would be growing more regressive, because that would allow wealthy citizens to retain more of their income. But the reality is likely the opposite. Despite the claims of undue influence of the rich, taxes in the United States appear to be becoming more progressive in terms of the amount paid by the rich.[48] Indeed, by some measures, the United States operates the most progressive national tax system among industrialized nations.[49] Prominent billionaires like Bill Gates and Warren Buffett openly advocate for higher taxes on the wealthy,[50] and organizations such as Patriotic Millionaires explicitly campaign for tax reform targeted at the affluent. In the context of restoring fiscal stability,[51] scholars at think tanks—funded by the rich and their foundations—also call for higher taxes.[52]

In any event, the study fails to address a critical question about the influence of the wealthy in a representative democracy: How would the views of the rich and the rest of the population differ if they possessed the same levels of understanding of social policy? Without this comparison, even apart from their benefits in countering other groups, the concern over the wealthy's clout overlooks the benefits that their more informed perspective may provide.

The question whether those with greater relevant knowledge should legitimately wield more influence in a democracy has long been a salient topic for political thinkers. John Stuart Mill, a towering figure in liberal thought, expressed reservations about extending the franchise to everyone, particularly those who lacked the educational background to grasp complex policy issues. Mill even considered the idea of imposing educational qualifications on voters.[53] Modern democracy has rejected this notion, as drawing a line between the educated and uneducated would be fraught with challenges, and politics gains buy-in from the participation of all adults, even if they are uninformed.

Mill's unease, however, should lead us to appreciate the compromise inherent in our representative democracy. While everyone has an equal vote, certain groups—those likely possessing a deeper understanding of the issues—naturally exert more influence. Critics of the wealthy's influence often accept the additional sway of the intelligentsia because of their claims to greater knowledge, despite that group's unrepresentative ideology and insularity from the broader citizenry and the practical workings of the world. The impact of the wealthy thus provides a crucial counterweight, especially in a commercial republic where the flourishing of the market not only drives prosperity but also strengthens democracy. The entrepreneurial spirit fuels both economic growth and the dynamism of democratic governance.

The alignment of politicians with the views of the wealthy may stem less from undue influence and more from the valuable information and feedback the wealthy provide. If the wealthy, by virtue of their experience, intelligence, and self-image of focusing on consequences, have a better grasp of the likely results of legislation, representatives are naturally inclined to heed their insights. This alignment benefits the public at large, as legislation that fosters economic growth and other positive outcomes tends to have widespread advantages. As Edmund Burke famously argued, a representative owes not just his industry but his judgment to his constituents,[54] and often those through whom he can best inform his judgment are the most influential.

Another concern is that the wealthy might use their power to entrench themselves in power, creating a self-perpetuating oligarchy. Classical political philosophers often worried that the power of the rich could lead to such outcomes.[55] However, ancient societies were far more economically static than modern market democracies.[56] In the past, wealth was primarily tied to land, passed down from generation to generation, with each generation living in much the same circumstances.

In contrast, the world we inhabit is far more fluid, both technologically and economically, than that of previous generations. The next wave of wealth will emerge from unforeseen innovations and entrepreneurial ventures, much like the last generation of wealthy entrepreneurs did. This constant evolution ensures that no single group of families will dominate politics for long, and the rich will change not only in name but also in outlook. Their wealth will be forged in different industries, and their upbringing will be shaped by radically different circumstances. The tech innovators of Silicon Valley, for instance, approach society with a mindset that diverges significantly from that of those who built fortunes in the commodities of the nineteenth century or the manufacturing giants of the early twentieth.

A society that continually mints new wealthy individuals, each earning their fortunes in novel ways, prevents old money from building an impenetrable fortress around itself. We have evidence of the fluidity among the very rich. For instance, a study of the Forbes 400 showed that almost 60 percent had not been on the list just twelve years ago.[57] Even in those previous generations, while descendants of the top 1 percent tended to be rich, 90 percent of the grandchildren of those in the top 1 percent in wealth failed to remain in that top tier.[58] Our age of technological acceleration likely will make that number even smaller.

This process, described by Joseph Schumpeter as "creative destruction," does not just bring forth new products in the economic realm; it also fosters fresh political insights.[59] It injects into the public sphere individuals who possess an understanding of the contemporary society that their innovations have helped to create. The rapid acceleration of technology, spurred by exponential increases in computational power, amplifies these phenomena. Startups today have the potential to create a class of first-generation wealthy more swiftly than ever before, ensuring that the wealthy remain an evolving group, far different from the closed and parochial class that they might constitute in a more static society.

Moreover, unlike the intelligentsia, the wealthy cannot easily exclude individuals with unorthodox views from joining their ranks. In academia, for example, professors collectively decide who receives tenure, often reinforcing prevailing intellectual trends and sidelining those who challenge the status quo. Outside of the natural sciences, where more objective standards are more likely to prevail, this gatekeeping limits the impact and career prospects of those who deviate from mainstream academic conversations. Similarly, while journalists with heterodox views may find employment at conservative outlets, the mainstream media tends to filter out dissenting voices, as evidenced by the lopsided ideological ratios within newsrooms. In comparison, the wealthy are less bound by these insular processes, making their influence an essential corrective to the potential oligarchic tendencies within intellectual circles.

Concerns about oligarchy extend beyond its power to distort governance. Robert Michels, an Italian sociologist, coined the phrase "iron law of oligarchy" to describe how elites inevitably gain control over even democratic and grassroots organizations.[60] To function efficiently, organizations require centralization, and this centralization fosters the rise of an elite. Once in power, this elite entrenches itself, shaping the organization's structure and goals to serve its own interests. However, the wealthy in a modern market democracy militate against this tendency.

The constant threat of market disruption disciplines corporate bureaucracies, ensuring they cannot become too complacent. Although this process may take time, even nonprofits are likely to be rejuvenated by the influx of new wealth. Nonprofits, dependent on fresh sources of funding, often find their boards invigorated by new donors who bring fresh perspectives and a willingness to challenge the status quo. Thus, the rich, far from being a static and self-serving class, contribute to the ongoing renewal of both economic and social institutions.

The rise of the newly rich in every generation is one of the greatest forces for the regeneration of institutions. To be sure, it is not a perfect elixir for rejuvenation. New people can be co-opted into old ways and may not speak up for fear of losing social status. But it is hard to think of better ways of battling entrenched oligarchies in market and civil society than allowing the new classes of rich who earned their money in competitive markets from shaking things up.

Given contemporary events, it is impossible to avoid address-ing another objection to the influence of the rich, which is based less on a principle than on a person. The recent prominence of Elon Musk in American politics has provoked widespread consternation, particularly given his once robust support for Donald Trump and his role as an informal adviser early in Trump's second presidential term. One needs to begin any analysis by disentangling the effect of wealth in Musk's dual roles as a political donor and a strategic confidant. His ability to fund political action committees on an extraordinary scale flows directly from his immense wealth, a characteristic shared by many of the rich who contribute to candidates across the ideological spectrum. Indeed, as previously noted, the wealthy have heterogeneous views, supporting both Democrats and Republicans. In the 2024 election, Kamala Harris outraised Trump, with more billionaires supporting her.[61] Her eventual loss was not the result of financial disadvantage but the lack of resonance of her message with voters. Through his financial support, Musk competed in moving voters with many other factors, including many Americans whose wealth, celebrity, or media status gave them an outsized presence. Moreover, in a democracy with free speech to publicize their sources, donations can prove counterproductive, as Musk found out more recently in a race for the Wisconsin Supreme Court. His intervention energized the base of the candidate he was opposing.[62]

However, Musk's standing as a political adviser was rooted not primarily in his wealth, given that Trump has a lot of wealthy people from whom to choose advisors. Instead, it came from his unmatched reputation as an upender of the status quo. His ventures, from revolutionizing the automobile industry with Tesla to private space exploration through SpaceX, epitomize technological audacity. Neuralink, his endeavor to integrate the human brain with the digital world, underscores his position at the frontier of progress. Musk's achievements are singular, a testament to the capacity of one individual to challenge and reshape the technological landscape. Few people, if any, have founded such a diverse array of companies, each pushing the boundaries of human capability.

These innovations also evoke a profound aspect of America's national identity. The American historian Frederick Jackson Turner famously argued that the American character was forged on the frontier, where the ethos of unbounded opportunity prevailed.[63] Turner noted that the closure of the physical frontier in the late nineteenth century posed a challenge to this defining ideal. Musk, however, reopens the frontier, by looking not westward but outward to the stars, and inward to the human mind. His endeavors rekindle the spirit of exploration and boundless possibility, reaffirming a core element of what many perceive as America's greatness.

Musk's early prominence in Trump's inner circle thus reflects more than mere personal alignment; it embodies the themes of Trump's electoral campaign. Trump rose to power on a promise to disrupt entrenched systems and restore a vision of greatness rooted in individual opportunity and national ambition. In Musk he has found a kindred spirit whose career exemplifies these ideals. Trump's slogan, "Make America Great Again," resonates with the imagery of new frontiers and unlimited potential, and Musk's presence symbolizes this ethos. Trump's many critics may find fault with Musk's approach, but it aligns with the vision that secured Trump's democratic mandate. Relying on an adviser who personifies the campaign's themes is not antidemocratic; instead, it reflects democracy. The voters chose disruption, and Musk, the quintessential disrupter, stands as a natural avatar of that choice.

The implementation of any advice that Musk provides remains firmly within the constraints of democratic governance. Musk's ideas, no matter how bold or imaginative, require the president or his agency heads to exercise executive authority, when permitted by law, or to persuade Congress to enact them into law when such authority is absent. In a representative government, democratically elected presidents must be free to seek counsel from whomever they choose. Leadership improves when it receives input from the most talented in society. This recognition does not require an endorsement of all the effects of Musk's advice. Democracy allows government to pursue ends with which many people disagree.

It is also undeniable that Musk commands authority beyond his relationship with President Trump. Yet not all authority in a democratic polity is or should be political. Political scientists have long recognized the concept of *non-constituted authority*—influence that derives not from formal office but from intellectual, moral, or cultural leadership.[64] Figures like Benjamin Franklin and Martin Luther King Jr. wielded such authority, shaping norms and inspiring change that ultimately found expression in laws enacted through democratic means. A healthy political system accommodates this form of influence, as it fosters the circulation of ideas and the organic evolution of social norms. Only in an authoritarian state would such contributions be dismissed as illegitimate.

To attribute Musk's non-constituted authority solely to his wealth would be a fundamental error. The United States is home to many wealthy individuals who lack the cultural resonance that Musk embodies. His authority arises not primarily from his fortune but from his embodiment of values that many Americans hold dear: boldness, ambition, and innovation. Just as Benjamin Franklin's experiments with electricity and inventions captured the spirit of the early republic, Musk's ventures into space, electric cars, and human-machine interfaces resonate with the contemporary imagination of many. In both cases, any popular awe stems mostly not from their material wealth but from their ability to push boundaries and expand horizons. Musk's authority, like Franklin's, reflects the ideals of the American society that prizes progress and daring.

This kind of authority, married with wealth, supports great independence of action. It allowed Musk to break with President Trump on a signature issue of his presidency—the so-called "big, beautiful bill." Musk denounced it "as an abomination," for its spending and lack of fiscal restraint[65] and has even considered breaking with Republicans to found a new political party. Without such wealth, presidential advisors are generally apparatchiks, fearful of breaking with their patron lest they sink into oblivion.

As Mancur Olson taught us, democracy carries within it a paradox: Its stability breeds interest-group entrenchment. Once organizations become effective at influencing the government, they have staying power, so the number of special interest groups grows until the next social upheaval cleanses society of their negative impact.[66] Thus, stable societies like our own accumulate ever more special-interest organizations over time. The rich are a social force that tempers this problem by disrupting the entrenched status quo and giving voice to diffuse interests that might otherwise be voiceless and ignored.

CHAPTER 6

◇◇◇◇◇◇◇◇◇◇◇◇◇◇◇◇

COUNTERACTING DEMOCRACY'S INHERENT FLAWS

By its nature, representative democracy grants substantial political and cultural power to the majority. As Tocqueville observed in *Democracy in America*, "The very essence of democratic government consists in the absolute sovereignty of the majority."[1] Since ancient times, political theorists have expressed concern that the people may exercise their power unwisely, with potentially dire consequences for the polity. Populism can oppress minorities, including the wealthy. It can hinder disfavored causes from gaining a fair hearing. Representative democracy often centers on middling talents, neglecting to cultivate excellence and instead fostering a culture of mediocrity. Furthermore, democracy's emphasis on equality can lead to demands for a paternalistic state, which undermines individual liberty and personal responsibility.

These flaws imperil the endurance of democracy itself. Majoritarian democracy's oppression of minorities can lead to injustice, social unrest, and upheaval, all of which put a republic at risk. The failure to nurture self-reliance can weaken democracy's defenses against both undemocratic domestic forces and foreign adversaries. Additionally, the tendency of democracy to overspend risks a fiscal crisis.

The actions of the wealthy within a democracy temper these flaws. First, the rich, with their independent means, are better positioned to resist democracy's proclivity to embrace conformity. Second, many wealthy people support excellence, particularly in the arts, arresting democracy's slide toward mediocrity. Because they are less dependent on the state, they have both the means and the interest to question the expansion of government power, counteracting democracy's tendency to create a paternalistic and fiscally unsustainable government. Their influence, in short, serves as a constraint on the natural excesses of majoritarian rule.

CONFORMITY AND OPPRESSION OF MINORITIES

Tocqueville offers the most insightful analysis of the problem of populist power in America. His key observation is that in a republic governed by the many, citizens have strong incentives to align with prevailing opinion to maintain popularity. This conformity makes social opinion more homogeneous and more docile, which in turn threatens the long-term health of society. A diverse range of thought is essential to democracy because it is more likely to produce novel ideas that can address the ever-changing challenges of social life.

As John Stuart Mill reminds us, ideas initially dismissed as incorrect often turn out to be true.[2] Even ideas that are only partially correct can serve to refine and improve existing knowledge. The contestation of ideas is crucial to freeing society from dogmatism, which can stifle further inquiry. For all of these reasons, our political order has a vested interest in encouraging dissenters and contrarians.

Although the First Amendment protects citizens from government retaliation when voicing unconventional or uncomfortable viewpoints, the contrarian still faces social risks. Speaking out can result in the loss of social connections and business opportunities, demonstrating that legal protections are often insufficient to encourage dissent.

Tocqueville coined the term "tyranny of the majority" to describe how majority opinion can dominate and oppress, even in nations with free speech protections.[3] He was particularly scathing in his assessment of how the American majority treated Native Americans and African Americans, highlighting the dangers of majoritarian rule when it turns the law into a tool of oppression.

The harm inflicted by the majority is not confined to unjust laws. Conformist majorities can also wield power outside the legal system to harm minorities. Tocqueville recalled how a mob lynched those who opposed the War of 1812, illustrating the peril that predominant sentiment poses during times of crisis.[4] Another mob in Pennsylvania intimidated free Black citizens to keep them from voting, demonstrating how the majority's failure to protect dissenters and minorities can be as damaging as codifying discrimination in law.[5]

The wealthy play a crucial role in pushing back against this democratic conformity. With their independent means, the rich possess the resources and networks to challenge popular opinion. The wealthy are not as vulnerable as those of modest means to being dismissed or losing their primary income. They also face less risk of ostracism. Their substantial resources free them from dependence on ordinary social networks for three reasons: First, their wealth removes the need to seek out new commercial opportunities; second, they can create their own social networks, as others are eager to interact with them because of the opportunities they offer; and, third, the wealthy often establish foundations that have the institutional autonomy to resist conformist pressures. Because these foundations often outlive their founders, they can better withstand attacks than a living individual can.

Some might argue that tenured academics can be equally independent, but that is a misconception. Academics depend heavily on the opinions of their peers for their stature. Thus, most are rationally cautious about straying too far from the majority opinion within their discipline or university. The pressures for conformity within academia have intensified over the years as ideological homogeneity has increased.[6] Professors are now more susceptible to social cancellation and even to university discipline for expressing unpopular views, particularly on sensitive topics like race or sex. Even in the absence of punishment, most professors avoid controversy for fear it will harm their ability to move to more prestigious posts. While courageous academics can sometimes buck these forces and affect public opinion over time through their writings, they lack the resources to swiftly establish a platform for views that are widely despised by the public.

In contrast, the rich, with their resources and networks, can more readily counter the pressures of conformity and provide a voice for dissent in the face of majoritarian tyranny. American history is replete with examples of the crucial role that the wealthiest 1 percent have played in fighting tyranny and supporting causes that were once unpopular but are now universally recognized as just and essential to our democracy.

Take the American Revolution, for instance. It is no exaggeration to say that without the financial support and acumen of the wealthiest Americans, the Revolution would likely have failed. Robert Morris, a Pennsylvania merchant and the wealthiest man on the continent in 1776, was instrumental in ensuring the success of the revolution.[7] Morris accumulated his wealth through trading goods in the Mediterranean and India.[8] He served on key committees in the Continental Congress and used his financial expertise to secure the funds needed to keep the troops supplied.[9] When neither Congress nor any state could provide sufficient credit, Morris used his own to sustain the revolutionary effort.[10] He was not alone; other wealthy elites also used their resources to support the cause. John Hancock, for example, spent the equivalent of $15 million in today's money to supply a regiment that played a crucial role in the Northern campaigns.[11]

Wealthy merchants also addressed a critical deficit in the war effort: the lack of an effective American navy. They outfitted privateers, pooling their resources and repaying themselves by taking shares of the prize money from captured British ships.[12] This large-scale effort significantly disrupted British supply lines. Instead of funding a large navy, which the colonists could not afford, the Continental Congress registered nearly seventeen hundred private vessels.[13] In the first year of the war, these privateers captured vessels and goods valued at what would be $270 million today. Even in the leaner year of 1778, they seized one hundred British ships,[14] and by 1779 they captured two hundred more.[15] The success of the American Revolution owes much to the crucial support provided by the wealthiest early Americans.

The wealthy also played a pivotal role in the abolition of slavery, the greatest stain on the nation's founding and a prime example of the tyranny of the majority oppressing a minority. In 1833, when most citizens did not favor abolition, Lewis and Arthur Tappan, among the wealthiest merchants in the nation, helped establish the American Anti-Slavery Society.[16] Their financial support allowed this antislavery organization to gain national reach. The Tappan brothers funded antislavery meetings and the Underground Railroad that helped the enslaved escape to freedom, supported speakers like Frederick Douglass, and published sophisticated pamphlets advocating for abolition.

So unpopular was the abolitionist cause that the Tappan brothers became targets of widespread hostility. Arthur Tappan's effigy was burned in South Carolina,[17] and during the anti-abolitionist riots of 1834, a mob sacked Lewis Tappan's home in New York.[18] Yet, despite these attacks on their reputation and property, the brothers persisted, using their wealth to continue funding the abolitionist movement. Their financial independence allowed them to withstand these blows and remain steadfast in their commitment to ending slavery.

Gerrit Smith, one of the wealthiest merchants in New York, was instrumental in bankrolling and organizing the Liberty Party.[19] While the Anti-Slavery Society made the moral case against slavery, the Liberty Party was the first to make the political case, setting off a chain of events that helped lead to slavery's demise.[20] By participating in state, local, and national elections, the Liberty Party forced politicians from the Democratic and Whig parties to confront the issue of slavery, a topic they had tried to avoid in order to protect their electoral prospects. This confrontation fractured both parties, splitting Democrats between Northern and Southern factions, and dividing Whigs into Conscience and Cotton Whigs.[21]

This division led to the death of the Whig Party and paved the way for the rise of the Free Soil Party and, eventually, the Republican Party.[22] The Liberty Party also advanced various constitutional arguments to limit slavery and challenge provisions like the Fugitive Slave Clause.[23] As an abolitionist party, it was a catalyst for the political and legal realignment of antebellum America, making slavery the dominant issue in national politics. The success of the Liberty Party, in no small part, hinged on the support of wealthy individuals like Gerrit Smith.

Beyond the contributions of wealthy individuals, the commercial society of the time played a crucial role in isolating slavery as a peculiar institution. The success of commerce in fostering industrialization, wealth, and social mobility made slavery appear increasingly backward and anachronistic. Commercial relations naturally emphasized the importance of self-ownership and voluntary agreements between individuals. The slogan "Free Labor, Free Men, Free Soil," which became the rallying cry of the Republican Party against slavery, encapsulates the contribution of a commercial society to the abolitionist movement.[24] The rich were a driving force behind this society, propelling the movement forward.

Acknowledging the pivotal role wealthy individuals played in ending slavery does not diminish the contributions of others with more modest means: those who voted for antislavery parties, slaves who escaped from bondage, and the hundreds of thousands of soldiers who died for the Union cause. However, the rich were catalysts, accelerating the process and leading to an earlier realization of freedom. The American Anti-Slavery Society and the Liberty Party were at the forefront, hastening the nation's new birth of freedom.

The movement for women's rights also found its roots largely in the upper class.[25] It was upper-class women who had the leisure and connections to put the issue of voting rights for women on the national agenda.[26] Alva Belmont, the former wife of a Vanderbilt descendant and married to a wealthy investment banker, financed key organizations such as the National Woman's Party, which played a crucial role in pushing the Nineteenth Amendment to ratification.[27] The commercial engine driven by the rich played an important role here as well. The Industrial Revolution drew women into paid work beyond the household, granting them fresh independence and wider networks for collective action. Their growing presence in the workforce also spurred the rise of new media outlets eager to broadcast their cause.[28]

The rich also made important contributions to the civil rights movement of the last century. After Reconstruction, there was a tremendous backsliding on civil rights for African Americans.[29] The cause of civil rights was opposed by the Democratic Party and only feebly supported by the Republican Party.[30] Wealthy individuals, however, provided resources that kept an infrastructure for future activism alive. For instance, Julius Rosenwald, part owner and president of Sears, Roebuck and Company, was particularly active in the education of African Americans.[31] He built schools for African Americans who were not being well educated by states throughout the South.[32] He contributed to historically Black colleges and scholarships at other colleges to educate what he hoped would be the next generation of leadership in the African American community.[33] In Chicago he supported the Michigan Boulevard Garden Apartments to provide housing to African Americans who had escaped from the conditions of the South in the Great Migration but still faced discrimination.[34] His total contributions can be estimated in the hundreds of millions of dollars today.[35]

Wealthy individuals also facilitated civil rights activism. Foundations established by the very rich, such as the Ford Foundation and the Taconic Foundation established by the Mellon family, helped fund the NAACP Legal Defense Fund and the strategy that won many court victories for civil rights.[36] In fact, at the time of litigating *Brown v. Board of Education*, the fund was nearly broke.[37] Marshall Field III, heir to a department store fortune, and his family foundation provided critical support.[38]

As the civil rights movement matured in the 1960s, melding together its disparate and fractious organizations became a central challenge. For instance, the radical Student Non-Violent Coordinating Committee and the more conservative

NAACP often sharply disagreed on tactics. Under the leadership and funding of Stephen Currier and his family foundation, an umbrella organization, the Council for United Civil Rights Leadership, was created as a central clearinghouse for donations and a forum for hashing out disagreements.[39] The council was key to planning 1963's March on Washington, the single most important demonstration of the civil rights movement, where Martin Luther King Jr. gave his "I Have a Dream" speech.[40]

Of course, the success of the civil rights movement depended not only on the rich but also, crucially, on the work of leaders in the Black community, churches, and thousands who participated in boycotts and marches. However, the argument for the utility of the rich to democracy is not that the rich alone are responsible for democracy's success. Instead, they play an important role in promoting and accelerating political movements that began in unfavorable circumstances.

One might argue that the wealthy have also supported causes that are less esteemed than antislavery, women's suffrage, and civil rights. For several reasons, the wealthy's support of good causes is more important than any support for those that are bad. First, in a democracy, the wealthy cannot unilaterally impose their will. Instead, their role is often to amplify ideas and provide the resources necessary to bring them to public attention. For movements to succeed, they must resonate with broader societal values and gain the support of democratic institutions or the majority. This mechanism creates a filter where only those movements that align with societal consensus or values are likely to endure. While the wealthy can fund both good and bad causes, the ultimate test of success lies in public approval and institutional endorsement, which skews outcomes toward movements that reflect the public interest.

Second, wealth enables individuals to take risks on unorthodox or unpopular causes that may not initially enjoy widespread support. Many of these causes detailed above, such as abolition, civil rights, and women's suffrage, were considered radical at their inception but later became foundational to American progress. Even when wealthy individuals support controversial or morally dubious movements, the ensuing debates can provoke societal introspection, indirectly contributing to the refinement of public values and the advancement of better causes.

Third, "good" movements often have a lasting positive impact on society, institutionalizing freedom, equality, and rights. For example, the abolition of slavery and the expansion of voting rights fundamentally altered the trajectory of the American republic. Conversely, movements viewed as "bad" often tend to be self-limiting, either because they are incompatible with democratic values or because they provoke strong countermovements that mitigate their harm.

Fourth, over time, the historical legacy of wealthy Americans' support has skewed toward movements that endure and comport with principles of freedom and justice. The wealthy generally have a vested interest in the continuing stability and flourishing of the society in which they live. This incentive tends to align them more with movements that promote sustainable progress rather than destructive agendas.

DEMOCRATIC MEDIOCRITY

Majorities in a democracy pose cultural as well as legal risks. Just as a king is surrounded by flatterers, the majority in America often indulges in what Tocqueville describes as "perpetual adoration of itself."[41] By definition, the majority represents the average, not the exceptional. Tocqueville warns that a culture dominated by the majority, as opposed to one influenced by aristocratic values, may lead to mediocrity in its output. This critique has been expanded by others who note that a culture shaped by mass taste can result in philistinism, particularly in the arts.

Beyond their contributions to civic associations and unpopular social causes, the wealthy play a crucial role in promoting excellence in the arts. Fine arts constitute an indispensable part of our civilization's heritage, yet new artistic movements often struggle to gain immediate popularity. For example, the Impressionists were once dismissed as amateurs and poor artists.[42] Their endurance was aided by a handful of farsighted buyers who had both means and nerve. Gustave Caillebotte, an independently wealthy painter, bought dozens of canvases from Monet, Renoir, and Degas, often advancing cash when his friends could not pay the rent.[43] Dealer Paul Durand-Ruel acquired and exhibited thousands of their works at a time when almost no one else would, even at the risk of bankruptcy.[44] Their confidence drew in other collectors so that by the 1890s wealthy patrons on both sides of the Atlantic were underwriting exhibitions and seeding what later became the Impressionist rooms of major museums. In short, while critics and middle-class admirers mattered, early capital from a small circle of buyers gave the movement breathing room to outlast ridicule and reshape modern art.

In America, wealthy art collectors similarly supported artists and later donated their collections to museums. Peggy Guggenheim became an early patron of Jackson Pollock and collected works by Max Ernst, Pablo Picasso, and other modernists.[45] Today these masterpieces are on display in the Guggenheim Museum in New York, alongside the collection of Peggy Guggenheim's uncle, Solomon Guggenheim, who endowed the museum with his own acquisitions.[46] Albert Barnes, who collected Post-Impressionist and early modernist art, left his collection to the Barnes Foundation, now housed on the Benjamin Franklin Parkway in Philadelphia.[47] Through their patronage and philanthropy, the wealthy have ensured that groundbreaking art, once unpopular and misunderstood, is preserved and celebrated as part of our common patrimony.

The Guggenheim Museum itself testifies to the role the wealthy have played in creating magnificent buildings that now offer the public a chance to experience some of the greatest architectural achievements of their time. Among the most prominent examples are Fallingwater, designed by Frank Lloyd Wright for Edgar and Liliane Kaufmann; the Breakers, crafted by Richard Morris Hunt for Cornelius Vanderbilt II; and Monticello, the iconic home that Thomas Jefferson, himself a wealthy man as well as a brilliant designer. These are just a few of the hundreds of architectural masterpieces built by the wealthy on display across almost every state in the Union.

Such examples illustrate a virtuous circle in the fine arts, where the wealthy once again play an indispensable role. The rich act as prospectors—not in search of gold but of artists and architects who possess originality and vision. Just as with business startups, not all innovative artistic movements succeed or gain critical acclaim, but those that do often receive essential backing from the wealthy. Ultimately, the general public reaps the benefits, as most of the greatest works of art and architecture eventually find their way to public display. Walking through any major museum, one can trace not only the history of great art but also the legacy of the entrepreneurs and industrialists who were its early patrons.

The enjoyment of these magnificent works, donated by business titans, exposes the fallacy in the criticisms like those of the political theorist Ingrid Robeyns, which claim that important art remains locked away in homes rather than displayed in museums.[48] Without the initial support of the wealthy, many of these masterpieces would not exist in the first place. Robeyns's critique falsely assumes that some undefined social mechanism could replicate the intricate process by which great art is encouraged, preserved, and eventually shared with the public. Could a committee of bureaucrats, dispensing money that is not their own, have accomplished anything comparable?

The discovery and preservation of great art, assured by the support of the rich, are vital not only for maintaining ideals of excellence but also for sustaining the national identity on which any democratic nation depends. As John Ruskin observed, "Great nations write their autobiographies in three manuscripts: the book of their deeds, the book of their words, and the book of their art. Not one of these books can be understood unless we read the two others, but of the three, the only trustworthy one is the last."[49] Democratic nations, perhaps even more than others, require a deep connection to their history, including their artistic history, which can offer a sense of shared communion amid the fragmenting turbulence of politics. The public veneration of great works and the inspiration they provide also counteract the culture of mediocrity, a characteristic risk inherent in egalitarian democracy.

Such artistic benefactions illustrate how the contributions of the wealthy evolve across generations. The consumer surplus generated by the rich, as inventors and industrialists, has historically elevated the material well-being of the masses. For example, the new weaving mechanisms developed by nineteenth-century industrialists clothed millions at prices more affordable than ever before.[50] As patrons of the arts, their descendants invested in original paintings and sculptures, and, ultimately donated much of their collections to museums. This generosity allows their fellow citizens to develop a deeper appreciation for and a lasting love of the great monuments of their civilization.

Free markets perpetually engage in a kind of alchemy, transforming the useful into the beautiful, the mundane into the unique, and material wealth into spiritual enrichment. Often, the wealthiest among us act as our alchemists, channeling their enthusiasm for the sublime into lasting legacies that enhance society as a whole.

The wealthy do not merely donate works of art to museums; they also provide essential support to museums and cultural institutions as independent nonprofit organizations, vital to civil society and free from government control. This independence should not be overlooked, as many nations see governments exercising direct control over cultural life. Such control can lead to partisan manipulation. For instance, just last year the ruling coalition in Slovakia dismissed leaders of state-controlled cultural institutions, including museums, for political reasons.[51]

The benefits of the rich supporting the nonprofit cultural sector, however, extend far beyond merely inhibiting partisan interference. The independence of these institutions ensures that decisions about exhibitions, acquisitions, and programming are driven more by artistic and scholarly values than by interest-group politics. This independence fosters an environment of creativity, intellectual rigor, and experimentation, unencumbered by governmental influence or censorship. Such institutions are more capable of pursuing long-term cultural objectives, maintaining consistency in their missions despite the vagaries of political cycles. Their nonprofit status generates public trust by signaling that they do not serve political interests, leading to increased engagement, philanthropic support from a broader demographic, and deeper community connections.

To be sure, nonprofits are not immune to biases or fads. Cultural institutions are also often shaped by the same intellectual trends that pervade academia and entertainment. And, unlike for-profit companies, they do not have shareholders who exercise some discipline on radical excesses. Yet, here too, even a few among the wealthy can serve as a corrective force. Their financial resources and independence enable them to act as gadflies, whistleblowers, or even founders of new institutions to challenge prevailing biases of old ones. Otherwise, our culture is even more likely to fall victim to the latest trends of the intelligentsia. Again, the rich are a mechanism for self-correction, a key necessity in democratic culture.

In assessing the role of the wealthy in cultural life, we must guard against what could be termed the "philanthropic fallacy." This fallacy mirrors the "nirvana fallacy" in economics. Just as it is erroneous to assume that government intervention will automatically improve market failures, it is equally incorrect to believe that reducing the influence of the wealthy, even in flawed cultural institutions, will lead to the emergence of more diverse and enlightened perspectives.

SOFT DESPOTISM AND THE FISCAL RISKS OF THE TRANSFER STATE

America's transfer state and its resulting fiscal challenges reflect a blend of weaknesses in democracy, as highlighted by Aristotle, Tocqueville, and modern public choice theorists. Aristotle warned that the numerous poor might seek to take from the rich, leading to the impoverishment of all and the potential for social conflict.[52] That remains a potential risk in some democracies. However, as public choice theory explains, the political process in advanced democracies is more complex. In particular, Mancur Olson's theories can help explain why the danger of a transfer state that crowds out public goods has grown.[53] Transfer programs are politically successful because they provide concentrated benefits to better organized groups, such as the elderly, while spreading the costs across the broader population through taxes or deficit spending.[54] Individual taxpayers bear a relatively small cost for each transfer program, making it less likely that they will mobilize against the program. In contrast, the beneficiaries of transfer programs experience significant, direct benefits, giving them strong incentives to advocate for the continuation or expansion of those programs. Over time, this process leads to an expansion of transfer payments at the expense of less politically organized constituencies that benefit from public goods.

The political power of the middle class often directs the bulk of entitlement spending toward itself. Consistent with the public choice view that democratic legislatures favor more defined groups over more diffuse ones, entitlement programs are typically directed toward groups defined by specific characteristics, such as age, occupation, or educational attainment. To be sure, other means-tested programs like food stamps have also been increasing, but programs without means testing still make up the bulk of transfers.

Both non-means-tested entitlements and means-tested spending that discourages work align with Tocqueville's prediction that democracy would eventually give rise to an administrative despotism where the state assumes control of personal affairs.[55] This expansion of state responsibilities discourages even capable citizens from managing their own affairs, eroding the liberty and sense of duty that are essential to human flourishing.

Over the past ninety years, the most striking trend in the federal budget has been the shift from providing public goods to providing transfers.[56] Public goods, as defined by political scientists and economists, are not simply anything that some members of the public desire. Rather, they are goods from which the public cannot be excluded and from which everyone benefits, such as national defense, law enforcement, and clean air.[57] Because markets and families cannot effectively provide these goods, they remain the core responsibility of the state.

Franklin D. Roosevelt's introduction of the Social Security program in 1935 marked the dawn of a new fiscal era, one that fundamentally transformed the federal budget. It is no coincidence that the largest transfers in American democracy remain directed toward a group defined by age. The elderly are the most consistent voters; in 2020, the turnout of those over sixty-five far exceeded that of those from eighteen to twenty-four.[58] Additionally, since most elderly citizens are no longer employed, they have no incentives to cap the taxes on labor that help fund Social Security. Yet the elderly as a class are far from the poorest demographic group in America.[59]

Subsidies to farmers soon followed as another staple of the federal budget, justified by the claim that they were necessary to raise and stabilize farm prices.[60] Support for these subsidies also benefited from the traditional respect for those who work the land. Lyndon Johnson then broadened middle-class entitlements, most notably through the 1965 Medicare Act, which provided non-means-tested medical care for those over sixty-five.[61]

President Biden's administration opened a new chapter in the story of federal transfers with student loan cancellation. His initial effort, which was later struck down by the Supreme Court, aimed to provide $20,000 in student debt relief to individuals earning under $125,000.[62] His subsequent plan, though more complex, still offered substantial loan forgiveness to many in the middle class. This broad loan forgiveness marked a significant departure from the traditional view that government-funded student financial aid should be reserved for the truly needy. Higher education generally increases earning potential, positioning graduates of undergraduate and graduate programs to be better off than most of the population.

The trajectory of entitlements in America demonstrates how one transfer program inevitably begets another as groups left out of the initial benefits clamor for their share. The most expensive entitlements—Social Security and Medicare—are currently funded by all workers, including those just starting their careers. Social Security, in particular, fosters the illusion that people are merely reclaiming what they paid into the system, but most recipients today receive far more than they contributed in taxes. Still, given that Social Security operates on a pay-as-you-go basis, many young people recognize that the benefits available to them upon retirement will likely be less generous. The Social Security Trust Fund is projected to be depleted around 2033; payroll taxes would cover about 77 percent of scheduled benefits thereafter.[63] This looming reality may change the political behavior of those who pay into a system that may fail. Why shouldn't younger generations demand their share of government largesse through student loan forgiveness while it's still available?

Transfers have expanded dramatically, both as a percentage of the federal budget and as a share of GDP. Before the advent of Social Security, the portion of the federal budget devoted to transfers was small. By the 1970s, it had swelled to 35 percent, reached 55 percent by the turn of the millennium, and soared to 60 percent by 2020.[64] Similarly, transfers have risen sharply as a percentage of GDP—from almost nothing in the 1930s to nearly 16 percent as of 2022.[65] Projections indicate that, with an aging population, transfers will continue to rise. To grasp the magnitude of this entitlement wave, the Penn Wharton Budget Model states that "current U.S. fiscal policy is in permanent imbalance as current debt plus projected future spending outstrips future tax revenue. Achieving fiscal balance would require the federal government to permanently increase tax revenues by over 40% or reduce expenditures by 30% or some combination of both."[66]

The costs of this ever-expanding transfer state to our republic are substantial. First, the tax burden required to fund these transfers would stifle growth and innovation. An excessively expanding transfer state also harms democracy because prosperity is crucial to its endurance. Second, this transformation makes it increasingly difficult to fund genuine public goods. As tax burdens rise, citizens become less willing to pay taxes, yet future threats may require increased spending on public goods. The challenges posed by China and Russia are prime examples. While isolationism may seem fiscally prudent in the short term, it is geopolitically dangerous in the long run. Additionally, investing now in reducing dependence on fossil fuels could prevent greater future expenditures needed to address the more severe consequences of climate change. Democracy survives only if it can meet future crises that will require major new spending. This is not an abstract concern. The United States had the fiscal capacity to greatly expand spending to fight World War II, not only for itself but for the entire free world. On the present trajectory, it may lack that capacity in the near future, perhaps making it impossible to save ourselves and others from crises of that magnitude.

As Rachel Lu observes, the costs of a transfer state that is not limited by considerations of need are spiritual as well as material.[67] A focus on material well-being and commerce naturally fosters interactions and attention to others. The responsibilities of caring for family members are fundamental to creating strong family bonds. However, as the state increasingly assumes these responsibilities, social connections have withered. The loneliness and despair seen today are in part the side effects of a state that has taken over functions once provided more personally and less bureaucratically by the family or private charity. In this way, the transfer state not only burdens our economy but also erodes the social fabric that binds us together.

A metastasizing transfer state flips John F. Kennedy's famous phrase on its head—"Ask not what you can do for your country, but what your country can do for you."[68] A culture driven by transfers that are not based on need turns governance into a zero-sum game, where what one person receives is inevitably at the expense of another—a reality the younger generation is beginning to recognize. This dynamic fosters a war of all against all within the state, a paradox considering that the modern state was originally conceived by thinkers like Thomas Hobbes as a mechanism to prevent such conflict. A republic focused on public goods unites its citizens, but one centered on transfers divides them.

The public consistently ranks federal budget problems among their top concerns, yet these issues remain largely unaddressed by either political party.[69] The 2024 presidential campaign provides an excellent example of malign neglect. Both Donald Trump and Kamala Harris were assiduous in proposing special interest tax breaks, such as eliminating taxes on tips and providing tax breaks for particular manufacturing sectors.[70] The announced plans of both candidates grew the deficit. Neither proposed plans to address the looming shortfalls in Medicare and Social Security. If electoral politics has difficulty addressing the fiscal and civic costs of the burgeoning transfer state, democracy must rely on civil society to do so.

The wealthy are the group with the greatest incentive and the most resources to push for solutions to this looming danger to our democracy. They have a direct interest in this matter, as they bear a very substantial share of the financial burden of the transfer state. While the bottom half of the income distribution contributes just over 2 percent of federal income taxes, the top 1 percent shoulders approximately 46 percent of this burden.[71] The top 10 percent collectively pay around three-quarters of federal income taxes.[72] Additionally, the wealthiest Americans bear the entire burden of estate taxes and are disproportionately affected by corporate taxes due to their greater equity holdings.[73]

Moreover, America's fiscal position is an example of an issue that may not have much short-term resonance but clearly will have a long-term impact. The wealthy tend to be better at looking at such issues, since their wealth is a buffer against being overly concerned with the short term. They also have the means to bring this issue to the political forefront. Politicians often avoid addressing the problem for fear of alienating large voting blocs. Nevertheless, the wealthy have funded initiatives to keep our fiscal challenges in the public eye. The Peterson Foundation, funded by the billionaire and former commerce secretary Peter Peterson, focuses almost exclusively on this issue.[74] Other think tanks, like the American Enterprise Institute and the Brookings Institution, which rely significantly on funding from wealthy donors, also offer programming on these topics. These efforts cannot be dismissed as representing a narrow ideological perspective; AEI leans center-right, while Brookings is center-left. Pete Peterson himself was a liberal Republican who was fired by the Nixon administration for refusing to toe the party line.[75]

These and similar organizations propose a variety of solutions, many of which include raising taxes on the wealthy while also curbing the growth of transfers. Once again, individuals of independent means, operating outside of government, perform a vital service to democracy; by highlighting the consequences of its inherent weaknesses, they keep hope alive for the necessary reforms that strengthen democracy in the long run.

Winston Churchill's quip that democracy is "the worst form of government—except for all the others" reminds us that its defects demand continual repair. The rich help mend three of its most important flaws. First, because their fortunes free them from the need to appease transient majorities, the wealthy can defy mass conformity and shield vulnerable minorities when popular passions turn oppressive. Second, their patronage of enterprise, science, and the arts sustains a culture of excellence whose achievements elevate civic pride and pull democracy upward from mediocrity. Third, as the citizens who underwrite the state and yet rely on its subventions least, the rich are best positioned to sound the alarm against budgetary imbalance, reinforcing fiscal restraint and, by extension, the personal responsibility upon which democratic endurance depends.

CHAPTER 7

◇◇◇◇◇◇◇◇◇◇◇◇◇◇◇

AMERICA'S COMMERCIAL REPUBLIC

The United States was founded as a commercial republic, reflecting the Enlightenment consensus that commerce improves society.[1] Drawing from these ideas, the Founders believed that an emphasis on commerce would restrain despotism, foster respect for the rule of law, refine social manners, and promote international peace.[2] Economic thinkers of the Enlightenment further argued that a commercial republic drives economic growth, continuously improving the lives of its citizens.[3] Farsighted theorists also implied that this economic dynamism would, in turn, strengthen democracy, as growth would give more people a vested interest in maintaining the democratic system that underpinned their prosperity. Thus, the substantial advantages of a commercial republic were seen not only in economic terms but also in political and moral dimensions.

THE FOUNDATIONS OF THE
COMMERCIAL REPUBLIC

The enthusiasm for a commercial society is embedded in the original federal Constitution and state constitutions, which contain provisions that protect and promote commerce. The wealthy are well positioned to defend the commercial society because they benefit from it and understand how its mechanisms affect prosperity.[4]

The Founders' confidence in the benefits of a commercial society traces back to Enlightenment thinkers who extolled the virtues of commerce.[5] Among these, Baron de Montesquieu was particularly influential; he was the most frequently quoted political theorist in *The Federalist Papers* and at the Constitutional Convention.[6] Montesquieu believed that commerce helps people get along by dissolving prejudices: "Commerce is a cure for the most destructive prejudices; for it is almost a general rule, that wherever we find agreeable manners, there commerce flourishes; and that wherever there is commerce, there we meet with agreeable manners."[7] While Montesquieu did not detail the mechanism by which commerce dissipates prejudice, other Enlightenment figures like Voltaire and Adam Smith clarified that the potential for mutual gain through trade and employment makes factors such as race, religion, and appearance less significant in social relations.

Montesquieu also argued that commerce has a moderating effect on the abuse of political power.[8] Commercial societies, he suggested, are less prone to extremism and violence because commercial activity demands cooperation, the rule of law, and stability. A commercial society is a more peaceful society, according to Montesquieu.[9] He extended this idea to the international sphere, noting, "Peace is the natural effect of trade. Two nations who traffic with one another, become mutually dependent."[10] This insight underscores the idea that commerce not only enriches a nation economically but also cultivates the social and political conditions necessary for lasting peace and stability with the rest of the world. These features of commerce help sustain democracy. The surplus that commerce creates, which Montesquieu refers to as "luxury," is also broadly beneficent to society. That luxury helps generate the development of science and art, which also has a civilizing effect.

Many of the Founders shared the belief that commerce was essential to sustaining the republic. George Washington regarded "commerce and industry as the best mines of a nation," seeing them as the true sources of wealth and prosperity.[11] Even Thomas Jefferson echoed this sentiment, stating that commerce, along with agriculture, manufacture, and navigation, formed the pillars of the nation.[12] Perhaps most eloquently, Gouverneur Morris, the drafter of the Constitution, proclaimed that commerce was the source of progress: "Now as Society is in itself Progressive as Commerce gives a mighty Spring to that progressive force."[13]

James Madison offered the most subtle view of how a commercial society supports the republic. He believed that the protection of the diverse and unequal faculties of men from which the acquisition of property arises was "the first object of government."[14] Madison had several reasons for this priority. First, he argued that a nation that fails to protect property rights would likely fail to protect other rights as well.[15] In his essay "On Property," Madison even analogizes civil rights, such as the right to free speech, to property rights, thus placing civil rights on a more solid foundation.[16]

Madison's ideas about factions also implicitly highlight some of the virtues of the wealthy, as the commercial republic creates different paths to wealth and therefore different interests. Multiplying the foundations of wealth addresses the problem of factions, which he saw as the primary threat to republican government.[17] James Madison defined a faction in "Federalist No. 10," today the most famous of his Federalist essays, as a group of citizens, whether a minority or majority, that is united by a common interest or passion adverse to the rights of other citizens or the common good. He was particularly concerned about factions because he believed they could lead to the oppression of minority groups and the destabilization of government. Madison feared that factions would pursue their own interests at the expense of the public good, creating conflict and division.

Madison also observed that different propertied groups have different particular interests depending on the sources of their wealth.[18] For example, the landed class naturally has different political objectives from those in the manufacturing class. Over time, the variety of ways to acquire property creates more distinct groups of the wealthy, leading to a beneficial fragmentation in politics. The economy that entrepreneurs and investors create reduces the danger of an entrenched faction with enduring power to dominate society.[19] The commercial republic then mints new business people who make their money in many different fields, because a dynamic economy is always opening up fundamentally new opportunities.[20] While Madison does not draw this corollary directly, this diversity makes it harder for the wealthy to form a faction pursuing special interests connected to their particular way of making money.

In comparison, the shared interests of the wealthy, such as a commitment to a rule of law that facilitates transactions and to economic growth that increases the value of their capital, align more closely with the broader interests of society. Regardless of how the wealthy have made their fortunes, they generally have a stake in a stable legal system to protect their assets and a thriving economy to secure good returns on their investments. As the commercial republic grows and diversifies, it creates a virtuous circle where the promotion of commerce strengthens the rule of law and fosters the conditions for further growth.

These implicit ideas about the role of commerce and the wealthy were the background of the explicit legal structures the Constitution's framers put in place. The structure of the U.S. Constitution itself reflects the view that commerce is the foundation of the good society, creating in essence a commercial republic. It is remarkable that except for national defense, almost all the enumerated powers of the federal government were meant to facilitate a continental market—to make commerce "regular," as the Commerce Clause authorizes Congress to do.[21] Other powers of the federal government also facilitated commerce, such as its authority to mint money, create uniform bankruptcy laws, and create copyrights and patents.[22]

The original Constitution put few constraints on the states, but most of those constraints prevented interference with commerce. For instance, the states were forbidden from impairing the obligations of contracts.[23] A particular concern animating this clause was debtor relief legislation that would make credit more expensive in the future and so cripple commerce.[24] Another prohibition prevented states from minting coins or issuing bills of credit.[25] The Framers feared that irresponsible monetary policy could spark inflation.[26] The states were also forbidden from imposing tariffs on goods coming from out of state, a practice that could inhibit trade among the states.[27]

There were far-reaching implications to the essentially commercial character of American society contemplated by the Constitution of 1789. The commercial republic envisioned by the Founders put a premium on self-control and honesty; it required citizens to pass judgment informally on one another's reliability and integrity, since many decisions would be based on reputation; and it required the free exchange of information and ideas so that opportunities could become known. Thus, commerce rewards virtues of self-restraint, fair judgment, and social interchange that are indispensable to republican life.

More than two centuries later, the wealthy still anchor the commercial republic and fuel its gains. The rich help sustain it in two ways. First, as entrepreneurs, they widen prosperity by seeing what others miss: new combinations of talent and tools, better uses of existing resources, and novel means of coordinating work.[28] They bear the uncertainty of trial and error, often fail, and are highly compensated when they succeed because their ventures are risky. Yet even then, the vast majority of the surplus their innovations generate accrues to consumers through lower prices, better quality, and greater variety, and to workers through new jobs of higher value. The wealthy are more inclined to make risky investments that drive innovation because their resources allow them to absorb large losses.[30] Much like drilling for oil, where many attempts fail before striking success, original ventures require numerous failures before breakthroughs are achieved.[31] While innovation has always been crucial to improving people's lives, in our digital era it also fosters greater equality by creating free or affordable goods that the vast majority can access.

A society with a growing economy is also more likely to sustain democracy. Economic growth strengthens democracy through several mechanisms. First, growth enables people to become better educated, making them more capable of accessing and using information to hold politicians accountable. Second, as people become more affluent, they develop a greater stake in preserving the political system.

Today democratic society thrives on growth, spurred by the rich. As the philosopher Ernest Gellner vividly describes, our modern industrial democracy "is the only society ever to live by and rely on sustained and perpetual growth, on an expected and continuous improvement.... Its favored mode of social control is universal Danegeld, buying off social aggression with material enhancement; its greatest weakness is its inability to survive any temporary reduction of the social bribery fund, and to weather the loss of legitimacy which befalls it if the cornucopia becomes temporarily jammed and the flow falters."[32] In this sense, economic growth not only fuels prosperity but also underpins the legitimacy and stability of democratic governance. And the rich are an indispensable engine of that growth and thus our stability.

THE RICH AND MODERN INNOVATION

The rich today remain primary drivers of innovation in the nation. A glance at the Forbes 400 reveals countless examples of individuals who have fundamentally transformed the world by introducing new services that were often unimaginable before they were created. The most obvious examples come from the technology sector. Bill Gates's Microsoft revolutionized personal computing, making it accessible and useful for hundreds of millions.[33] Mark Zuckerberg's Facebook connected billions across the globe.[34] Jeff Bezos's Amazon vastly expanded consumer choice, enabling shopping with a simple click and drastically reducing delivery times. The founders of Uber and Lyft redefined transportation, allowing almost anyone to summon a ride almost anytime, anywhere, with a smartphone—a device popularized by Steve Jobs, one of the greatest technological visionaries of our time.

Yet advances are not confined to technology. Founders of enterprises outside the tech industry have also reshaped business landscapes. Sam Walton revolutionized retail with Walmart, creating a big-box store with an efficient supply chain that lowered prices for consumers and provided jobs for those who previously struggled to find employment.[35] Bernard Marcus and Arthur Blank created Home Depot, making home improvement more accessible by offering one-stop shopping for supplies, thereby creating a new hobby for millions and enabling many others to start side businesses in renovating houses.[36] These are the household names. Thousands of other entrepreneurs have started companies that have enhanced our lives, leading to more flourishing and abundance. While they may not have reached billionaire status, they too have become wealthy by making life better for others.

All of these business leaders took substantial risks to create their ventures. Most startups fail,[37] and even well-managed ones can fall prey to bad timing or intense competition. Rewards must be commensurate with that risk. Those with the talent to start and manage such enterprises could have chosen a safer, still well-remunerated life at an established company, where they might have contributed to consumer value through incremental product improvements. The most successful of these individuals eventually join the ranks of the truly wealthy, but even top corporate jobs come with risks of bankruptcy and lawsuits. There are other lines of work with reasonable pay and minimal risk, work for state governments being a prime example. Without the prospect of substantial rewards, such jobs become more attractive to people who might otherwise be entrepreneurs.

But it is those who dare to take the greatest risks in pursuit of innovation who most dramatically shape our society, constantly renewing the dynamism of the commercial republic. While the rewards for innovators are substantial, often making founders multimillionaires or even billionaires, they typically capture only a fraction of the value their enterprises generate for consumers. Thus, the commercial republic, especially in our age of technological acceleration, remains a powerful mechanism for the commercially talented to enhance the lives of those who are less skilled or less inclined toward commerce.

THE RICH AND MODERN INVESTING

Even after accumulating wealth, the rich continue to play a crucial role in fostering a dynamic economy.[38] When it comes to investments, the wealthy are fundamentally different from the average person. Their greater resources allow them to invest in ways that are particularly beneficial to novel ventures. With longer investment horizons, they often invest with future generations in mind, including their children and grandchildren. This long-term perspective leads them to take on riskier investments, which are essential for fueling commerical advances.[39]

The rich, for example, pioneered venture capital and remain key players in this sector.[40] In hubs like California's Silicon Valley, a virtuous circle of innovation and investment thrives. Successful tech founders, after retiring, often transition into venture capitalists.[41] They bring not only their money but also their experience, helping to identify and fund promising startups. Their wealth also enables them to sustain reverses: Startups, by their very nature, require investors to be prepared for the possibility of total loss. The wealthy are thus uniquely positioned to make the high-risk investments that accelerate the development of new technology. This process of renewal rolls on through decades, sustained by the wealth and wisdom of those who have already succeeded.[42]

Charitable institutions, such as universities and foundations with large endowments, also contribute to this dynamic economy by making long-term investments. Over the past twenty years, inspired by university endowment managers like David Swensen of Yale University, these endowments have diversified into riskier alternative investments, including venture capital.[43] The funds they invest are mostly derived from donations by wealthy individuals who have made or inherited fortunes through entrepreneurial success. In addition to supporting public goods—which will be discussed in chapter 8 on the rich and civic life—these endowments play a vital role in creating a dynamic economy.

THE RICH AS EXEMPLARS FOR THE COMMERCIAL REPUBLIC

The wealthy also uphold the commercial republic through their presence in public life. A commercial republic encourages individuals to improve their economic status through entrepreneurship, hard work, and innovation. The wealthy serve as visible proof of the system's promise, embodying the possibility of upward mobility that motivates others to engage in productive efforts. Rooted in Enlightenment thought, particularly in thinkers like Adam Smith, is the idea that wealth, when earned through free-market competition, is a reward for virtues such as foresight, thrift, and industriousness.[44] Wealthy individuals exemplify these virtues, which are essential to the maintenance of the commercial republic.

In a capitalist society, the wealthy often achieve their status through risk-taking and creation. By doing so, they serve as role models, encouraging others to pursue similar ventures that spur economic growth and technological progress. Their prominence also supports the republican idea that citizens actively participate in shaping and enhancing society. A commercial democracy is founded on the notion that citizens manifest their equality not only through their franchise but also through their autonomy in the commercial realm as owners, workers, and consumers.

A commercial republic thrives on the widespread support of its citizens, even those not directly involved in commerce. In the United States, some wealthy entrepreneurs and innovators—figures such as Thomas Edison, Thomas Watson, and Steve Jobs—are still celebrated. While economists can demonstrate how markets outperform other systems in delivering goods, most people are not drawn to abstract economic theories. They rely on more personalized narratives of invention, ingenuity, and success. The contemporary media coverage of wealthy figures like Jeff Bezos and Bill Gates also reminds the public of the fruits of innovation in a commercial society and links them to the key business pioneers behind these advancements. In this way, the rich serve not only as financial engines driving economic progress but also as symbols reminding us of the benefits of a commercial republic.

THE RICH AND TODAY'S INEQUALITY

The wealthy have always served as a primary source of economic growth in market societies, propelling the commercial republic forward. However, their very success has generated a persistent concern about whether that success exacerbates inequality. Critics worry that even as the rich today drive innovation and economic expansion, their actions widen the gap between the wealthy and the rest of society. But even on their own terms, these criticisms are flawed. Equally important, they ignore the way the new ventures fueled by the wealthy promise to provide more equal access to experience and skills across the income scale.

Thomas Piketty and his colleagues have argued that inequality is on the rise, particularly in the industrialized world and most notably in the United States.[45] They claim that after a period of declining inequality from the early to mid-twentieth century, the gap has been widening once again. Piketty bases his argument on tax records and other financial data, suggesting that this trend is not a temporary aberration but a long-term trajectory.[46] He offers a theory to explain why this trend is occurring. He postulates that return on capital has tended to exceed economic growth, allowing those with capital to outpace the rest of society. He also encapsulates this claim in the formula $r > g$, where the rate of return on capital (r) consistently exceeds the rate of economic growth (g).[47] He is confident that this formula will continue to hold, predicting that as economic growth slows in industrial nations, the rich will continue to find profitable opportunities abroad, further increasing their wealth and, consequently, inequality within the nation.[48] Even on Piketty's own terms, such investment abroad likely reduced global inequality, helping the worst off in the world.

Piketty's view raises the concern that a significant increase in inequality could diminish the net benefits that the rich provide to democracy within a nation-state, even as it reduces global inequality. If, for example, the top 1 percent were to control 95 percent of the wealth, it might be argued that they would no longer act as catalysts for social movements that depend on broad popular support. Instead, they could become the sole arbiters of which movements succeed.

However, Piketty's arguments falter under closer empirical and theoretical scrutiny. Gerald Auten and David Splinter have critiqued Piketty's data on the United States in two significant ways.[49] First, Piketty's analysis relies heavily on tax returns, but, as he acknowledges, not all income is reported, and he assumes that most unreported income belongs to the rich. Auten and Splinter challenge this assumption, showing that Piketty largely overlooks unreported income in the gray and black markets, which often accrues to poorer individuals.[50] When this unreported income is accounted for, the increase in the top 1 percent's income over recent decades is relatively minor, about 2.6 percent.

Second, Auten and Splinter highlight the impact of transfer payments, which Piketty underemphasizes. These payments significantly raise the income of the poor,[51] and when they are included, the growth in inequality also appears much less dramatic.[52] While this assessment depends on considering income adjusted for taxes and government benefits, it offers a more accurate metric for evaluating how the rich influence democracy. In the United States, at least, the wealthy have not prevented democracy from addressing pre-tax inequality through new tax and benefit policies. This analysis is more consistent with the finding that inequality in consumption has not grown nearly as much as inequality in income.[53]

Former senator Phil Gramm observes that income inequality may at times be exacerbated by increasing transfer payments, because these payments can diminish incentives of the poor to work.[54] In a nation like the United States, focusing on inequality of all residents, including those who have come to this country recently, also can be misleading. Immigrants, who often arrive with fewer resources than the average citizen, temporarily increase inequality within the nation even as the boost in their income, compared with what they had earned in their home nations, reduces global inequality.

Just as his empirical evidence for the substantial growth of inequality in the United States has flaws, Piketty's equation—suggesting that the rate of return on capital will always outstrip economic growth—rests on shaky assumptions. It presumes that technological advances will stagnate; but if innovation accelerates, it would boost economic growth, undermining Piketty's premise. The rapid introduction of AI across society suggests that this acceleration may well be happening. For instance, the capabilities of large language models have grown tremendously. Just a few years ago, they wrote at the level of a primary schooler. Now they are passing graduate-level exams.

Additionally, this equation contradicts a fundamental economic principle: As the amount of capital increases, its returns should diminish, much like any other factor of production. Economist Tyler Cowen likens Piketty's argument to an updated version of David Ricardo's concern that landowners would become wealthier than others because land was essential for production.[55] Yet land values have plummeted relative to other factors of production, showing the dangers of extrapolation into the future. The substantial landowners of America's nineteenth century are not numbered among the ultra-wealthy of today.

Some also have suggested that inheritance is reclaiming its dominance as a source of American wealth, yet this assertion remains unproven. Indeed, among the most visible and wealthiest Americans, inheritance is clearly declining in significance. The evidence is stark: The proportion of individuals on the Forbes 400 list who come from wealthy families has plummeted from 60 percent in 1982 to just 32 percent today.[56] Broader analyses of American wealth similarly fail to reveal any dramatic inheritance boom.[57] Even if individual inheritances have modestly increased on average, this rise can be explained simply by declining family size, which naturally boosts each heir's proportional share without necessarily increasing inheritance's overall share of national wealth. Furthermore, inherited wealth can itself enrich the political order by underwriting philanthropy, fostering artistic excellence, encouraging long-term investment, and promoting innovation. Far from threatening democratic ideals, inherited wealth contributes substantially to sustaining a vibrant and forward-looking society.

In sum, while the wealthy continue to drive economic growth, fears that they are responsible for substantially worsening inequality do not hold up well against deeper analysis. Indeed, the digital revolution of our time tempers inequality in several ways. Technology affects equality not only by minting new billionaires but also by generating a continuous stream of new ideas and products that quickly become accessible to everyone. When we surf the web or use mobile devices we benefit from countless innovations, many of which are intangible yet immensely valuable. These ideas—rather than the limited material resources required to manufacture a tablet or transmit data—constitute the lion's share of the value these gadgets bring to our lives.

Our world is transitioning from an era of physical resources to one dominated by bits, where value is increasingly derived from the information that organizes material goods. Our digital age offers a stark contrast to the experience of most human beings throughout history. For most of history, wealth was tied to land or personal property, with value derived from the costs of scarce materials and the labor required for cultivation and production. Material resources, like crude oil or land, are inherently zero-sum: Five people cannot simultaneously own the same barrel of oil or the same hectare of land. Their deployment is similarly constrained: One barrel of crude cannot heat thousands of homes and power millions of cars across different continents at the same time.

Ideas and information, however, exist in a realm that defies these limitations. Unlike physical goods, information can be shared without diminishing its value. As Thomas Jefferson eloquently noted, "He who receives an idea from me, receives instruction himself without lessening mine; as he who lights his candle at mine, receives light without darkening me."[58] This shift means we now enjoy an ever-expanding common inheritance, generating widespread benefits that mitigate the impact of income inequality. The wealth of ideas and information enhances consumption for all, softening the blow of any disparities in income growth.

Because more resources are now ideas, income gaps matter less. An infinite number of people can access the same piece of information and apply it in countless different ways, all at the same moment. The accelerating pace of technological change continues to drive down the costs of these information-based products—so much so that some, like many computer apps or much online education, are immediately free, while others rapidly become more affordable. Many software programs are soon downloadable at no cost. In this digital age, a billionaire and a member of the middle class enjoy relatively equal access to the wonders of the internet, a stark contrast to the disparity in information access in centuries past.

Economists have noted this important fact: "New, sometimes very specialized, goods appear with increasing rapidity, and free goods (such as information and entertainment services) are increasingly available at zero price, reflecting the very low marginal costs of digital replication and distribution."[59] They note that these free digital goods mean GDP rises more than the statistics show.[60] One study estimates that adding the consumer surplus Americans receive from Facebook—a service they use free of charge—would raise measured U.S. GDP by 0.11 percent per year.[61] The proliferation of such free goods available to all also tempers claims of increasing inequality.[62]

Further, cheaper manufacturing and distribution processes mean that lower-income individuals now enjoy the benefits of the latest technologies much more rapidly.[63] It took centuries after the invention of the clock for timekeeping devices to become affordable to the middle class.[64] Even as recently as the last century, refrigerators and televisions were initially luxuries available only to the relatively well-to-do. Today new technologies permeate the population far more quickly. Just five years after the introduction of the smartphone, nearly half of America's population owned one.[65] This rapid diffusion quickly turns yesterday's luxuries into mass goods as scale and learning curves cut costs, spreading benefits widely and easing concerns about inequality.

One might argue that new products and services are not truly free, given that ideas are treated as intellectual property, protected by patents and copyrights. Inventors and authors can indeed charge for their creations. However, this perspective overlooks a crucial distinction: Only the expressions of ideas are subject to intellectual property laws; the ideas themselves are not. Once a concept like a big-box store or mobile telephony is introduced, it enters the public domain. Additionally, our laws impose limits on intellectual property protections—for instance, requiring that patents describing new ideas in detail be made fully public in exchange for their protection.[66] This public disclosure provides the foundation for further advances. Even these limited protections are temporary, ultimately allowing the ideas to enter a common pool accessible to everyone.

Moreover, the rapid pace of technological change helps keep the cost of accessing these ideas low, or even nonexistent. As new products emerge, the value of slightly older products—still perfectly functional—plummets, regardless of legal protections.[67] For instance, it is possible to get used laptops of a few years' vintage for little money. The rich get the most expensive smartphone only a few years before the rest of us gain a device of the same capacity.

Modern technology not only drives innovation but also opens broad access to its fruits, further moderating concerns about inequality. Today new advances have narrowed the gap between many of the everyday experiences of the wealthy and much of the middle class. Through the internet, people of modest means now have a vast private library at their fingertips and, through services like Uber and Lyft, a chauffeur available at their beck and call. Likewise through streaming services, ordinary families can summon Broadway and symphony performances into their living rooms. Through online platforms, they retain sophisticated financial advisers once reserved for the wealthy. Through smartphones, workers at every level enjoy the seamless global communication formerly confined to corporate executives.

The fabulously wealthy do still have striking material goods, like yachts and apartments with spectacular views. But as virtual reality technology improves, the distinction between a real, material experience and a far cheaper virtual one may well blur. One can now readily envision a future where someone can virtually experience the luxury of traveling on a large yacht, an experience that was once the exclusive domain of the superrich. Consumption is dematerializing before our eyes through products that the wealthy help create. As it does, the significance of material scarcity in driving inequality diminishes.

It is not only in consumption that technological tools are equalizing but in production as well. First, traditionally, access to high-quality education, tutoring, and professional advice has been expensive and geographically concentrated.[68] AI tools, such as ChatGPT, can provide instant access to information and personalized learning assistance at little or no cost. This development enables individuals from underprivileged backgrounds or remote areas to access the same knowledge as those from wealthier or urban areas, reducing educational and skill gaps. The diffusion of such capabilities equalizes human capital and opportunity.

Second, such tools can offer initial guidance on a wide range of complex subjects, such as law and regulation. Traditionally, access to such advice has been restricted by the cost of hiring expensive professionals, but increasingly, AI systems can provide assistance for free or at a low cost, making professional knowledge more accessible to those who cannot afford traditional services. This makes it easier for people of modest means to start companies.

Third, the rapid development of specific digital tools helps bridge the skills gap for those with limited educational or technical backgrounds. For instance, Google's Career Certificates offer an inviting pathway to narrow the competency deficits in tech, supplying innovative programs not often provided by traditional educational institutions in fields like information technology support, data analytics, project management, and design for user experience. A worker with a high school diploma can complete Google's IT Support Certificate in six months and qualify for entry-level support, with over 70 percent reporting positive career outcomes. Over one million have completed certificates, and a consortium of 150 employers considers graduates for entry-level roles. Low-cost, self-paced courses without degree prerequisites and partnerships with community colleges lower barriers for jobs in high demand. These results underscore how such credentials, which ultimately stem from innovations of the wealthy, expand opportunity.[69]

This example is just one of the numerous free or low-cost methods for upgrading skills. The drive of the wealthy thus not only fuels innovation but also helps to democratize the fruits of that innovation, ensuring that its benefits extend far beyond those who initially reap the rewards.

These developments reveal that the wealthy may supply the tools that soften meritocracy's costs. Compare the wealthy in this respect to university professors. We professors largely educate people with already high natural abilities that make them an even more elite class of citizens. Even K-12 teachers at good schools are partly engaged in a sorting process to reveal where students of various talents are best placed in the educational meritocracy.

To be sure, educators play a valuable role teaching the people who later create art, advance knowledge, and lead cultural life. But these achievements do little to temper a principal criticism of meritocracy: that it deepens natural inequality by providing the best education to those with the most talent, that it creates a regulatory world that is easily navigable and legible to such graduates but increasingly opaque to others, and that it sustains barriers to opportunity through an overemphasis on credentialism. In contrast, the wealthy have founded companies that provide some tools that equalize performance between the more and less talented, reduce the costs of professional advice necessary to navigate the modern world, and offer services that build skills without expensive credentials. These aspects of an educational market system, driven by innovations of the wealthy, provide an important complement to more traditional forms of education.

By paying premium prices, the wealthy also speed untested goods to market. For example, in 1983 the first cellular phones cost four thousand dollars (about thirteen thousand dollars in today's money).[70] Now smartphones with far greater capabilities can be purchased for a fraction of that price. The trajectory of flat-screen televisions follows a similar pattern. When they first appeared, around 1997, they were prohibitively expensive, costing several thousand dollars, but today they are available for only a few hundred dollars.[71] The stories of DVDs and digital cameras echo this same trend.

The value of early adoption by the wealthy goes beyond merely covering the high costs of new technology. Early adopters take on the risk of disappointment, buying products that may fail to live up to their hype. Consider Google Glass, an innovative device that was initially expensive but ultimately discontinued after poor reviews.[72] Most early adopters ended up discarding it, having purchased frustration rather than enjoyment.

The rich are pioneers in even more extreme and expensive forms of consumption that in the long run may advance human flourishing. For instance, Bryan Johnson, a wealthy retired tech entrepreneur, spends $2 million a year trying to hold back the process of aging through a regimen of diet, exercise, medications, and health technology devices.[73] He carefully measures the results of these various therapies. Most people would have neither the resources nor the willpower to engage in his strenuous regimen. And sometimes he discontinues therapies that have proved harmful.[74] But any discoveries he makes will benefit the longevity of others.

To be sure, some social critics still believe that the consumption of the rich is dividing society more than ever. The most eloquent exponent of this view is the political philosopher Michael Sandel, who contends that wealth exacerbates social divisions and erodes the shared experiences that sustain a healthy democracy, using the metaphor of skyboxes to dramatize his argument.[75] Skyboxes, which are suites perched high above the common seating in sports stadiums, reflect, for Sandel, the physical and social segregation of the affluent from the general public. He suggests that this spatial division epitomizes a broader retreat of the wealthy from shared public life. Spaces that were once egalitarian then become stratified domains. Sandel believes that privatized goods and tiered services like first-class airline seating, gated communities, and private schools are other recent examples of this trend. These social structures, he argues, weaken the fraternity and solidarity necessary for democratic cohesion. Society then becomes more atomistic and less empathetic.

But Sandel's critique rests on an overly romantic and historically tenuous premise. The affluent have always enjoyed enclaves and status symbols that distinguish them from others. In the past, exclusive private clubs served as symbols of wealth. In fact, ships and railroads operated with explicit class divisions.[76] Such distinctions are hardly novel. Instead, they evolve with the times. Today the markers of wealth are less visible in many spaces. Silicon Valley billionaires in hoodies and jeans mingle on sidewalks. It is harder to tell the status of someone just by looking than at any time in modern history. While skyboxes may display economic stratification, the claim that they uniquely or disproportionately undermine solidarity neglects these broader cultural trends toward integration in everyday life.

Sandel overlooks the economic role that tiered services like skyboxes play in enhancing the shared experiences he values. Revenues from skyboxes subsidize the broader stadium experience. They enable teams to recruit better players and build superior facilities that benefit all fans. Ironically, skyboxes themselves often lack the best views of the game, which may be provided by seats closer to the field. Moreover, what truly unites fans is not the amenities of their seats but their shared enthusiasm for the game. Skyboxes indirectly help sustain that collective experience. The game itself, as a locus of communal feeling, remains the central thread of civic solidarity, and skyboxes, far from undermining it, contribute to its vitality.

Sandel's focus on skyboxes also misjudges the broader contributions of the wealthy to shared societal goods. While he laments the social distance of the stands, he discounts a deeper civic influence: the rich shape public life through entrepreneurship, philanthropy, and technological innovation. The medical breakthroughs, educational initiatives, and rapidly affordable technologies that they help finance generate a prosperity in which many participate. This outweighs the camaraderie of rubbing shoulders at a sporting event. Sandel's nostalgia for bygone fellowship thus risks neglecting the more important social roles of wealthy citizens.[77] It is these enduring contributions, not the seating arrangements at stadiums, that define the true democratic dividends of wealth.

One final critique of the idea that the wealthy help limit effective inequality in our technological society through the market is the claim that a more effective approach would be to improve education, thereby giving everyone an equal chance to create innovations rather than merely enjoying them. However, this argument, in its strong form, is utopian. Education certainly can and should be improved, and the wealthy, as discussed in chapter 5, are making great efforts to do so. But gaps in achievement often stem from differences in natural endowments and family environments, factors that precede formal education.[78] Intelligence, like other traits, is substantially inherited,[79] and families vary significantly in the time they devote to education-related activities at home. School performance is more closely linked to the number of books in a home than to parental income levels.[80]

Therefore, in a world where natural endowments and family environments play a substantial and intractable role in maintaining inequality in ability, the most effective way to reduce inequality in lived experience is to continue fostering innovations that make life more equitable. Ensuring the dynamism of capitalism, in which the wealthy play a pivotal role, is essential to this strategy. By driving technological progress and embracing the risks associated with early adoption, the wealthy help create a world where the benefits of novel products are increasingly accessible to all, thereby narrowing the difference in lived experience across social classes.

THE RICH AND THE SOCIAL DYNAMISM OF TECHNOLOGY

Rapid technological progress, often funded by the rich, keeps wealth from hardening into a closed elite. Innovation constantly creates new and diverse classes of wealth, each with distinct perspectives and approaches.[81] It is worth briefly detailing the enduring reasons for technological acceleration and showing how the wealthy class will remain open to newcomers.

This technological acceleration is founded on the relentless increase in the power of raw computation. The exponential growth of this capacity has reshaped journalism, the military, energy, medicine, and countless other sectors. Moore's law—named after Gordon Moore, a cofounder of Intel—captures this phenomenon by noting that the number of transistors on a computer chip doubles approximately every eighteen months to two years.[82] This observation, made in the mid-1960s, has accurately predicted the explosive growth in all aspects of the digital world, from processing power to memory capacity.[83]

Despite repeated predictions of its demise, this exponential growth has continued largely unabated.[84] The computer scientist Ray Kurzweil plausibly argues that even when silicon-based technologies reach their limits, new advances—such as those in optical or quantum computing that we are now witnessing—will sustain this growth, pushing the boundaries of what is possible even further.[85] Changes in software and connectivity magnify the overall increase in computational power, creating a cascade of advancements.

The power of this growth is difficult to overstate. As the economist Robert Lucas aptly remarked, once a person begins to grasp the implications of exponential growth, it becomes difficult to think about anything else.[86] To appreciate its impact, consider this: The smartphones of today are five thousand times faster than the supercomputers of the early 1980s.[87] This staggering increase in capability underscores the transformative force of technological advancement, driving social dynamism and reshaping the landscape of wealth and power in ways previously unimaginable.

In the 1960s, mainframes dominated computing. The 1970s saw the rise of "minicomputers," which were soon overtaken by personal computers in the 1980s. The 1990s introduced laptops, and by the 2000s smartphones emerged as the primary computing devices. It is likely that by the 2030s computers will become small enough to be routinely implanted as medical devices within the human body, further integrating technology into our very beings.[88] The computer is a revolutionary machine unlike any other, because it can enhance almost every device and nearly every human function by harnessing additional intelligence and data manipulation.

It takes great skill to be neither too early nor too late in judging whether increased computational capacity is sufficient to create a transformative product like a personal computer, internet search, or large language model. In bottling computational power into widely varying products, tech entrepreneurs generate not only economic dynamism but also social dynamism, which makes it increasingly difficult for any group—whether old money or entrenched interest groups—to manipulate the government for their own gain at the expense of others.

Unlike the rich of previous generations, today's wealthy individuals are also more likely to have interests that align with innovation and disruption, providing fresh perspectives. Their fortunes are tied to the success of new technologies that can benefit broader society. Consider how tech entrepreneurs invest both directly and philanthropically in education, renewable energy, and health care technologies. Younger people can make wealth more rapidly in the technological age. As generational attitudes shift, a new generation of the wealthy adds a new perspective.

The vigor of technological progress driven by the wealthy also helps prevent the stagnation by which established interest groups can manipulate government for their own benefit. Interest groups are often structured around existing technologies, and when these technologies evolve, it becomes more difficult for these groups to maintain their advantageous positions at the public's expense.

Take, for example, the legal profession. State bar associations have traditionally enforced rules against the practice of law by those who do not have law licenses, partly to shield lawyers from competition. However, the advent of online legal services like LegalZoom has democratized access to basic legal services, such as drafting wills, at a fraction of the usual cost. When the State Bar of Texas attempted to ban individuals from using computer software to provide basic legal services, the Texas legislature swiftly overruled the bar.[89] This is an example of how technological change disrupts entrenched interests, making it more difficult for them to resist innovations that benefit the broader public.

Similarly, platforms like Uber and Airbnb have challenged traditional industries such as taxi services and hotels. Established companies had strong lobbying power and regulatory protections. However, the emergence of these platforms mobilized consumers to demand changes in regulations, often forcing traditional players to adapt or innovate. In many cities, regulations that favored established companies were overturned in favor of more competitive and consumer-friendly options.

The rise of telemedicine has challenged traditional health care delivery models.[90] Established health care providers often resisted changes that would disrupt their business models. However, the COVID-19 pandemic accelerated the adoption of telehealth, leading to increased access for patients and new regulatory frameworks that prioritize convenience and cost-effectiveness. This shift has prompted traditional health care systems to experiment and adapt to remain competitive. In all of these ways, the wealthy translate technological progress into a social landscape where vested interests find it increasingly challenging to block the widespread distribution of the benefits of these innovations.

The rich are indispensable to the vitality of America's commercial republic. They renew its foundations again and again. They finance bold experiments that become common tools. Those bets catalyze breakthroughs, diffusing privilege and pulling yesterday's luxuries into everyday life. Their ventures seed competition and keep markets fluid. Incumbents cannot coast; no dynasty holds the field for long. That dynamism protects liberty and expands opportunity. They also model the virtues a commercial society needs: independence, prudence, ambition, and a willingness to invest in the future.

CHAPTER 8

◇◇◇◇◇◇◇◇◇◇◇◇◇◇◇◇

AMERICA'S PHILANTHROPIC REPUBLIC

America was founded not only as a commercial republic but also as a nation where civil society would play an important role in strengthening democracy and delivering public goods. America's philanthropic republic stemmed naturally from both the structural and sociological features of its democracy. Structurally, the federal government and most state governments were designed to move slowly and deliberately. Mandating bicameralism and the presidential veto requires consensus before the government can provide public goods, and that consensus takes time and sometimes cannot be achieved.

Sociologically, American culture is associative. As Alexis de Tocqueville observed, it was uniquely shaped by voluntary civil associations.[1] These associations often supply public goods and confer further essential benefits. Tocqueville noted, and contemporary political theorists continue to emphasize, that civic associations advance democracy by making people fitter for democratic life.[2] Through hands-on involvement in public-spirited missions, individuals become more tolerant and engaged citizens. These associations also supplement state action, providing essential public goods in education and social welfare. Civil society can often be more innovative and efficient than a bureaucratic state.

Today, as in Tocqueville's day, the wealthy remain central in providing services and maintaining civic associations across the country. The rich possess not only the financial assets but also the extensive networks necessary to overcome the free-rider problem that hinders both the private provision of public goods and the formation of associations. Far from detracting from democracy, the wealthy provide a significant benefit by supporting one of its most essential foundations. The importance of the rich in sustaining civic associations and public goods may be greater today than ever before for two reasons. First, the time spent on entertainment in modern society routinely drains away the time and energy needed to bolster civic enterprises. Second, the scale at which many civic associations and public goods must now operate has expanded, requiring resources that only the wealthy can readily provide, both as a substitute for volunteer time and to sustain the necessary size and scope of these organizations. This chapter first considers the rich and civic associations, then the rich and public goods more generally.

HOW CIVIC ASSOCIATIONS HELP CONSTITUTE AMERICA

Several forces made civil society far more vital in America than in Europe, from which the founders of our nation originally came.

First, the necessity of privately associating was born of material conditions. America was a frontier society where government was often absent, and people had to rely on themselves and their communities. As an immigrant society, America also saw various ethnic groups forming associations to provide mutual support in an unfamiliar and sometimes hostile world.

Second, the timing of America's birth played a significant role. The United States was founded during the Enlightenment, an era that emphasized individual liberty, reason, and self-improvement. These values naturally led to a focus on voluntary associations for social uplift, particularly in areas like education, seen as essential for fostering reason and progress.

The U.S. Constitution further contributed to this civic dynamism by fragmenting government both horizontally and vertically. Federalism allowed for competition among states, enabling citizens to relocate to states whose government provided a better environment for their families and businesses. This mobility ensured that while government overreach could be curtailed, voluntary civil society could still provide necessary public goods without driving people away. Additionally, the separation of powers at the national level often leads to divided government, making it difficult for the federal government to reach a consensus on new public initiatives. Civil society, however, remains unaffected by these governmental stalemates, continuing to provide public goods and sustain the community even when the state cannot.

Famously, Alexis de Tocqueville regarded civic associations as the lifeblood of American democracy. Tocqueville argued that America was unique in its citizens' "continuous use of the right of association in civil life," through which they secured "all the goods that civilization can offer."[3] This propensity for forming civic associations yielded numerous benefits for democracy. Voluntary civil associations equipped citizens with the habits and skills necessary to resist tyranny. As Tocqueville observed, "If each citizen...does not learn the art of uniting with those like him to defend [democracy], tyranny will necessarily grow with equality."[4] Only associations formed in civil life—a core element of civil society—could effectively serve this protective role.

These organizations also instilled the habits of collaboration for common enterprises, fostering a sense of fellow feeling and sympathy among participants that transcends politics. Tocqueville warned that if men in democratic societies possessed neither the right nor the inclination to unite in pursuit of political goals, their independence would be at great risk.[5] Indeed, if citizens failed to "acquire the practice of associating with each other in ordinary life, civilization itself would be in peril."[6] Civic associations were thus inextricably linked to the progress of civilization because, as Tocqueville put it, "the science of association is the mother science; the progress of all the others depends on the progress of that one."[7]

As Tocqueville observed, civic associations, both religious and secular, also temper the materialism and self-interested individualism of a commercial republic by requiring people to work together toward aims that rise above personal gain. Harvey Mansfield succinctly captured this idea: "Associations draw men from the private ease of individualism into public activity, engaging their self-interest and their ambition while promoting the public good."[8]

Tocqueville also recognized the commercial corporation as another kind of association where individuals acquire the habits of cooperating for shared ends, thereby modeling the mores essential to a democratic society.[9] This advantage of association in enterprise extends beyond wealth creation, for it cultivates the civic virtues that sustain democratic flourishing. In this way, civic associations and corporations alike reinforce the moral and social fabric of a free society, ensuring that citizens remain active participants in the common enterprise of self-governance.[10]

Tocqueville was thus skeptical that government could ever replicate the benefits provided by associations: "A government could take the place of some of the greatest American associations, and within the Union several particular states already have attempted it. But what political power would ever be in a state to suffice for the innumerable multitude of small undertakings that American citizens execute every day with the aid of an association?"[11]

When Alexis de Tocqueville toured America in the 1830s, he was struck by the nation's do-it-yourself spirit; townspeople formed reading clubs, fire brigades, and school committees with hardly a penny from government coffers.[12] But much has changed. Formal volunteering has drifted downward for half a century, and Americans are now ten percentage points less likely to volunteer than they were in the mid-1970s. Civic engagement more generally has also fallen.

As a result, the actions of the rich are more important than ever to fill the gap and to provide the infrastructure for civic associations as well as public goods. Households in the top 1 percent now supply about one-third of all charitable dollars in the United States, and private foundations send more than $100 billion a year to nonprofit groups across the nation.[13] In effect, the wealthy underwrite projects that Tocqueville's neighborhood committees once shouldered and supply focal points for connection and association among citizens. By building firms such as Google with distinctive cultures and strong employee ties, they add another node of association.

THE RICH, CIVIC ASSOCIATIONS, AND PUBLIC GOODS IN EARLY AMERICA

Throughout the early history of the United States, the wealthy played a pivotal role in using civic associations to provide important public goods. One striking example is the Pennsylvania Hospital, founded in 1751 by a group of affluent merchants, including Dr. Thomas Bond and Benjamin Franklin. This institution was the first hospital in the nation, created "to care for the sick-poor and insane who were wandering the streets of Philadelphia."[14] The hospital quickly became a beacon of medical progress, housing the first surgical amphitheater, hospital apothecary, and medical library in the country.[15] Massachusetts General Hospital followed soon after, with wealthy citizens once again at the helm. Their contributions went beyond mere financial support; they were instrumental in conceptualizing a solution to a collective problem, providing both the vision and the means for the community to build the hospital.[16] These early examples demonstrate how the rich used their resources not just for personal gain but also to address the pressing needs of society.

The Metropolitan Museum of Art in New York traces its origins to 1866 in Paris, where a group of wealthy Americans resolved to create a "national institution and gallery of art" to bring art and art education to the American people. John Jay II, the grandson of John Jay, the first chief justice, spearheaded the project upon his return from France. Under his leadership, the Union League Club in New York rallied businessmen, art collectors, and philanthropists to the cause, ultimately realizing the vision of a great American art institution.[17]

Beyond founding hospitals and museums, the wealthy were also critical in founding associations for causes that were, at the time, deeply unpopular. The Manumission Society, which sought the end of slavery in New York, was supported by some of the wealthiest merchants of the era, including John Murray Jr. and John Jay. It was a precursor to the abolitionist movement discussed in chapter 6. The work of the society began with protests against the widespread practice of kidnapping Black New Yorkers—both enslaved and free—and selling them into slavery elsewhere. Its advocacy culminated in the passage of the 1799 law granting gradual manumission to New York's slaves. The society also provided legal assistance to both free and enslaved Blacks who were subjected to abuse, showing how the rich often leveraged their influence and resources to champion associations for justice and equality, even when the weight of opinion was massed against such causes.[18]

While many of these civic associations were elite and supported public goods and causes largely favored by elite opinion, the rich have provided the infrastructure for civic associations that drew in volunteerism and activism from the broader population. For instance, the Young Men's Christian Association was an example of a nineteenth-century association that spanned classes, but often depended on the support of the wealthy. In Philadelphia, the department-store innovator John Wanamaker underwrote the handsome six-story Arch Street branch completed in 1907.[19] In my own city of Chicago, the first YMCA building, Farwell Hall, was paid for by dry-goods wholesaler John V. Farwell.[20] The wealthy were important to local associations. Hull House in Chicago became a society of volunteers from all classes who helped immigrants and other groups living at the margins of respectability.[21] The house itself was donated by Helen Culver, cousin of the original owner, and the society was supported by other wealthy contributors.[22]

The rich also provided money for local institutions for educational and cultural self-improvement. For instance, George Peabody established an eponymous institution that included a free public library, an art gallery, a lecture hall, and a music conservatory open to all.[23] When it opened in the early 1860s, the Peabody Institute offered concerts, art exhibits, and lectures that attracted Baltimoreans of every social class.[24] On the other side of the country, the Mechanics' Institute of San Francisco had many of the same functions.[25] Its initial flourishing was supported by the major real-estate developer, James Lick.[26]

These examples underscore the profound impact of the wealthy in shaping the public institutions and moral direction of the early United States. Their contributions were not merely acts of charity but were foundational in building the civic infrastructure. Through their efforts, they helped establish a culture of philanthropy and public service that continues to benefit society today.

THE RICH AND TODAY'S CIVIC ASSOCIATIONS

Civic associations remain as vital today as they were in Tocqueville's time, serving as crucial checks on government power
and providing public goods that the state cannot match in
efficiency or innovation. However, the volunteerism that once
fueled a vibrant array of nonprofit organizations and civic
associations has waned in the modern era. Robert Putnam, in
Bowling Alone, meticulously documented this decline in communal engagement. He observed that "for the first two-thirds
of the twentieth century a powerful tide bore Americans into
ever deeper engagement in the life of their communities, but a
few decades ago—silently, without warning—that tide reversed,
and we were overtaken by a treacherous rip current."[27] This
retreat from collective action poses a significant challenge to
the continued vitality of civic associations and the democratic
values they uphold.

The reasons for the decline in civic engagement are complex
and multifaceted. Putnam attributes much of this shift to the
rise of entertainment, an explanation he offered even before the
pervasive presence of cell phones and streaming services.[28] Today
our virtual world is more isolating and less communal than the
physical spaces we once shared. Some suggest that people are
simply working harder and have less time to volunteer. But
this claim conflicts with evidence showing that Americans, on
average, now have more discretionary time than ever before,
particularly with labor-saving devices for household chores.[29]

In response to the decline of volunteering, the role of
the wealthy in founding and sustaining civic associations has
grown more crucial than ever as financial resources increasingly

substitute for the time that people are less willing or able to give. For example, the more funding a hospital receives, the less it needs volunteers for staffing children's playrooms and other auxiliary activities, as paid staff can be hired to fill these roles. However, though money can provide essential public goods like health care, it cannot wholly replicate the civic engagement that fosters and sustains democratic participation.

Nonetheless, philanthropy can still play a beneficent role in revitalizing volunteerism by making it more enjoyable and personally rewarding. Civic organizations can invest in volunteer training, equipping individuals with skills that benefit both their charitable work and personal lives. For instance, Habitat for Humanity offers extensive training in construction and repair, skills that volunteers can apply beyond their community service.[30] Additionally, financial resources can be used to recognize and reward volunteers, offering gifts and creating pleasant environments for networking activities. The Nature Conservancy, for example, leads its volunteers on nature walks and organizes forums where participants can learn from leading scientists and experts.[31] Wealthy foundations, such as the Chan Zuckerberg Initiative, also contribute by providing paid time off for employees to volunteer, thereby encouraging civic engagement through both time and resources.[32] In this way, philanthropy helps compensate for the decline in volunteerism.

The wealthy not support only existing civic organizations but have also founded new ones. For instance, Paul Tudor Jones, a billionaire hedge fund manager, established the Robin Hood Foundation to combat poverty and provide economic opportunity in New York.[33] This foundation not only provides grants to community groups but also organizes tens of thousands of volunteers to further its mission.

The Boys and Girls Clubs of America, originally founded as the Boys Clubs of America over 150 years ago to nurture youth, has continued to evolve and expand its mission. However, to remain relevant in the modern world, it has needed new resources. Foundations like those established by DeWitt and Lila Acheson Wallace, founders of *Reader's Digest*, and Charles Schwab, founder of the eponymous brokerage house, have contributed significantly to this cause.[34] Like the Robin Hood Foundation, the Boys and Girls Clubs of America serves as a hub for volunteerism, a role that would be greatly diminished without such substantial financial contributions. Similarly, MacKenzie Scott, the former wife of Amazon founder Jeff Bezos, gave $281 million to the Boys and Girls Clubs of America, making it the largest gift in their 160-year history.[35] She parceled out $400 million among more than forty YMCA associations.[36] Just as wealthy philanthropists in the nineteenth century built up the YMCA, they sustain it in the twenty-first century.

THE RICH AND CHARITABLE PUBLIC GOODS

Even beyond strengthening civic organizations, the wealthy create charities that address needs both local and national. Private charitable initiatives often possess distinct advantages over government programs when it comes to providing public goods and addressing social issues. While both private and public sectors aim to enhance societal welfare, private charity can fill gaps that government programs, constrained by bureaucracy, cannot reach.

Private support for public goods can meet needs that state programs too often leave unmet. First, private organizations enjoy greater flexibility. Private actors are better able to mobilize resources with dispatch because they do not have bureaucratic mandates.[37] As a result, where government agencies are slowed down by red tape, private charities can deliver aid better when speed matters most. They have more adaptability and can quickly reset priorities to track evolving community needs. Their capacity to recalibrate lets them make changes in their programs more rapidly. They can scale up or discontinue initiatives as conditions warrant. By contrast, public programs can be slow and resistant to revision. Political incentives and entrenched interests thwart all-too-many initiatives. Thus, private charity can often get more things done with a similar amount of money.

Second, such nonprofits typically operate with superior efficiency.[38] Accountable to donors who closely scrutinize their performance, these organizations face pressure to minimize overhead and maximize effectiveness, ensuring that resources reach their intended beneficiaries. In foundations funded and governed by a small number of individuals, the incentive for careful oversight is especially pronounced. More inspired by business than government, private charities adopt streamlined operations and employ rigorous metrics to assess both inputs and results. They function as a sharpened scalpel compared with government's blunter instruments.

Third, charities can have longer time horizons than government. Government may look for short-term payoffs because politicians must face reelection. But the wealthy and their foundations have the independence to take the longer view.[39] Some public goods, like medical and scientific research, take a long time to bear fruit.

A fourth advantage of private provision lies in its insulation from political disruption. Even when political shifts reduce official commitments, Gates Foundation resources sustained immunization efforts without significant interruptions, advancing the fight against polio and other diseases in developing nations. While private resources alone cannot replace governmental support, they can buffer critical programs from political volatility.

Finally, the ability to innovate and take risks further distinguishes private charity. Wealthy donors and their foundations are often willing to invest in experimental solutions to social problems, venturing into uncharted territory that government programs, beholden to taxpayers and voters, hesitate to explore. When a foundation remains under the guidance of its entrepreneurial founder, it frequently mirrors the bold, risk-taking spirit that originally amassed the wealth. This mindset drives private charities to test new approaches to public goods, much like it did to transform industries, while government programs, constrained by political caution, remain rooted in conventional methods.

The wealthy are the linchpin of private charity. They continue to provide immense philanthropic support, significantly aiding both the production of public goods and the promotion of volunteer activities through various organizations. The top 1.4 percent contribute 86 percent of all charitable bequests.[40] Notably, around one hundred American billionaires, including some of the wealthiest, such as Elon Musk, Bill Gates, and Warren Buffett, have pledged to give away the majority of their fortunes.[41] This commitment aligns with the perspective of early modern political philosophers who welcomed the growth of private wealth, believing it fosters the virtue of magnanimity.[42]

These raw numbers, however, understate the true impact of the rich on philanthropy. The very wealthy have the capacity to give large sums that can ignite the creation of new organizations or revitalize those that have fallen on hard times. They can make long-term commitments, providing a stable foundation around which civic and charitable organizations can plan their future endeavors. Such long-term commitments make it more likely that others of more modest means will give because they become more confident that charity has long-term viability.

A prime national example of charitable experimentation from the wealthy comes from Michael Bloomberg. Bloomberg's time as mayor of New York City infused his philanthropic strategy with a special focus on cities, given his commitment to urban reform.[43] His foundation's central mission is to equip cities with the tools to implement evidence-based policies that transform public services. One initiative, What Works Cities, epitomizes Bloomberg's campaign to make governance empirical. The program equips municipalities to use metrics to discipline policy, improving the efficiency and results of public services.[44] A companion effort, the Mayor's Challenge, invites cities to test novel answers to urban problems and backs the most promising entries with money and support.[45] In combination, Bloomberg's philanthropy presses city halls to convert ambition into measurable gains.

The wealthy do not confine their philanthropy to the national or international stage; they also invest deeply in localities to which they are personally connected. Take the Gateses' efforts to combat homelessness in Seattle, the city where Bill Gates was raised.[46] Characteristically, Gates Foundation initiatives brought new ideas to the forefront. Among its original contributions was the coordination of housing services for homeless families.[47] Its system does not shunt families through fragmented referrals. Instead, a single entry point now assesses needs. The reform improved on the former bureaucratic maze for families, even if general homelessness persisted. No less notable was the program's focus on data. Real-time metrics tested which interventions worked and doubled annual exits of families to permanent housing. Over time, that information may help deliver services with greater care and precision.[48] Gates, a tech billionaire, naturally emphasized data transparency and accountability, ensuring that public and nonprofit agencies could pivot their strategies based on hard evidence. As Gates has done in the tech world, so too in philanthropy. This kind of focus illustrates the benefits of permitting the wealthy to transfer to the public sphere the energies and talents that brought them riches.

Headquartered in Battle Creek, Michigan—the birthplace of the fortune that seeded it—the Kellogg Foundation shows the same kind of local focus, concentrating on early childhood education and supports for families. It has invested heavily in high-quality preschool to close achievement gaps in its home community.[49] One of the most striking innovations of the Kellogg Foundation's work in Battle Creek is its holistic approach to community development. Unlike government efforts that may be hobbled by bureaucratic fiefdoms, the foundation addresses interwoven challenges—education, health, and economic opportunity—not in isolation but as parts of a unified whole.[50]

To describe such initiatives is not to endorse all of their programs. But social policy improves by trial and error. The wealthy expand the range of public goods that permit progress in policy over time. Their current focus on rigorous evaluation of results makes it even more likely that their initiatives will have beneficial effects beyond the citizens directly served by their programs. And the rich also provide public goods whose benefits hardly need evaluation. For instance, recently a group of wealthy donors from New York contributed the lion's share of funds for creating a pool and skating complex at the north end of Central Park, the city's premier public land. The recreation area is a public good that serves a largely poor and minority community, far from the area where affluent New Yorkers live. This project, like many other recent ones in the city, shows how the philanthropy of the rich is not limited to public goods that cater chiefly to the well-off.[51]

THE RICH AND AMERICAN UNIVERSITIES

American universities, in particular, owe much of their global preeminence to the generosity of the wealthy. Regularly topping world rankings, these institutions, including sixteen of the top twenty universities in the *U.S. News & World Report* survey,[52] thrive in no small part due to their substantial endowments.

Harvard, with its nearly $50 billion endowment, is among the richest nonprofit institutions in the world by liquid financial assets.[53] Many other top universities boast endowments exceeding $10 billion.[54] Even some state universities, like the University of California and University of Texas, manage very significant endowments.

These financial reserves enable universities to attract leading scholars from across the globe and to invest in long-term projects that allow them to adapt to rapid changes in the world. To be sure, as discussed in chapter 3, many universities do not nurture and model civic discourse as they once did, because of their ideological monoculture. Yet, at least in the natural sciences, American universities still deliver the goods. These institutions dominate in producing Nobel laureates whose groundbreaking research lays the foundation for technological advancements that enrich society and extend human life.[55] For producing and disseminating knowledge, the private nonprofit status of most great American universities has proved to be a superior model to the government control that characterizes most other universities across the globe.

Maintaining America's leadership in technological innovation is not merely an academic concern but a matter of national security. As China rapidly advances in both basic research and technology, securing more patents each year and earning recognition for its universities, the stakes are high.[56] The most important war between China and the United States is the knowledge contest, and funding our private universities through philanthropy is as important a weapon as any in the contemporary arsenal of democracy.

The wealthy are essential to sustaining the strength of America's elite universities. Their philanthropy ensures that American institutions continue to top global rankings, providing public goods through scientific education, discovery, and the preparation of future civic and democratic leaders. However, the influence of the wealthy extends beyond mere funding; they are crucial in overseeing these institutions, ensuring they remain true to their missions. Unlike for-profit organizations, nonprofits lack the clear metrics of profit and loss to gauge success, making it challenging to hold leaders accountable. This absence of financial benchmarks can lead to mission drift as various stakeholders, including students, faculty, and administrators, attempt to steer the organization toward their own interests. Wealthy donors and patrons, with their financial resources and social clout, possess the unique ability to intervene, fostering debates and refocusing attention when an organization strays from its intended purpose.

Recent events have highlighted the importance of this oversight, particularly at elite universities. These institutions face significant governance challenges, exacerbated by their immense wealth. The reputations of these universities are so entrenched that market forces can change their behavior at only a glacial pace.

In this context, the role of the wealthy becomes even more vital. Their involvement is not just about providing financial support but also about ensuring that these institutions adhere to the principles of academic freedom, diversity of thought, and intellectual rigor. By doing so, they help preserve the integrity of the very institutions that are foundational to a thriving democratic society.

The governance structures at many elite private universities are so insular that genuine accountability from within the institution is nearly nonexistent. Boards of trustees, which are supposed to provide oversight, are often self-perpetuating entities. When a trustee retires, the remaining members handpick the successor, ensuring the continuation of a closed circle. While a few elite institutions reserve some trustee positions for alumni elections, these elections are not truly open. Candidates are typically selected by nominating committees that are closely aligned with the university administration. Although it is technically possible for an insurgent candidate to challenge the slate, the chances of success are slim. For instance, Yale saw its first such challenge in 2021—after nearly two decades of uncontested elections.[57]

This restricted selection process results in boards that are often ideologically homogeneous, despite superficial diversity in ethnicity or gender. Elite universities, sitting on vast endowments, have not historically had to appease their largest donors by offering them trustee positions. Instead, they can curate their boards much like an exclusive club, wary of admitting anyone who might disrupt the consensus with fundamental disagreements. Without the profit motive, trustees derive satisfaction from social reinforcement—the comfort of being surrounded by like-minded individuals who share their worldview. Furthermore, the allure of serving on the board of trustees at such prestigious institutions can lead to inherent conflicts of interest. Trustees may hesitate to challenge the status quo, motivated by the desire to maintain good relationships with fellow board members or secure preferential admissions for their children and grandchildren.

Consider the example of Harvard, where the twelve-member Harvard Corporation hired Claudine Gay as president in 2023. The board included President Obama's former commerce secretary, another former Obama official, and a Democratic appointee to the California Supreme Court, now leading a left-wing foundation.[58] Ninety-nine percent of campaign contributions from the corporation's members went to Democrats.[59] Such homogeneity breeds the potential for serious mistakes, as the lack of diverse ideological and experiential perspectives can lead to poor decision-making. In these circumstances, outside pressure from wealthy alumni is the most likely source of corrective action. Though the media could theoretically serve as another check, the modern mainstream press often shares the same ideological leanings as university administrators and faculty. Consequently, while they may report on university controversies, they are less inclined to engage in the kind of investigative journalism they reserve for for-profit corporations and government institutions.

Recent events at Harvard and the University of Pennsylvania vividly illustrate how external pressure, particularly from the wealthy, can hold university leadership accountable. At Harvard, Claudine Gay's January 2024 resignation was precipitated in no small part by billionaire Bill Ackman, who publicly challenged her leadership on multiple fronts. First, he criticized her tepid response to the October 2023 Hamas attack on Israel, especially when contrasted with her much stronger statements regarding the killing of George Floyd. Second, Ackman pointed out Gay's attempts to defend hate speech against Israel as potentially protected by free speech, even as Harvard was ranked last among major universities in defending free speech overall. Third, possible instances of plagiarism were discovered in her academic work, which was already less prolific and impressive compared with that of her Harvard colleagues, let alone past presidents. Ackman's campaign against Gay was amplified by the social media platform X, demonstrating how wealthy individuals can leverage their resources and influence to expose inadequacies that might otherwise remain hidden.[60]

Harvard's board made a poor choice in appointing Gay as president, seemingly prioritizing the promotion of diversity, equity, and inclusion over Harvard's core mission of truth-seeking through rigorous meritocracy. Ackman's example highlights how the rich, unencumbered by fears of job loss or social ostracization, can take on the difficult task of monitoring elite institutions, often succeeding where others cannot. To be sure, others, like Aaron Sibarium of the *Washington Free Beacon*, played a role in changing the leadership at Harvard. But without Ackman's relentless social media campaign, Harvard might still be struggling under this misguided leadership.

A similar dynamic unfolded at the University of Pennsylvania. There, President Liz Magill contended she was following free speech principles in permitting slogans on campus that could be construed as calls for the destruction of Israel. But the claim of acting on principle appeared to be undermined by her actions. For instance, it was revealed that she had approved harsh penalties against Amy Wax, a professor at the university's law school and an outspoken critic of racial preferences, in part, for making statements protected by free speech, exposing a double standard in the university's approach that depended on the ideological valence of expression.[61] In the aftermath of her testimony, major donors, from Marc Rowan to Ronald Lauder, were successful in calling for her resignation.[62]

The structure of university governance often makes it difficult to hold leaders accountable without external pressure. The forced changes in leadership at these two prestigious universities have sent a clear message throughout the world of higher education, altering the incentives for university presidents and compelling boards of trustees to reevaluate how well their administrations are fulfilling their core missions.

But, again, the rich do not only support causes at universities that are favored by the political right. When the Trump administration threatened to withhold grants from Harvard University, wealthy supporters became sources of support for Harvard.[63] Their independence made possible by their resources supports the independence of universities from the government—on this occasion a government that donors saw as pressing for another kind of conformity.

Private mediating institutions in areas like education and the arts play an essential role in democracy by distributing power beyond government, providing public goods, and promoting excellence. However, mediating institutions can sometimes lose sight of their missions or fall prey to corruption. In such cases, the wealthy, with their independence and resources, are uniquely positioned to serve as self-correcting mechanisms for institutions that have strayed from their core purpose under the pressure of their administrators or employees. Unlike government, whose coercive power is ill-suited for tasks requiring judgment and nuance, the rich can better provide the oversight and support needed to maintain the integrity of these vital civic organizations.

CRITICISM OF THE RICH IN PHILANTHROPY

Following the ousters of the college presidents at Harvard and the University of Pennsylvania, some journalists decried the clout of "loud billionaires" who, in their view, wielded their wealth as a form of undue power.[64] They lamented that figures like Gay and Magill, with less job security in their roles as university presidents, were at a disadvantage, suggesting an uneven playing field. However, such complaints are misguided. Gay and Magill, despite stepping down from their presidencies, continue to enjoy highly compensated positions as professors at elite institutions. More crucially, the criticism overlooks the significant accountability issues inherent in the governance of nonprofit organizations, particularly at our most prestigious universities. Without the intervention of the wealthy, who are often the only ones with the freedom and resources to raise alarms, universities are far less likely to correct course when they stray from their missions. One cannot depend on professors, who are often ideologically aligned with current administrations, have more to lose professionally, and are not as inclined to challenge the status quo.

Some critics argue more generally that substantial philanthropy from the wealthy is inherently undemocratic. This argument, however, is difficult to credit. The United States has allowed charitable donations since its founding, with no significant public outcry against this practice.[65] In fact, tax laws have encouraged charitable giving by permitting deductions since the beginning of the income tax, and these laws are, of course, democratically enacted.[66] The criticism also neglects the many benefits that Tocqueville identified in the provision of public goods by civic associations, which often rely on the support of the wealthy to flourish.

Moreover, there is no reason to accept the assumption underlying this criticism: that government alone should or could effectively fund all necessary public goods if it had more resources. While the government indeed plays a crucial role in providing certain public goods, the question is not whether government provision should be eliminated but whether private contributions offer additional advantages. Both theory and evidence suggest that a combination of government and private provision of public goods is superior to government action alone. Private individuals often possess knowledge of specific needs that government may overlook, and private organizations can operate without the bureaucratic constraints that sometimes hamper government efficiency. Furthermore, private philanthropy can circumvent very powerful special interest groups that might obstruct the provision of valuable public goods. For example, school choice programs, which have been supported by wealthy philanthropists, might never have received government funding due to opposition from powerful teachers' unions if they had not gotten seed capital from the wealthy.

Private charities also often possess a keener ability to monitor their performance than government initiatives. While it is true that nonprofit organizations can drift from their missions, government is often at great risk of failure. The government, beset by bureaucratic inertia, frequently does not effectively monitor programs or dismantle those that underperform. Government provision of public goods creates a web of beneficiaries and stakeholders—classic concentrated interests—that can sustain a program even when it no longer serves the public interest.

Consider farm subsidies, which have long cost taxpayers money, distorted markets, and benefited wealthy farmers.[67] Yet they have resisted termination for decades due to entrenched interests. Similarly, the U.S. Department of Commerce's Advanced Technology Program, established in 1993, persisted for nearly two decades despite clear evidence that it funded projects with little commercial viability.[68] A visit to any post office reveals a kind of time warp, where outdated equipment and a stagnant atmosphere underscore the U.S. Postal Service's inability to adapt to innovations in the digital age, hamstrung by special interests and a lack of accountability.

Other critics argue that allowing the rich to direct their vast resources toward charitable initiatives grants them disproportionate sway over the trajectory of social change. The philanthropy of the rich is also said to merely address the superficial symptoms of social injustice rather than the deeper mechanisms of inequality that facilitate wealth accumulation.

These critiques, however, are merely modern iterations of age-old complaints about the impact of the wealthy—complaints that have been addressed in preceding chapters. The concern about influence erroneously assumes that in the absence of the wealthy, no other group would dominate the public square. Yet, as is evident, many other groups, such as academics, journalists, and special interest groups, exert equal or greater influence on public discourse. In this context, the wealthy provide a necessary counterweight. Notably, philanthropic efforts by the rich—whether funding university centers for heterodox thought or advocating for labor-market deregulation—offer a balancing force against the entrenched agendas of these powerful groups.

Additionally, the claim that the wealthy address only surface-level issues while ignoring the root causes of inequality is itself a matter of profound dispute. The question of what truly constitutes the "root causes" of social problems is highly contested, and the influence of academics and activists often skews this debate. Without the financial support of the rich, our range of ideas and initiatives to solve social problems would be impoverished. Moreover, contrary to claims that the rich avoid systemic critiques, many of their foundations fund initiatives aligned with left-wing ideals that advocate for deep societal changes. Consider George Soros's Open Society Foundations, which supports the Movement for Black Lives and other groups advocating for radical reform in policing and incarceration,[69] or the Ford Foundation, which funds left-leaning social justice movements, including those for workers' rights and gender equality.[70] Their openness to such causes is not surprising, because the wealthy have diverse views about politics and society, including views that accept the need to get at the "root causes" that left-liberals believe are the sources of injustice.

Democracy is not built at the polls alone. It thrives in the Tocquevillian web of associations that stand between citizen and state. The wealthy sustain these mediating institutions. They fund public goods, thicken social trust, and school the virtues of self-rule. Their part is not mere largesse. Their independence guards these bodies from political pressure, and their stewardship recalls them to mission when they drift. Without that support, our civic lattice frays and democracy weakens.

CHAPTER 9

⟨⟨⟨⟨⟨⟨⟨⟨⟨⟨⟨⟨⟨⟨⟨⟨⟨

THE RICH IN LIBERAL
AND ILLIBERAL DEMOCRACY

The American political order is not merely a democracy but a liberal democracy. The rich contribute even more significantly to this compound system than to democracy narrowly conceived. However, the question arises whether conservatives, particularly those aligned with the New Right, who have become skeptical of liberal democracy, should be wary of the wealthy's influence in preserving its liberal nature. At least for now, such conservatives may have little choice but to rely on the rich, as they lack another elite class that may advance their objectives.

THE RICH AND LIBERAL DEMOCRACY

Marrying liberalism and democracy is a complex endeavor because it requires balancing two forces that can strengthen one another and yet be at odds. Liberalism is primarily concerned with safeguarding individual rights and nurturing a culture that allows those rights to flourish. In contrast, democracy is about empowering governance by the people and cultivating the culture necessary for collective decision-making. Yet, America's social system has long been described as a liberal democracy, not merely a democracy, because it strives to protect both individual rights and collective self-government. Liberalism and democracy as a practical matter can reinforce one another. Democracy protects rights by diffusing power across a wide array of citizens. Conversely, rights help protect democracy by giving citizens the independent resources and capacities to check rulers who might undermine it.

Since the eighteenth century, liberalism has pursued inter-related projects aimed at its overarching goal: human autonomy in the ordinary course of life.[1] One such project is the scientific and technological effort to free humans from nature's constraints, expanding autonomy across space, time, and public and private domains.[2] Another is preserving a free market that enables entrepreneurial autonomy and supports technology by fostering innovation and spreading its fruits more widely.[3] A third is limited government, which not only shields the market from predation but, in some circumstances, also facilitates and guides its proper functioning within modern constitutional orders.[4] Last, liberalism cultivates a culture of tolerance, respect for rights, and the rule of law, norms that temper majorities and sustain liberty. This culture underpins autonomy by allowing individuals to plan their lives while maintaining the necessary constraints on governmental power.[5]

In a liberal democracy, individuals enjoy the freedom to pursue their own ventures as long as they do not harm others. Contrary to claims that the wealthy undermine liberal democracy, the wealthy, in fact, continuously bring the ideals of liberalism to life in service of a democratic culture. As discussed in chapter 7, they generate wealth, thereby stabilizing democracy. They help sustain civic life, providing the essential infrastructure of democracy. They also model greatness through their achievements and support for the arts, countering the culture of mediocrity that theorists like Tocqueville have long warned is an inherent risk of the egalitarian impulse that accompanies democracy.

Liberal democracy rests on the twin pillars of civil rights and property rights. The influence of the wealthy, when combined with that of academics, journalists, and entertainers, provides a robust foundation for upholding both sets of rights. By their nature and interests, the knowledge class tends to champion civil rights, such as those enshrined in the First Amendment. Free speech, after all, is crucial to their livelihood and sustains the culture of discourse they hold dear. Conversely, the wealthy, who benefit from and are deeply familiar with property rights in their daily lives, are more inclined to use their power to protect that aspect of democracy. This is not to suggest that individuals from both groups cannot care about both types of rights but rather, that this division of focus and interest helps guarantee that there will always be a strong social foundation for supporting both categories of rights.

Some recent attacks on the wealthy are less concerned with the harm they might cause and more focused on the personal ventures that their wealth enables. These critiques, which target the very autonomy that liberalism seeks to protect, are worth examining closely because they may signal a broader threat to individual freedom in liberal democracy. The rich, being easily scapegoated, may well be the first group whose pursuits are restricted without evidence of harm—canaries in the coal mine warning of danger to others. Ingrid Robeyns, for example, expresses hostility to some personal projects of the rich in her book *Limitarianism*, calling for a ceiling on personal wealth. She prides herself on living modestly as an academic, and dismisses people with different ambitions. She labels endeavors like buying Twitter (now X) or developing space tourism as "absurd."[6] However, in a liberal society, the state should not curb people's enterprises merely because others find them absurd.

There are, in fact, thoughtful and substantial reasons behind these so-called absurd ventures. Elon Musk acquired Twitter with the serious intent of promoting free speech and inquiry among his fellow citizens. Jeff Bezos, through his company Blue Origin, aims to democratize space travel. While initial flights in his spacecraft have been expensive, the high cost is typical of early-stage technologies. Over time, Bezos envisions making the transformative experience of seeing Earth from space accessible to more people. These projects are not merely exercises in personal autonomy—an intrinsic liberal value—but also contribute to broader liberal objectives. Musk's efforts bolster free speech and inquiry, cornerstones of a liberal society. Bezos's ambition aligns with liberalism's technocratic project of liberating humanity from the physical constraints of nature, allowing us to "slip the surly bonds of Earth."[7]

A liberal, pluralistic society thrives on moxie and verve, where individuals pursue their passions in unpredictable ways. This freedom has led to unprecedented wealth, diversity of vocations and avocations, and artistic expression—outcomes that past illiberal societies could scarcely imagine. Opponents of the liberal order, however, seek to impose a predetermined end-state based on aesthetic or dogmatic preferences, disregarding whether these preferences harm others. Their vision, particularly when tinged with disdain for the wealthy, resembles a Procrustean bed of enforced equality—one that prioritizes certain projects while denying others the freedom to pursue their own. It is fine for Robeyns to enjoy bicycling through the Dutch countryside, but it is both wrong and contrary to the evidence of human progress to prevent others from pursuing grander schemes.

Robeyns also complains that the wealthy consume more energy than the average citizen, but rationing consumption is also inconsistent with liberal principles unless there are no other ways to address a crisis. However, Robeyns fails to demonstrate that personal consumption by the rich significantly contributes to greenhouse gas emissions compared with industrial consumption. And even if it were a substantial factor, governments could address this issue through a progressive consumption tax, thereby both curbing energy use among the wealthy and using the proceeds to mitigate climate change. Assuming that climate change is as serious a problem as Robeyns believes, she also overlooks how the rich contribute to combating climate change and other public goods by fostering innovation and investment, particularly in technologies like AI. For instance, Elon Musk's introduction of Teslas—electric vehicles that consumers genuinely desire—has likely reduced carbon emissions far more than the combined personal emissions of the top 1 percent.[8] In

2022 alone, Tesla users avoided releasing approximately 13.4 million metric tons of carbon dioxide equivalent.[9]

Numerous startups, supported by venture capital, are tackling environmental issues. For example, many companies have recently been founded to focus on extracting carbon from the atmosphere, reducing carbon dioxide levels.[10] Novoloop is converting hard-to-recycle plastics into useful materials, addressing waste and the demand for new plastics.[11] Form Energy, backed significantly by Bill Gates and Jeff Bezos, is developing long-lasting batteries that could make renewable energy more viable.[12] These are just a few examples of the many startups striving to combat climate change. While many of these ventures may not succeed, the wealthy have the resources to take on these high-risk but potentially transformative bets. Creating fixed carbon allowances for every person would create obstacles to fight climate change by curbing their activities. Particularly given the difficulty of making and enforcing an international agreement to limit emissions, an essential part of any solution to climate change is technological progress—the kind of progress that the rich in liberal democracies help generate.

THE RICH AND ILLIBERAL DEMOCRACY

Most criticism of the influence of the rich in American democracy comes from the left. Recently, however, elements of the New Right have joined the chorus, adding their own distinctive critiques. While much of the New Right still upholds the value of democracy, it takes issue with "liberal democracy." Viktor Orban, the long-serving prime minister of Hungary, has even advocated for what he calls "illiberal democracy."[13] An illiberal democracy is a society that elects its rulers but lacks a strong commitment to individual rights, including minority rights.[14] One part of the New Right's critique of liberal democracy is the belief that the rich have taken advantage of their liberty to betray the working class. This claim prompts an assessment of the New Right's critiques against the wealthy.

The first charge is that the rich have led society into a decadent cul-de-sac. Some among the wealthy live lives of moral disorder, serving as terrible role models, particularly for the less fortunate, who lack the resources to endure the consequences of poor decisions. Even more troubling, others among the rich may live conventionally upright lives, focusing appropriately on work and family, yet they preach a political catechism that is resolutely nonjudgmental about the choices individuals make regarding family and work. This stance effectively undermines the conservative valorization of marriage, thrift, and self-reliance, eroding the traditional framework that is essential for human flourishing. In this view, the rich often become affluent social wreckers, seducing the less well-off with luxury beliefs that only the rich can afford and generally know better than to follow themselves.[15]

The second critique is that the rich are globalists who neglect their nation and local communities in favor of the wider world. They see themselves first as cosmopolitans rather than as citizens of the United States or members of their local communities. As a result, they invest abroad, often at the expense of American workers. Like Mrs. Jellyby in Dickens's *Bleak House*, whose charity is more concerned with distant causes than with her own family, these wealthy individuals focus their philanthropy on people they have never met in distant lands rather than on their needy neighbors. Their favored immigration policies, which tend toward open borders, secure a supply of cheap labor—including domestic help—while depressing wages for the least educated and least skilled. All of these policies weaken the sense of fraternity necessary to maintain community and the patriotism required to sustain the nation.

A third criticism leveled against the wealthy is that they wield their clout to promote favoritism toward privilege, from crony capitalism to legacy admissions at our most prestigious universities. They thrive in a world that is opaque to most, manipulating the levers of power to entrench their status as the ultimate insiders. In doing so, they build barriers to social mobility, resisting transparency and true meritocracy to the detriment of those striving to rise from humble beginnings.

Conservatives of various stripes have voiced similar critiques of the wealthy for centuries, if not millennia. The notion that luxury corrupts virtue is as old as classical philosophy.[16] The charge that society's elites are insufficiently patriotic harks back to criticisms of aristocrats who mingled with their international peers rather than their own countrymen.[17] Cronyism has long been the rallying cry of the "country party" against the "court party" in emerging democracies.[18] This historical complaint easily translates to the modern rich, who appear to enjoy privileged access to the contemporary equivalent of the monarch's court: the administrative state and elite educational institutions.

Just as some leftist critiques target the rich as a stepping stone to a broader attack on the liberal constitutional order that sustains them, certain conservatives today view the wealthy with suspicion as part of a larger indictment of liberalism itself. These critics do not differentiate between the classical liberalism of the eighteenth and nineteenth centuries and the modern left-leaning liberalism. They see liberalism in any form as having led to an overemphasis on individualism over community, on freedom over duty, and on a detached rationalism over a sustaining faith. If liberalism is indeed destructive, then the rich—who have most visibly benefited from the freedoms it has championed—are naturally cast as adherents of a false idol.

However, the conservative critique of the rich today may be less easy to translate into political action than previously. Conservatives who seek radical cultural and institutional transformation find themselves with no class other than the wealthy to support these changes. As the most astute critics of our liberal regime acknowledge—and as sensible conservatives have long understood—governing without elites is an impossibility. Patrick Deneen, for instance, in his 2023 book, *Regime Change*, calls for an "aristopopulism," a fusion of the working class and a new elite, to supplant the current order.[19] Thus, any attempt to create a more conservative nation, along any of the lines described, will need the backing of some elite faction.

When nineteenth-century theorists like Joseph de Maistre criticized the emerging bourgeoisie in the wake of the French Revolution, they could still appeal to the remnants of established hierarchies—those loyal to the throne and altar.[20] Even without a king in the United States, organized religion wielded significant power. But today, these traditional hierarchies have largely faded into the background. The aristocracy of Europe has no political salience, and the WASP (White Anglo-Saxon Protestant) elite that once dominated American social governance no longer holds sway.[21] Even the most substantial and organized religion in America—the Catholic Church—is deeply divided, with conservative and liberal factions clashing over social issues ranging from same-sex marriage to capitalism.[22] Meanwhile, most evangelical groups lack the formal structure and intellectual leadership to gain elite political heft.

In the absence of these traditional forces, the New Right will rely on the wealthy to build its movement. While the rich are not generally aligned with their cause, this group is heterogeneous enough to provide the resources necessary to create associations, institutes, universities, and publications that can disseminate their ideas and begin the process of building a counter-elite. As previously discussed, a relatively small but concentrated amount of support can go a long way in amplifying ideas that resonate with the public. The New Right's essential premise is that if their ideas can only be aired, they will find favor with the many. They seek to mobilize a democracy currently stymied by elite roadblocks.

Certainly, the New Right is more likely to find potent allies among the wealthy than within the intelligentsia. Few intellectuals lean right, and those who do are generally libertarians or classical liberals who reject the New Right's ideological direction. Indeed, these classical liberals are sometimes the New Right's fiercest opponents. Bureaucrats are also on the left-liberal side. While a new regime with a more right-leaning bureaucracy might exist in a possible future world, that regime would require time and money to construct.

In contrast, the New Right currently receives substantial support from various wealthy donors. Tom Monaghan, the founder of Domino's Pizza, established a town centered on a conservative Catholic University that bans pornography, creating a model for an integralist community.[23] Thomas Klingenstein, an American hedge fund manager, along with foundations like the Sarah Scaife Foundation, supports the Claremont Institute, a California think tank for many New Right thinkers.[24] The New Right is often concerned with increasing the presence of religion in the public sphere. As described in chapter 4, religious groups are able to get their political message out because of the wealthy.[25] Without the support of the rich, such groups would have great difficulty in getting their voices heard around election time. These wealthy supporters are indispensable for amplifying traditional conservative ideas. Without intellectual resources such as magazines and websites, the New Right movement will struggle to refine its ideas, respond to current events, and apply them to new social problems. And without campaign support to encourage candidates to challenge well-funded incumbents and more established right-leaning candidates, insurgent movements will fail to take root.

Beyond the New Right's need for the rich to help launch their new brand of conservatism, both intellectually and politically, the wealthy are essential to implementing their program on the ground. Unlike the left, the New Right rejects an abstract egalitarianism requiring cutting down the rich. Indeed, the rich can play a constructive role in their envisioned regime. And again unlike the left, the New Right is enthusiastic about business as long as its benefits are concentrated within the United States.

They may advocate for tariffs to protect domestic industries and stronger immigration laws to support American workers, but they also want productive businesses to thrive under these protections.[26] Entrepreneurs seeking riches and wealthy investors are as crucial to the program of the New Right as they are to sustaining the commercial republic more broadly.

Similarly, conservatives who are concerned about the excesses of individualism leading to cultural decadence call for more civic associations as a way to foster community and temper individualism. Engagement in such associations can strengthen citizens' commitment to virtues by encouraging and monitoring their behavior within a supportive group. This is particularly true of religious associations, but throughout American history, other civic associations have also promoted virtues like temperance and charity. As Tocqueville observed, associations temper individualism by fostering a sense of common purpose. However, in our age of distraction, as discussed in chapter 8, associations are more dependent on the wealthy than ever before. Large donations help overcome the free-rider problem that impedes the formation of civic associations. These contributions provide the financial stability that allows these organizations to plan for the future. Even if the New Right does not embrace libertarianism and classical liberalism, the building blocks of their social order rely on the participation of the rich and cannot be replicated by a society that has cut down the rich through state intervention.

The attacks on the rich as the source of cronyism and barriers to social mobility are largely misplaced. The greatest forces for cronyism are special interest groups of all sorts, from trade associations to unions, which seek to secure privileges for their members, thereby harming mobility for others. Individual wealthy people do not create these interest groups; they are too diverse in ideology and interest. Even without their presence, special interests would continue to operate in much the same way. In fact, wealthy individuals often fund various groups that aim to break down the barriers established by special interest groups.

Legacy admissions at colleges are often criticized, but they are decisions that universities make to secure resources for themselves. It is not obvious that eliminating legacy admissions for the rich would benefit the working class. The donor class to universities provides funds for scholarship and other public goods, such as scientific research and student aid. Universities would still need to raise funds for their operations, and without contributions from the wealthy, they might expand legacy admissions to the merely affluent, broadening the pool of potential donors. This could dilute the focus on socioeconomic diversity and maintain a system that still privileges certain groups, just with a different emphasis. In any event, California, a state with a high concentration of the very wealthy, has banned legacy admissions even at private colleges that receive state funds.[27] Other states have similar bills pending.[28] The rich currently do not seem to have the political capital to ensure that any advantages they have in the college admission process will continue.

The New Right may seem opposed to the wealthy, yet they have little hope of establishing a new regime without their support. Indeed, the participation of the wealthy could help it achieve its goals.

CHAPTER 10

◇◇◇◇◇◇◇◇◇◇◇◇◇◇

THE RICH AND THE FUTURE

Artificial intelligence is the most important technology of our time. By manufacturing intelligence from electricity, AI will contribute to prosperity by allowing more efficient production of established goods and the discovery of new ones. These innovations include medical technologies that cure disease and extend life. It is also a public good because advances in AI are crucial to national security and to other objectives, from combating climate change to preventing asteroid strikes.[1]

Yet while the United States' progress in AI remains crucial to its prosperity and security, AI comes with risks both immediate and long-term. Foremost is the existential risk that AI will slip from human control and harm humans.[2] But as AI becomes more capable, other risks arise when bad actors employ AI to carry out all-too-human misdeeds, from violence to fraud. What once required organizations can now be done by a lone malefactor. The wealthy are vital to both maintaining the United States' leadership in AI and mitigating its risks, underscoring their utility to the American republic.

Government alone cannot efficiently advance AI because it lacks both the market system's distributed intelligence and the incentives for risk-taking in innovation where most ideas fail. In contrast, as in the past, new entrepreneurs will push technology forward. The wealth that successful entrepreneurship generates provides incentives to pursue novel ideas despite the likelihood of failure. Wealthy investors provide substantial capital for the new ventures that will be needed.

American advances in AI are necessary to the nation's security. Like transformative technologies throughout history, AI is reshaping the battlefield.[3] It enables new autonomous weapons, such as drones, and its algorithms are critical to both defensive and offensive cyber operations.[4] AI enhances information analysis, making good intelligence a force multiplier on the battlefield. It streamlines the logistics of supply chains, ensuring that resources are efficiently deployed. The United States must stay ahead of other nations, particularly authoritarian regimes like Russia and totalitarian powers like China, not only for its own security but also for the protection of other democracies. Moreover, a lead in AI will be essential for combating asymmetric threats by helping our government predict terrorist behavior and devise new ways to fight it. The United States is not just any democracy. It is the world's hegemon, providing the public goods of global peace and security. By helping to drive AI research, wealthy Americans contribute not only to national security but also to the peace and prosperity of the world.

Advances in AI also yield other significant public goods. AI was indispensable during the COVID-19 pandemic—crucial in discovering vaccines, improving projections to guide policy, and developing medical treatments.[5] Recently developed digital tools, like Zoom, maintained productivity during the crisis. Had COVID struck just twenty years earlier, before significant AI advancements, vaccine deployment would have been slower, treatments less effective, and society would have faced the grim choice between massive productivity losses or far more deaths. The virtual solutions enabled by AI allowed for continuity in education, work, and social interaction.

The rich, either directly or through venture capital, have played a crucial role in launching AI ventures that are poised to benefit democracy. OpenAI, for example, was initially conceived and significantly funded by Elon Musk. Jeff Bezos has invested in Perplexity, a new type of smart search engine.[6] Peter Thiel was a key figure behind Palantir, a firm that uses AI to analyze information, enabling sophisticated simulations and predictions.[7]

Such advancements in AI are poised to enhance modern democracy, as information and its analysis are the lifeblood of a functioning political system. Democracy thrives on accurate information and analysis, allowing politicians and voters to make informed policy decisions. By aggregating data, AI can help government better discern public preferences and thus become more responsive. By simulating the effects of potential policies before implementation, AI can help prevent costly missteps. Additionally, AI's ability to analyze data post-implementation of policy offers social scientists a robust tool to assess outcomes, providing a solid foundation for continuous improvement. Democracy, in essence, operates like a series of experiments; AI amplifies this process by accelerating the feedback loop for evaluation.

As the volume of information that we generate continues to grow, the role of AI becomes even more critical. The rapid accumulation of data in our world necessitates advanced mechanisms for sorting and analysis. For example, the military already struggles to process the vast amounts of information it receives from drones, lacking the necessary capacity to sort and analyze it.[8] AI, in this context, is not just a tool but a necessity for managing the deluge of information.

The military's dilemma serves as a metaphor for social decision-making at large. As technology accelerates, it spawns complexity at an unprecedented pace in fields like nanotechnology, biotechnology, and robotics—domains that were scarcely imaginable a few decades ago. Social decision-making now faces the daunting task of analyzing this ever-growing tide of new phenomena. Societies thrive when they can effectively harness and analyze all available information to make sound decisions. Yet, the deluge of data may soon surpass human capacity to manage it without the assistance of AI.

Certainly, better information does not always sway people's decisions, especially if they are deeply partisan or have already made up their minds. However, affecting the views of the undecided or those open to persuasion can significantly improve decision-making. Swing voters and moderate representatives can still be decisive.

Observers worry that AI-generated deepfakes could flood the information space with lies. However, AI also holds the potential to purify the very well that it could poison. Algorithms are being developed to detect deepfakes, and AI systems can trace the origins of information and verify or debunk it as necessary.[9]

AI can also analyze the behavior of accounts on social media, identifying bots and coordinated misinformation campaigns.

AI can serve as an invaluable tool for humans in the pursuit of truth. By cross-referencing information at unprecedented speeds, AI can significantly enhance the efforts of human fact-checkers. Perhaps more critically, it can help these fact-checkers recognize their own biases by ensuring they consider all relevant data. There is already substantial evidence that AI can assist in de-biasing citizens more broadly. For example, conversations with the computer program GPT-4 (Generative Pre-trained Transformer 4) have been shown to reduce belief in conspiracy theories among those who initially subscribed to them.[10]

Some argue that AI itself poses an existential threat by being poised to take over the world and potentially destroy humanity, but even if this were true, direct government regulation is likely to do more harm than good. Regulation for existential risk in this rapidly evolving field faces challenges that are difficult, if not impossible, to surmount. The pace and unpredictability of AI advancements make it impossible to govern research with a detailed regulatory code.[11] If regulations are instead based on broad standards, the resulting vagueness and regulatory discretion could stifle innovation and deter investment, as researchers may fear that their work could be abruptly halted by unpredictable government action. Another challenge lies in the bureaucracy tasked with enforcement. The government would struggle to attract experts of the same caliber as those driving AI breakthroughs, given the competitive salaries in the private sector.

Moreover, regulating AI creates an intractable national security dilemma. United States regulation to mitigate existential threats would likely prove counterproductive and indeed dangerous. Research in such a lucrative and critical area would simply shift to other countries, including adversaries and rogue nations. But international regulation would be virtually impossible to enforce; monitoring AI research is more difficult than tracking nuclear activities because AI requires less infrastructure. Again, our adversaries and rogue nations would be the least likely to comply.

Because regulation often backfires, private action is the better path. Private actors can establish AI companies committed to addressing existential risks, as some are already doing. Organizations can also be formed to guide the development of AI that avoids such dangers. By accelerating the development of "friendly AI," we can potentially prevent harmful AI by ensuring that friendly AI is more powerful and capable of monitoring and neutralizing risks. To be sure, the government may prod companies to undertake such activities through subsidies or mandates, but ultimately success may well depend on private initiatives. It stands to reason that the wealthy would lead this effort. They have a history of advancing philanthropy in science and education and in creating the tech companies that will need to figure out how to make AI safer. Their resources and influence make them natural leaders in the quest to mitigate the existential risks posed by AI.

The wealthy are already trying to shape a better AI future, investing heavily in nonprofit and for-profit ventures aimed at ensuring AI remains a force for good. For instance, both the

Center for Human-Compatible Artificial Intelligence at the University of California, Berkeley, and the Machine Intelligence Research Institute receive significant funding from Open Philanthropy,[12] a foundation supported by Dustin Moskovitz, a billionaire cofounder of Facebook. Following ideas pioneered by Ray Kurzweil, Elon Musk envisions the melding of mind and machine intelligence as a safeguard against AI's potentially surpassing human intelligence in dangerous ways. This is one reason he founded Neuralink, a company devoted to developing interfaces between the brain and computation.[13]

Thus, the contributions of the rich extend beyond merely aiding in the development of AI. They are pursuing projects aimed at keeping AI safe, especially in a world where the pace and global nature of innovation outstrip the capacity of national regulation to keep up. That backing is now essential. The wealthy lead the effort to blunt AI's risks to democracy and keep the technology an asset, not a liability.

CONCLUSION

The wealthy are not merely adjuncts to the machinery of a market economy. They secure essential ballast for a robust democracy. The left often caricatures the rich as antagonists to egalitarian governance. The right sometimes reduces their role to that of economic engines threatened by an overweening state. Both views are wrong. The wealthy, far from being democracy's contradiction, are its indispensable collaborators. They enrich not just the coffers of the nation but also the fabric of its political life.

Democracy is often envisioned as the equal distribution of political power among citizens. Yet, as practical governance reveals, influence is inherently uneven. The natural and intractable differences in talents, positions, and ambitions among the citizenry demand a more nuanced understanding of how disparate forces advance democracy's higher aims. The wealthy inject pluralism into the political bloodstream, counterbalancing the ideological conformity of the knowledge class and bureaucracy. By financing innovative policies and diverse causes, they ensure that democracy remains a dynamic exchange of ideas, not an echo chamber.

The wealthy also stand as bulwarks against the power of special interests. They advocate for public goods—particularly education—that serve as the twin engines of mobility and progress. By doing so, they combat a successful and stable democracy's tendency to drift toward special-interest sclerosis, reminding us that enduring governance requires both reform and renewal.

Throughout American history, the wealthy have also tempered the inherent flaws of majoritarian democracy. They have championed justice and experimentation. They have amplified the voices of the marginalized. They have promoted movements that sought to perfect the nation's promises, from abolition to women's suffrage. They also safeguard excellence, resisting democracy's drift toward mediocrity and supporting artistic greatness. These efforts make the polity prouder and more stable in the long term. In short, they fortify democracy against some of its latent fragilities.

What sets American democracy apart from many others is its dual character as a commercial and civic republic. This rare synthesis, generated by the Constitution, which restrains central authority, fosters both economic and civil liberties. But the Constitution is an old document. For it to remain vibrant, it must enjoy support from a culture that reflects its values and reinforces its objectives. The wealthy, through their living example of enterprise and achievement, inspire others to participate in the American tradition of commercial enterprise and self-reliance, fostering a culture of ambition and innovation that is compatible with maintaining the Constitution. Our limited government also relies on the wealthy to bridge its inherent gaps. Where government falters in providing public goods, the wealthy innovate, funding parks, museums, and scientific advances that enrich both mind and spirit. They are stewards of a public-private partnership that exemplifies the American experiment.

Today the contributions of the wealthy are more vital than ever. Their fortunes infuse democracy with fresh perspectives because they derive from diverse and dynamic sources. Rapid turnover among wealthy citizens diminishes the specter of entrenched oligarchies. Their investments drive technological revolutions that democratize power itself. From AI to the internet, the tools that the rich help create often enable more equal consumption for the middle class and the better-off. They empower the speech of ordinary citizens in ways that were unimaginable even a generation ago.

In a time when civic associations struggle against a tide of distractions, the wealthy possess a capacity to reinvigorate community life. Through philanthropy, they can help civic institutions become vibrant spaces of fellowship and purpose. A well-funded civic association does more than convene citizens. It also energizes them and cultivates a civil atmosphere of belonging and engagement.

Wealth, then, is not democracy's rival but one of its catalysts: the reserve of independence that checks conformity, the counterweight that steadies the scale against rival elites, the reservoir that funds excellence, and the restless engine that helps renew liberal democracy, generation after generation.

ACKNOWLEDGMENTS

I am rich in colleagues, friends, and family. This book has benefited greatly from all these quarters. A workshop at Northwestern Law elicited insightful comments from many colleagues. Andy Koppelman and Jide Nzelibe went further, offering detailed written suggestions that sharpened my arguments. Friends outside the law school played a crucial role as well. Nelson Lund and Mark Movsesian provided extensive and thoughtful feedback on earlier drafts. Walter Stahr, a former high school classmate and biographer of rare talent, reminded me to always write with an audience beyond academics in mind. Gary Libecap, a friend from my days at the International Centre for Economic Research in Turin, provided helpful pointers to relevant articles.

At home, my wife and nine-year-old daughter patiently endured my long days at the office and the inevitable distractions of research. My daughter's youth reminds me of the stakes for the future in keeping democracy fit for its purpose—an open-order system that is self-perpetuating where ideas and experiments percolate from many perspectives.

My late father, who, sadly, did not live to see this book completed, remains a guiding spirit of the project. A master of contrarian ideas, he never hesitated to defend unpopular positions. If I share that inclination, it is largely his legacy. My late mother, more the diplomat, encouraged me to present ideas in ways that minimized unnecessary offense to those who disagreed. I have sought to honor her wisdom by following that counsel.

I am also grateful to my student research assistants, including Jesse Albrecht, Quianyu Chen, Farah Mavrakis, and Breana Spight, who provided valuable help, as well as to Northwestern Law librarians Tom Gaylord and Clare Gaynor Willis. Emilio Lehoucq, a data scientist at Northwestern's Research Computing and Data Services, was a great help, offering advice on data and providing a supporting memo and map on migration trends. I am a poor proofreader, and thus am particularly grateful to Cannon Labrie and Jill Hughes for their fine work. I owe an enormous debt to Elizabeth Bachmann at Encounter for patiently and carefully overseeing the production from beginning to end.

This book explores the essential role of the wealthy in sustaining democracy, and in a fitting parallel, the institutions they have built and funded have helped sustain the intellectual work behind it. Some of its arguments first took shape in essays published by *Law & Liberty* and *City Journal*. *Law & Liberty*, a project of the Liberty Fund, exists entirely because Pierre Goodrich, one of Indiana's most successful businessmen, dedicated his fortune to an endowment that advances classical liberal ideas by supporting symposia, republishing classic texts, and fostering debate. *City Journal*, in turn, is an initiative of the Manhattan Institute, a think tank made possible by the philanthropy of wealthy individuals and foundations. I am grateful to all of my editors at these institutions: Brian Anderson, Paul Beston, John Grove, Michael Lucchese, and Brian Smith. I also wish to thank the *William & Mary Law Review* for printing earlier versions of arguments discussed here: "Laws for Learning in an Age of Acceleration" (2011), and "Neutral Principles and Some Campaign Finance Problems" (2015).

Even in the later stages of this project, the contributions of the wealthy have left their mark. ChatGPT, which has helped refine my research and editing, owes its origins to an initial infusion of funds from Elon Musk. It continues to expand, powered by venture capital that depends on wealthy investors willing to take risks on transformative ideas.

This is my book. It is not a product of the very wealthy. But the institutions they have built, funded, and sustained have served as a catalyst for its creation. Their role in facilitating it mirrors the broader argument of the book: Democracy flourishes not in opposition to wealth but because of the opportunities and institutions that wealth makes possible.

ABOUT THE AUTHOR

John O. McGinnis is the George C. Dix Professor in Constitutional Law at Northwestern University. He is also a contributing editor at *City Journal* and *Law & Liberty* as well as a contributor to such periodicals as the *Wall Street Journal*, *National Review*, and *National Affairs*. He was previously a deputy assistant attorney general at the Department of Justice in its Office of Legal Counsel.

NOTES

INTRODUCTION

1   Christian Britschgi, "Bernie Sanders Thinks Every Billionaire Is a Policy Failure," *Reason*, Sept. 24, 2019.

2   Chelsia Rose Marcius, "We Shouldn't Have Billionaires, Mamdani Says," *New York Times*, June 29, 2025, www.nytimes.com/2025/06/29/nyregion/zohran-mamdani-nyc-affordability-billionaires.html.

3   See Ingrid Robeyns, *Limitarianism: The Case Against Extreme Wealth* (New York: Astra House, 2024), xvii–xviii.

4   Vanessa Sumo, "Most Billionaires Are Self-Made, Not Heirs," *Chicago Booth Review*, Aug. 22, 2014, https://www.chicagobooth.edu/review/billionaires-self-made.

5   Alex Tabarrok, "Why CEOs Earn Big Paychecks," Marginal Revolution, Aug. 20, 2024, https://marginalrevolution.com/marginalrevolution/2024/08/why-top-ceos-earn-big-paychecks.html.

6   See John Rentoul, "Intensely Relaxed About People Getting Filthy Rich," *Eagle Eye* (blog), Feb. 14, 2013, https://independentblogposts.wordpress.com/2018/01/21/intensely-relaxed-about-people-getting-filthy-rich/.

7   T. M. Scanlon, *Why Does Inequality Matter?* (New York: Oxford University Press, 2018), 74–95.

8   See Jacob S. Hacker and Nathaniel Loewentheil, "Prosperity Economics: Building an Economy for All," Economic Policy Institute (2012): 2, 32, https://isps.yale.edu/sites/default/files/publication/2013/01/2012-prosperity-for-all.pdf.

9   Zeke Miller et al., "Biden Warns in Farewell Address That 'Oligarchy' of Ultrarich in US Threatens Future of Democracy," Associated Press, Jan. 15, 2025.

10 Mancur Olson, *The Rise and Decline of Nations: Economic Growth, Stagflation, and Social Rigidities* (New Haven, CT: Yale University Press, 1982), 41.

11 Olson, *Rise and Decline of Nations*, 2.

12 Christopher Harper Till, "Max Weber, Capitalism, and the Rational Attitude," *This Is Not a Sociology Blog*, Oct. 19, 2016, https://thisisnotasociology.blog/2016/10/19/max-weber-capitalism-and-the-

rational-attitude/. For an excellent discussion of Weber and rationality, see Jerry Z. Muller, *The Mind and the Market: Capitalism and Western Thought* (New York: Alfred A. Knopf, 2003), 208.

13 *Max Weber on Capitalism, Bureaucracy and Religion*, ed. and trans. Stanislav Andreski (London: Allen & Unwin, 1983), 117. This point is made in Muller, *The Mind and the Market: Capitalism and Western Thought*, 208.

14 Angel Au-Yeung, "Jack Dorsey Moves More Than $600 Million of Square Stock After His Promise to Donate $1 Billion to Coronavirus Relief." *Forbes*, April 14, 2020, www.forbes.com/sites/angelauyeung/2020/04/14/jack-dorsey-moves-more-than-600-million-of-square-stock-after-his-promise-to-donate-1-billion-to-coronavirus-relief/.

15 Quentin Skinner, *The Foundations of Modern Political Thought*, vol. 1: *The Renaissance* (Cambridge: Cambridge University Press, 1978), 42.

16 See James Brown Scott, "John Jay, First Chief Justice of the United States," *Columbia Law Review* 6, no. 5 (1906): 299.

17 Alexander Hamilton et al., "Federalist No. 51," in *The Federalist Papers*, ed. Clinton Rossiter (New York: Signet Classics, 1961), 322.

18 Nicholas Capaldi, *John Stuart Mill: A Biography* (Cambridge: Cambridge University Press, 2004), 193.

CHAPTER 1. WHAT IS DEMOCRACY AND WHO ARE THE RICH?

1 "GDP per Capita Current Prices," International Monetary Fund, https://www.imf.org/external/datamapper/NGDPDPC@WEO/OEMDC/ADVEC/WEOWORLD?year=2024; "Median Income by Country, 2024," World Population Review, https://worldpopulationreview.com/country-rankings/median-income-by-country.

2 "International Migrant Stock," *United Nations: Population Division*, https://www.un.org/development/desa/pd/content/international-migrant-stock. According to an analysis of Emilio Lehoucq, a data scientist at Northwestern University, "There are six countries that, at some point between 1995 and 2020, have had more emigrants from the U.S. than immigrants to the U.S.: Libya, Bangladesh, United Arab Emirates, Norway, Australia, and Micronesia. For the most part, the differences are small. Micronesia and Australia are the only exceptions with a relevant difference."

3 "Indian-Americans: A Data Snapshot," Pew Research Survey, https://www.pewresearch.org/2024/08/06/indian-americans-a-survey-data-snapshot/.

4 World Bank, via Our World in Data. "Median Income or Consumption per Day—World Bank (PIP)." Last updated August 7, 2025.

5 Alexis de Tocqueville, *Democracy in America*, trans. Harvey Mansfield and Delba Winthrop (Chicago: University of Chicago Press, 2012), 13.

6 John Stuart Mill, "Armand Carrel" (1837), reprinted in *The Collected Works of John Stuart Mill*, vol. 20: *Essays on French History and*

Historians, ed. J. M. Robson, introduction by John C. Cairns, 183–84 (Toronto: Toronto University Press, 1985).

7 Alex Tabarrock, "Democracy, Capitalism, and Monarchy (Yarvin)," *Marginal Revolution*, Jan. 22, 2025, https://marginalrevolution.com/marginalrevolution/2025/01/democracy-capitalism-and-monarchy.html.

8 Tocqueville, *Democracy in America*, lxxii.

9 Robert D. Putnam, *Bowling Alone: The Collapse and Revival of American Community* (New York: Simon & Schuster, 2000), 19.

10 Tocqueville, *Democracy in America*, 331–34.

11 Tocqueville, *Democracy in America*, 12.

12 Tocqueville, *Democracy in America*, 662.

13 Guido Alfani, *As Gods Among Men: A History of the Rich in the West* (Princeton, NJ: Princeton University Press, 2023), 8.

14 Neale Godfrey, "Are You Rich? U.S. Net Worth Percentiles Can Provide Answers," *Kiplinger*, Aug. 21, 2024, https://www.kiplinger.com/personal-finance/605075/are-you-rich.

15 Emmanuel Saez and Gabriel Zucman, "Progressive Wealth Taxation," *Brookings Papers on Economic Activity* (Fall 2019): 441.

16 Jon Bakija, Adam Cole, and Bradley T. Heim, "Jobs and Income Growth of Top Earners and the Causes of Changing Income Inequality: Evidence from U.S. Tax Return Data," Department of Economics Working Papers 2010-22, Department of Economics, Williams College, April 2012, https://web.williams.edu/Economics/wp/BakijaColeHeimJobsIncomeGrowthTopEarners.pdf.

17 Matthew Smith et al., "How Top Earners Make Money: Often, from Running a Business," April 16, 2019, *The Digest*, National Bureau of Economic Research, https://www.nber.org/digest/may19/how-top-earners-make-money-often-running-business.

18 Steven N. Kaplan and Joshua D. Rauh, "Family, Education and Sources of Wealth among the Richest Americans, 1982–2012, *American Economic Review: Papers and Proceedings*, no. 3 (2013): 161.

19 Kaplan and Rauh, "Family, Education and Sources of Wealth," 161.

20 Tom Nicholas and Vasiliki Fouka, "John D. Rockefeller: The Richest Man in the World," Harvard Business School Case 815-088, Dec. 2014 (revised March 2018), https://www.hbs.edu/faculty/Pages/item.aspx?num=47167.

21 As of early October 2025, Musk's worth was about $490 billion. "The World's Real-Time Billionaires List," *Forbes*, 2024, https://www.forbes.com/real-time-billionaires/#11cae1a43d78. GDP was approximately $30.5 trillion. in second quarter of 2025. FRED, Federal Reserve Bank St. Louis, https://fred.stlouisfed.org/series/GDP.

CHAPTER 2. AMERICAN REPRESENTATIVE DEMOCRACY AND THE RICH

1 Aristotle, *Politics*, trans. Benjamin Jowett (Oxford: Clarendon Press, 1885), book 4.

2 *Congressional Register*, vol. 2 (1789): 195, "Amendments to the Constitution, [15 August] 1789," Founders Online, National Archives, https://founders.archives.gov/documents/Madison/01-12-02-0224.

3 Rachel Bernhard and Sean Freeder, "The More You Know: Voter Heuristics and the Information Search," *Political Behavior* 42, no. 2 (2018): 603–23, https://doi.org/10.1007/s11109-018-9512-2.

4 On the advantage of economic growth for incumbents, see R. C. Fair, "The Effect of Economic Events on Votes for President," *Review of Economic Statistics* 60 (1978): 159–73.

5 Mancur Olson, *The Logic of Collective Action: Public Goods and the Theory of Groups* (Cambridge: Harvard University Press, 1965), 132–36.

6 Olson, *Logic of Collective Action*, 143–45.

7 *Eastern Railroad Presidents Conference v. Noerr Motor Freight, Inc.*, 365 U.S. 127 (1961).

8 James M. Buchanan, *The Calculus of Consent: Logical Foundations of Constitutional Democracy* (Ann Arbor: University of Michigan Press, 1962), 256–58.

9 *Buckley v. Valeo*, 424 U.S. 1 (1976).

10 *Citizens United v. Federal Election Commission*, 558 U.S. 310 (2010).

11 Aristotle, *Politics*, 127–30.

12 Harvey C. Mansfield, "Liberal Democracy as a Mixed Regime" reprinted in *The Spirit of Liberalism* (Cambridge, MA: Harvard University Press, 1979), 1.

13 Mansfield, "Liberal Democracy as a Mixed Regime," 9–16.

CHAPTER 3. PROFESSIONAL INFLUENCERS: JOURNALISTS, ACADEMICS, ENTERTAINERS, AND BUREAUCRATS

1 Samuel Taylor Coleridge, *On the Constitution of the Church and State According to the Idea of Each* (London: Hurst, Chance, and Co., 1830), 30–32.

2 "Bottom Line Pressures Now Hurting Coverage, Say Journalists: Press Going too Easy on Bush," Pew Research Center for the People and the Press (May 23, 2004): 24. https://web.archive.org/web/20040603115508/http:/people-press.org/reports/.

3 "Media Bias: Pretty Much All of Journalism Now Leans Left, Study Shows," editorial, *Investor's Business Daily*, Nov. 16, 2018, https://www.investors.com/politics/editorials/media-bias-left-study/.

4 S. Robert Lichter et al., *The Media Elite: America's New Powerbrokers* (Norwalk, CT: Hastings House, 1986), 30.

5 Lichter, *Media Elite*, 30.

6 Elaine Povich, *Partners and Adversaries: The Contentious Connection Between Congress and the Media* (Washington, DC: Freedom Forum, 1996), 315–16, appendix D.

7 "Key Findings from the 2022 American Journalist Study," *American Journalist*, 2022, https://www.theamericanjournalist.org/post/american-journalist-findings.

8 Lichter, *Media Elite*, 47.

9 Lichter, *Media Elite*, 47.

10 Tim Groseclose, *Left Turn: How the Liberal Media Bias Distorts the American Mind* (New York: St. Martin's Griffin, 2011), 17.

11 Groseclose, *Left Turn*, 17.

12 Maxwell E. McCombs and Donald L. Shaw, "The Agenda-Setting Function of Mass Media," *Public Opinion Quarterly* 36, no. 2 (1972): 176–87, https://www.jstor.org/stable/2747787.

13 Robert M. Entman, "Framing: Toward Clarification of a Fractured Paradigm," *Journal of Communication* 43, no. 4 (1993): 51–58, https://doi.org/10.1111/j.1460-2466.1993.tb01304.x.

14 Marshall Cohen, "The Steele Dossier: A Reckoning," CNN, Nov. 18, 2021, https://www.cnn.com/2021/11/18/politics/steele-dossier-reckoning/index.html.

15 Robby Soave, "The Mainstream Media Is Still in Denial about Hunter Biden's Laptop," *Reason*, June 13, 2024, https://reason.com/2024/06/13/the-mainstream-media-is-still-in-denial-about-hunter-bidens-laptop/.

16 Katie Glueck et al., "How Misleading Videos Are Trailing Biden as He Battles Age Doubts," *New York Times*, June 21, 2024, https://www.nytimes.com/2024/06/21/us/politics/biden-age-videos.html.

17 Nico Grant, "Google's Gemini AI Produces Historically Inaccurate Images of German Soldiers," *New York Times*, Feb. 22, 2024, https://www.nytimes.com/2024/02/22/technology/google-gemini-german-uniforms.html.

18 See Gerard Alexander, "Getting the Right All Wrong," *Claremont Review of Books*, vol. 15, no. 1, https://claremontreviewofbooks.com/getting-the-right-all-wrong/

19 "Is the New York Times Bestseller List Politically Biased?" *The Economist*, June 11, 2024, 71–73, www.economist.com/culture/2024/06/11/is-the-new-york-times-bestseller-list-politically-biased.

20 "How Journalists Documented America's Inequality Crisis in 2020," Center for Public Integrity, Dec. 18, 2020, https://publicintegrity.org/inside-publici/newsletters/watchdog-newsletter/how-journalists-documented-americas-inequality-crisis-in-2020/.

21 Adam Liptak, "Supreme Court Limits E.P.A.'s Power to Address Water Pollution," *New York Times*, May 25, 2023, www.nytimes.com/2023/05/25/us/supreme-court-epa-water-pollution.html.

22 Rishika Dugyala, "NYT Opinion Editor Resigns After Outrage over Tom Cotton Op-Ed," *Politico*, June 7, 2020, www.politico.com/news/2020/06/07/nyt-opinion-bennet-resigns-cotton-op-ed-306317.

23 Joseph A. Wulfsohn, "NY Times Editorial Board Member Who Opposed Tom Cotton Op-Ed Now Supports Hochul Sending Troops to NYC," Fox News, March 7, 2024, www.foxnews.com/media/ny-times-editorial-board-member-opposed-tom-cotton-op-ed-supports-hochul-sending-troops-nyc.

24 M. J. Lee, "Murdoch, Ailes Mark 15 Years of Fox," *Politico*, Oct. 7, 2011, www.politico.com/story/2011/10/murdoch-ailes-mark-15-years-of-fox-065414.

25 Pew Research Center, "Cable News Fact Sheet," Pew Research Center, June 27, 2023, https://www.pewresearch.org/journalism/fact-sheet/cable-news/.

26 Pew Research Center, "Cable News Fact Sheet."

27 Pew Research Center, "Cable News Fact Sheet."
    As this book went to press, Paramount acquired the Free Press with the expectation that its editor, Bari Weiss, would take over as head of CBS News. This one change does not transform the overwhelming left-wing political orientation of mainstream journalists. And Bari Weiss is not a conservative herself, but an eclectic centrist, having voted for Romney in 2012, Clinton in 2016, and Biden in 2020. She also holds a variety of liberal views on social issues like abortion and gun control. Stephen Battaglio, "Here Comes Bari Weiss. What Does It Mean for CBS News?" *Los Angeles Times*, October 3, 2025, https://www.latimes.com/entertainment-arts/business/story/2025-10-03/bari-weiss-is-coming-to-cbs-news-heres-what-it-means

28 Hongbin Cai and Joseph Tao-Yi Wang, "Overcommunication in Strategic Information Transmission Games," *Games and Economic Behavior* 56, no. 1 (2006): 7–36, https://doi.org/10.1016/j.geb.2005.04.001.

29 Groseclose, *Left Turn*, 220 (relying on Alan S. Gerber, Dean Karlan, and Daniel Bergan, "Does the Media Matter? A Field Experiment Measuring the Effect of Newspapers on Voting Behavior and Political Opinions," *American Economic Journal: Applied Economics* 1, no. 2 [2009]: 35–52, https://doi.org/10.1257/app.1.2.35.

30 Martin Tolchin, "Press Is Condemned by a Federal Judge for Court Coverage," *New York Times*, June 15, 1992, www.nytimes.com/1992/06/15/us/press-is-condemned-by-a-federal-judge-for-court-coverage.html.

31 Stephen J. Farnsworth and S. Robert Lichter, *The Nightly News Nightmare: Media Coverage of U.S. Presidential Elections, 1988–2008*, 2nd ed. (Lanham, MD: Rowman & Littlefield, 2011), 113.

32 David Rozado "Wikipedia's Neutrality: Myth or Reality," *City Journal*, June 24, 2024, www.city-journal.org/article/wikipedias-neutrality-myth-or-reality.

33 Mitchell Langbert, Anthony J. Quain, and Daniel B. Klein, "Faculty Voter Registration in Economics, History, Journalism, Law, and Psychology," *Academic Questions* 29, no. 3 (2016): 320, https://econjwatch.org/File+download/944/LangbertQuainKleinSept2016.pdf.

34 John O. McGinnis, Matthew A. Schwartz, and Benjamin Tisdell, "The Patterns and Implications of Political Contributions by Elite Law School Faculty," *Georgetown Law Journal* 93, no. 4 (2005): 1167–1212.

35 Derek T. Muller, "Law School Faculty Monetary Contributions to Political Candidates, 2017 to Early 2023," *Excess of Democracy* (blog), March 11, 2024, https://excessofdemocracy.com/blog/2024/3/law-school-faculty-monetary-contributions-to-political-candidates-

2017-to-early-2023; Adam Bonica, Adam S. Chilton, Kyle Rozema, and Maya Sen, "The Legal Academy's Ideological Uniformity," *Journal of Legal Studies* 47, no. 1 (2018): 4 (finding that male law professors are roughly twice as likely to be conservative as female professors and that nonminority professors are roughly one-and-a-half times as likely to be conservative as minority professors).

36   Ed Yong, "Psychology's Replication Crisis Is Running Out of Excuses," *The Atlantic*, Nov. 19, 2018, www.theatlantic.com/science/archive/2018/11/psychologys-replication-crisis-real/576223/.

37   Mirko Bagaric, Dan Hunter, and Jennifer Svilar, "Prison Abolition: From Naïve Idealism to Technological Pragmatism," *Journal of Criminal Law and Criminology* 111 (2021): 351–406, https://scholarlycommons.law.northwestern.edu/jclc/vol111/iss2/1/.

38   "The Overton Window: How Politics Change," Mackinac Center for Public Policy, www.mackinac.org/OvertonWindow.

39   Devon W. Carbado and L. Song Richardson, "The Black Police: Policing Our Own," *Harvard Law Review* 131, no. 7 (2018): 1741–62, https://harvardlawreview.org/print/vol-131/the-black-police-policing-our-own/.

40   Henry Adams, *The Education of Henry Adams* (Boston: Houghton Mifflin, 1907), ch. 20.

41   The most notorious is the widely used book by Howard Zinn, *A People's History of the United States* (New York: HarperCollins, 1999). Analyses of syllabi at universities have also shown ideological bias and lack of viewpoint diversity. See Jon A. Shields and Yuval Avnur, "Evidence Backs Trump on Higher Ed's Bias," The Wall Street Journal, August 13, 2025, https://www.wsj.com/opinion/evidence-backs-trump-on-higher-eds-bias-politics-13d4fec0.

42   Fox News Poll, July 19, 2020, https://static.foxnews.com/foxnews.com/content/uploads/2020/07/Fox_July-12-15-2020_Complete_National_Topline_July-19-Release.pdf.

43   Jerry Z. Muller, *The Mind and the Market: Capitalism and Western Thought* (New York: Alfred A. Knopf, 2003), 208.

44   Muller, *Mind and the Market*, 14.

45   Robert Nozick, "Why Do Intellectuals Oppose Capitalism?" *Cato Policy Report* 20, no. 1 (Jan./Feb. 1998): 1–6.

46   Scott, "John Jay, First Chief Justice," 95.

47   Todd D. Kendall, "An Empirical Analysis of Political Activity in Hollywood," *Journal of Cultural Economics* 33 no. 1 (2009): 19–47.

48   Sarah Begley, "90% of Hollywood Political Donations Are Going to Clinton," *Time*, Oct. 23, 2015, https://time.com/4084807/hollywood-political-donors-hillary-clinton/.

49   Mahita Gajanan, "What to Know About Murphy Brown's History of Making Real-World News," *Time*, Sept. 27, 2018, https://time.com/5405100/murphy-brown-cultural-importance-reboot/.

50   Calder McHugh, "Why Late Night Shows Won't Roast Joe Biden," *Politico*, May 3, 2024, www.politico.com/news/magazine/2024/05/03/late-night-goes-soft-on-biden-00154694.

51   James Poniewozik, "In 'Succession,' the Very Rich Are Very, Very Different," *New York Times*, May 26, 2023, www.nytimes.com/2023/05/26/arts/television/succession-finale.html.

52   "Welcome to Moneyland," *The Economist*, Sept. 14, 2024, 76. See also Andy Kessler, "The People's Republic of Hollywood," *Wall Street Journal*, August 24, 2025, https://www.wsj.com/opinion/the-peoples-republic-of-hollywood (showing how many well-known contemporary movies glorify socialism).

53   Steven J. Hoffman and Charlie Tan, "Biological, Psychological and Social Processes That Explain Celebrities' Influence on Patients' Health-Related Behaviors," *Archives of Public Health* 73, no. 1 (2015), https://doi.org/10.1186/2049-3258-73-3.

54   Darian Harff, "Political Content from Virtual 'Friends': How Influencers Arouse Young Women's Political Interest via Parasocial Relationships," *Journal of Social Media in Society* 11, no. 2 (2022), https://thejsms.org/index.php/JSMS/article/view/1053.

55   "Opinion: The Media's Mea Culpa after the Election," *New York Times*, Jan. 3, 2017, www.nytimes.com/2017/01/03/opinion/the-medias-mea-culpa-after-the-election.html.

56   Richard Pipes, *The Russian Revolution* (New York: Alfred A. Knopf, 1990), 130 (quoting Cochin).

57   Muller, *Mind and the Market*, 111.

58   John O. McGinnis and Michael B. Rappaport, "Presidential Polarization," *Ohio State Law Journal* 83, no. 1 (2022): 5–60, https://kb.osu.edu/items/961d5677-3605-4507-ad0e-883fcd172bcc.

59   Muller, *Mind and the Market*, 164.

60   Harold H. Bruff, "Reflections on Calabresi and Yoo's Unitary Executive," *University of Pennsylvania Journal of Constitutional Law* 12 (2010): 446.

61   Bruff, "Reflections," 446.

62   Jonathan Swan, "Government Workers Shun Trump, Give Big Money to Clinton," *The Hill*, Oct. 16, 2016, https://thehill.com/homenews/campaign/302817-government-workers-shun-trump-give-big-money-to-clinton-campaign/.

63   Joel D. Aberbach and Bert A. Rockman, *In the Web of Politics: Three Decades of the U.S. Federal Executive* (Washington, DC: Brookings Institution Press, 2000), 168.

64   Joel D. Aberbach et al., *Bureaucrats and Politicians in Western Democracy* (Cambridge, MA: Harvard University Press, 1981), 124.

65   Aberbach et al., *Bureaucrats and Politicians*, 245.

66   Jens Blom Hansen et al. "How Bureaucrats Shape Political Decisions: The Role of Policy Information," *Public Administration* 99, no.2 (2021): 658–77, https://onlinelibrary.wiley.com/doi/full/10.1111/padm.12709.

67   Aberbach et al., *Bureaucrats and Politicians*, 260.

68   "*Yes Minister*," BBC Two, 1980–84, created by Antony Jay and Jonathan Lynn, www.bbc.co.uk/programmes/b006x8f6.

69   James Sherk, "Tales from the Swamp: How Federal Bureaucrats

Resisted President Trump," Center for American Freedom (Jan. 8, 2025), America First Policy Institute, https://americafirstpolicy.com/issues/20222702-federal-bureaucrats-resisted-president-trump.

CHAPTER 4: COUNTERBALANCING
THE PROFESSIONAL INFLUENCERS

1 Muller, *Mind and the Market*, 309.
2 Michael Barone, "Which Party Is the Party of the 1 Percent?" Capital Research Center, Jan. 10, 2017, https://capitalresearch.org/article/party-one-percent/.
3 Barone, "Which Party Is the Party?"
4 Schumpeter recognized the centrality of "creative elites," including entrepreneurs, to the progress of capitalism. Muller, *Mind and the Market*, 291.
5 American Enterprise Institute, "Board of Trustees," Aug. 13, 2024, https://www.aei.org/about/board-of-trustees/.
6 "Manhattan Institute for Policy Studies," Influence Watch, https://www.influencewatch.org/non-profit/manhattan-institute-for-policy-research/.
7 "International Economics," Rockefeller Archive Center Research Reports (June 25, 2019), https://rockarch.issuelab.org/resource/austrian-economists-the-rockefeller-foundation-and-international-economics.html.
8 James Madison Program in American Ideals and Institutions, https://jmp.princeton.edu/.
9 Michael T. Nietzel, "Walton Heirs to Start a New STEM-Focused University in Arkansas," *Forbes*, May 8, 2025, www.forbes.com/sites/michaeltnietzel/2025/05/08/walton-heirs-to-start-a-new-stem-focused-university-in-arkansas/.
10 Art Carden et al., "The Vital Two: Retail Innovation by Sol Price and Sam Walton," *Essays in Economic & Business History* 40 (2022): 85–112. The authors devote an entire section to how "Walton . . . used the knowledge he acquired from studying retail logistics to develop a supply chain that dramatically lowered costs and passed those savings on to consumers."
11 I serve on the Federalist Society's board of directors.
12 Northwestern Pritzker School of Law hosted a multidisciplinary panel discussion in partnership with Feinberg School of Medicine and Medill School of Journalism, Media, Integrated Marketing Communications. Dr. Cassing Hammond (Feinberg), Doreen Weisenhaus (Medill), Dean Hari Osofsky, Paul Gowder, Heidi Kitrosser, Andrew M. Koppelman (Pritzker), "Law School Hosts Panel on the Implications of *Dobbs v. Jackson*," online panel, July 22, 2022, https://news.law.northwestern.edu/law-school-hosts-panel-on-the-implications-of-dobbs-v-jackson/.
13 "An(other) Post-AALS Post on Dobbs Etc.," *PrawfsBlawg* (blog), Jan. 13, 2023, https://prawfsblawg.blogs.com/prawfsblawg/rick_garnett/.
14 Steven Teles, *The Rise of the Conservative Legal Movement* (Princeton, NJ: Princeton University Press, 2009), 181–220.

15 Tocqueville, *Democracy in America*, 257.
16 David Morgan, "Former Twitter Execs Tell Republicans They Erred on Hunter Biden Laptop Story," Reuters, Feb. 8, 2023, www.reuters.com/world/us/republican-led-us-house-panel-probes-twitter-block-hunter-biden-story-2023-02-08/.
17 Peter Suciu, "The Babylon Bee's Twitter Account Was Suspended, but That Made Its Story Go Viral," *Forbes*, March 23, 2022, www.forbes.com/sites/petersuciu/2022/03/21/the-babylon-bees-twitter-account-was-suspended-but-that-made-its-story-go-viral/.
18 Joe Schoffstall, "Twitter Employees Still Flooding Democrats with 99 Percent of Their Donations for Midterm Elections," Fox News, April 27, 2022, www.foxnews.com/politics/twitter-employees-democrats-99-percent-donations-midterm-elections.
19 Gnaneshwar Rajan and Nandita Bose, "Zuckerberg Says Biden Administration Pressured Meta to Censor COVID-19 Content," Reuters, Aug. 27, 2024, www.reuters.com/technology/zuckerberg-says-biden-administration-pressured-meta-censor-covid-19-content-2024-08-27/.
20 "Plea of Guild of Paris Booksellers," quoted in Carla Hesse, "Economic Upheavals in Paris Publishing," in Robert Darnton and Daniel Roche, eds., *Revolution in Print: The Press in France, 1775–1800* (Berkeley: University of California Press, 1988), 77–78.
21 Pipes, *Russian Revolution*, 125.
22 Pipes, *Russian Revolution*, 125.
23 James Madison, "For the *National Gazette*, 27 March 1792, Property," Founders Online, National Archives, https://founders.archives.gov/documents/Madison/01-14-02-0238. [Original source: *The Papers of James Madison*, vol. 14, *6 April 1791–16 March 1793*, ed. Robert A. Rutland and Thomas A. Mason (Charlottesville: University Press of Virginia, 1983), 266–68.]
24 F. D. Flam, "Elon Musk's Community Notes Feature on X Is Working," *Bloomberg*, May 23, 2024, www.bloomberg.com/opinion/articles/2024-05-22/elon-musk-s-community-notes-feature-on-x-is-working.
25 Ashley Capoot, "Twitter Suspends Account Dedicated to Tracking Elon Musk's Private Jet," CNBC, Dec. 15, 2022, www.cnbc.com/2022/12/14/twitter-suspends-elonjet-account-that-tracks-elon-musks-private-jet-.html.
26 Joseph A. Wulfsohn, "Elon Musk, Self-Described 'Free Speech Absolutist,' Limits Free Speech Since Taking over Twitter," Fox News, April 13, 2023, www.foxnews.com/media/elon-musk-self-described-free-speech-absolutist-limits-free-speech-since-taking-over-twitter.
27 Russell Brandom, "Twitter Is Complying with More Government Demands Under Elon Musk," *Rest of World*, April 27, 2023, https://restofworld.org/2023/elon-musk-twitter-government-orders/.
28 Kevin Roose, "Bluesky, Smiling at Me," *New York Times*, Nov. 22, 2024, https://www.nytimes.com/2024/11/22/technology/bluesky-x-alternative.html.

29 Oliver Darcy, "The Washington Post Publisher Disclosed the Paper Lost $77 Million Last Year. Here's His Plan to Turn It Around," CNN, May 23, 2024, www.cnn.com/2024/05/23/media/washington-post-will-lewis-turnaround-plan/index.html.

30 Jeff Bezos, "The Hard Truth: Americans Don't Trust the Media," *Washington Post*, Oct. 28, 2024.

31 Sean Sullivan, "The Politics of Jeff Bezos," *Washington Post*, Aug. 7, 2013, https://www.washingtonpost.com/news/the-fix/wp/2013/08/07/the-politics-of-jeff-bezos/.

32 Gregory Svirnovskiy, "Washington Post Announces New Editor of Opinions Desk Overhauled by Jeff Bezos," *Politico*, June 11, 2025, www.politico.com/news/2025/06/11/washington-post-opinions-jeff-bezos-00401399.

33 James Bennett, "When the New York Times Lost Its Way," *1843 Magazine*, Dec. 14, 2023, https://www.economist.com/1843/2023/12/14/when-the-new-york-times-lost-its-way.

34 "ProPublica Bias: Skews Left," Ad Fontes Media, https://adfontesmedia.com/propublica-bias-and-reliability/.

35 "The Secret IRS Files: Inside the Tax Records of the .001%," *ProPublica*, June 8, 2021, https://www.propublica.org/series/the-secret-irs-files.

36 Ira Stoll, "Following the Money, the Associated Press Moves Left," *Wall Street Journal*, Feb. 27, 2025, www.wsj.com/opinion/following-the-money-ap-moves-left-financial-assistant-omidyar-bias-80a3d31b.

37 Max Tani, "Democrats, Influencers Huddle for a New Media Strategy," *Semafor*, Feb. 16, 2025, https://www.semafor.com/article/02/16/2025/democrats-influencers-huddle-for-a-new-new-media-strategy.

38 "Contribution Limits," Federal Election Commission, https://www.fec.gov/help-candidates-and-committees/candidate-taking-receipts/contribution-limits/.

39 Lee Drutman, "The Political One Percent of the One Percent," Sunlight Foundation, Dec. 13, 2011, https://sunlightfoundation.com/2011/12/13/the-political-one-percent-of-the-one-percent/.

40 Douglas Martin, "Stewart R. Mott, Longtime Patron of Liberal and Offbeat Causes, Dies at 70," *New York Times*, June 14, 2008.

41 Andy Kroll, "This Secret Club of Super-Rich Christians Are Ready to Rule Over You Now," *ProPublica*, July 16, 2024.

42 See Maggie Koerth, "How Money Affects Elections," FiveThirtyEight, Sept. 10, 2018, https://fivethirtyeight.com/features/money-and-elections-a-complicated-love-story/.

43 Christopher Magee, "The Incumbent Spending Puzzle," *Social Science Quarterly* 93, no. 4 (2012): 943.

44 Emily Stewart, "Donald Trump Rode $5 Billion in Free Media to the White House," *The Street*, Nov. 20, 2016, www.thestreet.com/politics/donald-trump-rode-5-billion-in-free-media-to-the-white-house-13896916.

45 William H. Riker and Peter C. Ordeshook, "A Theory of the Calculus of Voting," *American Political Science Review* 62, no. 1 (1968): 25–42.

46 Geoffrey Brennan and Loren Lomasky, *Democracy and Decision: The Pure Theory of Electoral Preference* (Cambridge: Cambridge University Press 1993), 24.

47 Edmund Burke, "Thoughts and Details on Scarcity: Originally Presented to the Right Hon. William Pitt, in the Month of November, 1795. By the Late . . . Edmund Burke," Eighteenth Century Collections Online, University of Michigan Library Digital Collections, https://name.umdl.umich.edu/004903053.0001.000, accessed Aug. 8, 2024.

48 Jerry Z. Muller, "The Threat of Democracy to Capitalism," *Journal of Applied Corporate Finance* 36, no. 2 (2024): 2.

49 Bryan Caplan, *The Myth of the Rational Voter: Why Democracies Choose Bad Policies* (Princeton, NJ: Princeton University Press, 2007), 30.

50 Caplan, *Myth of the Rational Voter*.

51 Richard Pipes, *Communism: A History* (New York: Modern Library, 2001), 94, 108–10.

52 Daniel B. Turban and Daniel W. Greening. "Corporate Social Performance and Organizational Attractiveness to Prospective Employees," *Academy of Management Journal* 40, no. 3 (1997): 658–72, https://www.jstor.org/stable/257057?seq=1; Kristin B. Backhaus, Brett A. Stone, and Karl Heiner, "Exploring the Relationship Between Corporate Social Performance and Employer Attractiveness," *Business & Society* 41, no. 3 (2002): 292–318, https://doi.org/10.1177/0007650302041003003.

53 See James Burnham, *The Managerial Revolution: What Is Happening in the World* (London: Lume Books, 2021); originally published 1941.

54 According to Salary.com, the average salary of a CEO in the United States as of July 29, 2024, was $874,992, and the typical range was between $656,700 and $1,117,814. "Chief Executive Officer Salary in the United States, Salary.com, accessed Aug. 14, 2024, https://www.salary.com/research/salary/benchmark/chief-executive-officer-salary.

CHAPTER 5. COUNTERBALANCING SPECIAL INTERESTS

1 Jonathan R. Macey, "Promoting Public-Regarding Legislation Through Statutory Interpretation: An Interest Group Model," *Columbia Law Review* 86 (1986): 230–32.

2 See, e.g., "Time for a U-Turn: Automakers' History of Intransigence and an Opportunity for Change," Union of Concerned Scientists, Dec. 6, 2017, https://www.ucs.org/resources/time-u-turn.

3 Rachel Carson, *Silent Spring* (Boston: Houghton Mifflin, 1962).

4 "Our History," Rockefeller Foundation, accessed Aug. 13, 2024, https://www.rockefellerfoundation.org/.

5 Ford Foundation, Annual Report 1970, pp. 28–30, https://www.fordfoundation.org/wp-content/uploads/2015/05/1970-annual-report.pdf.

6 See "Grantees," David and Lucile Packard Foundation, accessed Aug. 13, 2024, https://www.packard.org/grantees/search-our-grants.

7 "W. Alton Jones Foundation," Envirosource, https://www.envirosource.com/domino/thielen/envrsrc.nsf/BookSearch/FBEC538346F9BDDB86256622005D25D7?OpenDocument.

8 "U.S. Conservation," Pew Trusts, accessed Aug. 13, 2024, https://www.pewtrusts.org/en/projects/us-conservation.

9 "The Nature Conservancy," Gordon and Betty Moore Foundation, https://www.moore.org/grantee-detail?granteeId=26.

10 Kerry A. Dolan, "Salesforce Billionaire Marc Benioff Pledges $200 Million for Reforestation, Climate Entrepreneurs," *Forbes*, October 28, 2021, https://www.forbes.com/sites/kerryadolan/2021/10/28/salesforce-billionaire-marc-benioff-pledges-200-million-for-reforestation-climate-entrepreneurs/.

11 See United States, National Commission on Excellence in Education, *A Nation at Risk: The Imperative for Educational Reform* (Washington, DC: National Commission on Excellence in Education, 1983).

12 Robert J. Barro, "How Teachers' Unions Let Kids Down," Hoover Institution, Jan. 30, 1997, https://www.hoover.org/research/how-teachers-unions-let-kids-down.

13 Neal P. McCluskey, *Feds in the Classroom: How Big Government Corrupts, Cripples, and Compromises American Education* (Lanham, MD: Rowman & Littlefield, 2007).

14 Holly Hall, "2 Businessmen Pledge $100-Million to Send Poor Children to Private Schools," *Chronicle of Philanthropy*, June 18, 1998, https://www.philanthropy.com/article/2-businessmen-pledge-100-million-to-send-poor-children-to-private-schools/.

15 Tyler Kingkade, "A Betsy DeVos–Backed Group Helps Fuel a Rapid Expansion of Public Money for Private Schools," NBC News, March 30, 2023, www.nbcnews.com/politics/politics-news/betsy-devos-american-federation-children-private-school-rcna76307.

16 "About," Charter School Growth Fund, https://chartergrowthfund.org/about/.

17 "About Us," Eli and Edythe Broad Foundation, https://broadfoundation.org/about-us/.

18 Julie Landry, "Investment to Accelerate Creation of Strong Charter Schools," Gates Foundation, accessed Aug. 13, 2024, https://www.gatesfoundation.org/ideas/media-center/press-releases/2003/06/investing-in-highquality-charter-schools.

19 "Public Charter Startup Grants," Walton Family Foundation, accessed Aug. 13, 2024, https://www.waltonfamilyfoundation.org/grants/public-charter-startup-grants; "Laura and John Arnold Foundation," Influence Watch, https://www.influencewatch.org/non-profit/laura-and-john-arnold-foundation.

20 "Challenging Inequality," Ford Foundation, accessed Aug. 13, 2024, https://www.fordfoundation.org/work/challenging-inequality/.

21 "Education," Emerson Collective, accessed Aug. 13, 2024, https://www.emersoncollective.com/our-work/education.

22 Mark Chin et al., "Assessing the Impact of the Newark Education Reforms: The Role of Within-School Improvement vs. Between-School Shifts in Enrollment," Center for Education Policy Research, Harvard University (Oct. 2017), https://cepr.harvard.edu/files/cepr/files/newark_ed_reform_report_final.pdf.

23 See Dale Russakoff, *The Prize: Who's in Charge of America's Schools?*

(Boston: Houghton Mifflin Harcourt, 2015) (observing that $30 million went to backpay for the teachers union).

24 Matt Barnum, "Do School Vouchers 'Work'? As the Debate Heats Up, Here's What Research Really Says," *Chalkbeat*, July 12, 2017, www.chalkbeat.org/2017/7/12/21108235/school-choice-vouchers-system-pros-and-cons-research/.

25 Matthew Chingos et al., "The Effects of Ohio's Ed Choice Program on College, Enrollment and Graduation," *Urban Institute*, April 22, 2025, www.urban.org/research/publication/effects-ohios-edchoice-voucher-program-college-enrollment-and-graduation

26 Margaret E. Raymond et al, "As a Matter of Fact: The National Charter School Study III 2023", *Credo*, https://ncss3.stanford.edu/wp-content/uploads/2023/06/Credo-NCSS3-Report.pdf

27 "Education Program Evaluation Reports," Gates Foundation, https://docs.gatesfoundation.org/Documents/Evaluations.pdf.

28 John Dewey, "Democracy and Educational Administration," reprinted in *The Later Works of John Dewey, 1925–1953*, vol. 11, 1935–1937, ed. Jo Ann Boydston (Carbondale: Southern Illinois University Press, 1987): 296–97.

29 "How Cap and Trade Works," Environmental Defense Fund, Jan. 22, 2020, https://www.edf.org/climate/how-cap-and-trade-works.

30 Dylan Scott, "Cory Booker's Massive Overhaul of Newark Schools, Explained," *Vox*, March 13, 2020, https://www.vox.com/policy-and-politics/2019/3/13/18223129/2020-presidential-candidates-policies-cory-booker-newark-schools-2020.

31 "Occupational Licensing: A Framework for Policymakers," Department of the Treasury Office of Economic Policy, the Council of Economic Advisers, and the Department of Labor (July 2015), https://obamawhitehouse.archives.gov/sites/default/files/docs/licensing_report_final_nonembargo.pdf.

32 "Occupational Licensing," 17.

33 Adam Thierer and Trace Mitchell, "Occupational Licensing Reform and the Right to Earn a Living: A Blueprint for Action," Mercatus Center, George Mason University, April 20, 2020, https://www.mercatus.org/research/policy-briefs/occupational-licensing-reform-and-right-earn-living-blueprint-action.

34 "Mercatus Center," Center for Media and Democracy, https://www.sourcewatch.org/index.php/Mercatus_Center.

35 "Institute for Justice," Influence Watch, https://www.influencewatch.org/non-profit/institute-for-justice/.

36 Brooke Adams, "African Hair Braider Gets Federal Court Win," *Salt Lake Tribune*, August 10, 2012, https://archive.sltrib.com/article.php?id=54668494&itype=CMSID.

37 *Locke v. Shore*, 634 F.3d 1185 (2011).

38 "Inflation, Health Costs, Partisan Cooperation Among the Nation's Top Problems," Pew Research Center, June 12, 2023, https://www.pewresearch.org/politics/2023/06/21/inflation-health-costs-partisan-cooperation-among-the-nations-top-problems/.

39 Kathryn Fink et al., "Rockefellers Profited on Fossil Fuels. These Days, They're Taking Aim at the Industry," NPR, May 28, 2024, www.npr. org/2024/05/28/nx-s1-4977572/rockefellers-profited-on-fossil-fuels-these-days-theyre-taking-aim-at-the-industry.

40 Erin Shannon "When It Comes to Minimum Wage, Nick Hanauer 'Would Pay You Less, But Then I'd Go to Prison'" *Washington Policy Center*, March 9, 2016, www.washingtonpolicy.org/publications/detail/when-it-comes-to-minimum-wage-nick-hanauer-would-pay-you-less-but-then-id-go-to-prison.

41 Marissa Martino Golden, "Interest Groups in the Rulemaking Process: Who Participates? Whose Voices Get Heard?" *Journal of Public Administration Research and Theory* 8 (1998): 245, 250, 252 (with examples).

42 Benjamin Page, Larry M. Bartels, and Jason Seawright, "Democracy and the Policy Preferences of Wealthy Americans," *Perspectives on Politics* 11, no. 1 (2013): 51–73.

43 Page et al., "Democracy and the Policy Preferences," 57, 60.

44 Page et al., "Democracy and the Policy Preferences," 66–68.

45 "Indicators of Higher Education Equity in the United States 2024: 50-Year Historical Trend Report," Pell Institute, accessed Aug. 13, 2024, https://www.pellinstitute.org/the-indicators-of-higher-education-equity-in-the-united-states-2024-50-year-historical-trend-report/.

46 Jonathan Wai, "Investigating America's Elite: Cognitive Ability, Education, and Sex Differences," *Intelligence* 41, no. 4 (2013): 203–11, https://doi.org/10.1016/j.intell.2013.03.005.

47 Page et al., "Democracy and the Policy Preferences," 76.

48 Thomas Coleman and David A. Weisbach, "How Much Does the U.S. Fiscal System Redistribute," *University of Chicago Coase-Sandor Institute for Law & Economics Research Paper, 991* (2023), https://papers.ssrn.com/sol3/papers.cfm?abstract_id=4647122.

49 Kevin A. Hassett, "The Progressive U.S. Tax Code," *National Review*, Jan. 14, 2013, https://www.aei.org/articles/the-progressive-us-tax-code/.

50 Emmie Martin, "Warren Buffett and Bill Gates Agree That the Rich Should Pay Higher Taxes—Here's What They Suggest," CNBC, Feb. 26, 2019, www.cnbc.com/2019/02/25/warren-buffett-and-bill-gates-the-rich-should-pay-higher-taxes.html.

51 "Tax the Rich," Patriotic Millionaires, https://patrioticmillionaires.org/priorities/tax-the-rich/.

52 The United States' comparatively smaller welfare state, sometimes also cited as evidence of wealthy influence, is not well explained by plutocratic machinations, because the wealthy should be most concerned about who pays for government spending rather than its level. Moreover, historical and cultural factors are better explanations. Ethnically diverse societies like the United States often display less support for redistributive policies than more homogeneous nations. Moreover, the American story, woven from the experiences of

immigrants seeking opportunity and self-reliance, is imbued with a narrative of meritocracy that prioritizes individual effort over state support. Welfare, in this cultural context, is often seen as antithetical to the ethos of self-made success.

The absence of a feudal past further differentiates the United States from nations with entrenched welfare systems. In Europe the welfare state often arose as a response to the rigid class hierarchies of feudalism, addressing historical inequities baked into the social order. By contrast, America was born in an era that celebrated liberty and personal responsibility.

53 Nicholas Capaldi, *John Stuart Mill: A Biography* (Cambridge: Cambridge University Press, 2004), 297.

54 Edmund Burke, "Mr. Burke's Speech to the Electors of Bristol," in *The Works of Edmund Burke*, vol. 2 (Boston: Little and Brown, 1839), 7, 12–13.

55 See, e.g., Plato, *The Republic*, book 8, trans. Desmond Lee, 2nd ed. (London: Penguin, 2007).

56 Moses I. Finley, *The Ancient Economy* (New York: Penguin Books, 1992).

57 "A Rolling Tide: Changes in the Distribution of Wealth in the U.S., 1989-2001," Board of Governors Federal Reserve System (July 2003), https://www.federalreserve.gov/econres/feds/a-rolling-tide-changes-in-the-distribution-of-wealth-in-the-us-1989-2001.htm.

58 Priti Kalsi and Zachary Ward, "The Gilded Age and Beyond: The Persistence of Elite Wealth in American History," Working Paper 33555 (Jan. 2025), National Bureau of Economics Research.

59 Joseph Schumpeter, *Capitalism, Socialism, and Democracy* (New York: Harper Perennial Modern Thought, 2008).

60 Robert Michels, *Political Parties: A Sociological Study of the Oligarchical Tendencies of Modern Democracy*, trans. Eden and Cedar Paul (New York: Hearst's International Library Company, 1915).

61 Derek Saul, "Kamala Harris Has More Billionaires Prominently Backing Her Than Trump," *Forbes*, Oct. 30, 2024, www.forbes.com/sites/dereksaul/2024/10/30/kamala-harris-has-more-billionaires-prominently-backing-her-than-trump-bezos-and-griffin-weigh-in-updated/.

62 Alexandra Ulmer, "In Wisconsin Court Race, Megadonor Musk Helps Fuel Democratic Turnout," Reuters, April 2, 2025, https://www.reuters.com/world/us/wisconsin-court-race-megadonor-musks-role-helps-fuel-democratic-turnout-2025-04-02/.

63 Frederick Jackson Turner, *The Significance of the Frontier in American History* (Madison: State Historical Society of Wisconsin, 1893).

64 Richard A. Couto, in *The Oxford Handbook of Political Leadership*, ed. R. A. W. Rhodes and Paul t'Hart, 347–61 (Oxford: Oxford University Press, 2014). I am grateful to James Hankin for this point.

65 Giselle Ruhiyyih Ewing, "'Disgusting Abomination': Musk Goes Nuclear on Trump's 'Big Beautiful Bill,'" *Politico*, June 3, 2025, https://www.politico.com/news/2025/06/03/elon-musk-trump-bill-00382653,

66 Mancur Olson, *The Rise and Decline of Nations: Economic Growth, Stagflation, and Social Rigidities* (New Haven, CT: Yale University Press, 1984), 40.

CHAPTER 6. COUNTERACTING DEMOCRACY'S INHERENT FLAWS

1 Tocqueville, *Democracy in America*, trans. Harvey Mansfield and Delba Winthrop (Chicago: University of Chicago Press, 2012), 238.

2 John Stuart Mill, *On Liberty* (Mineola, NY: Dover, 2002), ch. 2; originally published 1859.

3 Tocqueville, *Democracy in America*, 239.

4 Tocqueville, *Democracy in America*, 241n4.

5 Tocqueville, *Democracy in America*, 241n4.

6 Mark Moyar, "A Conservative Professor on Academe's Political Conformity," *Chronicle of Higher Education*, July 30, 2024, https://www.chronicle.com/article/a-conservative-professor-on-academes-political-conformity.

7 Willard Sterne Randall, *The Founders' Fortunes: How Money Shaped the Birth of America* (New York: Dutton, 2022), 203.

8 Randall, *Founders' Fortunes*, 202; Adam E. Zielinski, "Robert Morris: The Financier of the American Revolution," *American Battlefield Trust*, March 18, 2020 (updated June 14, 2024), https://www.battlefields.org/learn/articles/robert-morris-financier-american-revolution.

9 Zielinski, "Robert Morris."

10 Randall, *Founders' Fortunes*, 203.

11 Randall, *Founders' Fortunes*, 137.

12 Randall, *Founders' Fortunes*, 173.

13 Thomas J. Cutler, "The Importance of Sea Power in the American Revolution," *Naval History* (Feb. 2024), https://www.usni.org/magazines/naval-history-magazine/2024/february/importance-sea-power-american-revolution.

14 Randall, *Founders' Fortunes*, 173.

15 Randall, *Founders' Fortunes*, 173.

16 "Tappan Brothers," Mapping the African American Past, Columbia University, https://maap.columbia.edu/mbl_place/5.html.

17 Doug Linder, "Stamped with Glory: Lewis Tappan and the Africans of the *Amistad*," University of Missouri–Kansas City School of Law, 2000, http://law2.umkc.edu/faculty/projects/ftrials/trialheroes/Tappanessay.html.

18 "Tappan Brothers."

19 "Tappan Brothers."

20 Charles Weisenberger, "Liberty Party," Special Collections and University Archives, University of Massachusetts Amherst, 2014, http://scua.library.umass.edu/exhibits/hudson/Liberty%20Party.html.

21 "About Parties and Leadership," United States Senate, https://www.senate.gov/about/parties-leadership.htm.

22 A. James Fuller, "The Free Soil Party," Bill of Rights Institute, https://billofrightsinstitute.org/essays/the-free-soil-party.

23 James Mack Henry Frederick, *National Party Platforms of the United States: Presidential Candidates and Electoral and Popular Votes* (N.p.: Werner Company, 2007), 22; originally published 1896, www.google.com/books/edition/National_Party_Platforms_of_the_United_S/4Ig0AAAAIAAJ?hl=en&gbpv=1.

24 Susan Martin, "'Free Soil, Free Speech, Free Labor, Free Men': Charles Sumner and the Massachusetts Free Soil Party," *The Beehive* (blog), Massachusetts Historical Society, Jan. 25, 2017, www.masshist.org/beehiveblog/2017/01/free-soil-free-speech-free-labor-free-men-charles-sumner-and-the-massachusetts-free-soil-party/.

25 Joan Marie Johnson, "Following the Money: Wealthy Women, Feminism, and the American Suffrage Movement," *Journal of Women's History* 27, no. 3 (2015): 62, https://muse.jhu.edu/article/605149.

26 Johnson, "Following the Money," 69.

27 Johnson, "Following the Money," 71–74.

28 "Women's Rights," University of Maryland Libraries Exhibitions, https://exhibitions.lib.umd.edu/unions/social/womens-rights.

29 "Jim Crow & Reconstruction," African American Heritage, National Park Service, https://www.nps.gov/subjects/africanamericanheritage/reconstruction.htm.

30 Russell G. Brooker, "Political Parties in Black and White," America's Black Holocaust Museum, https://www.abhmuseum.org/political-parties-in-black-and-white/.

31 "The Rosenwald Schools: Progressive Era Philanthropy in the Segregated South," Teaching with Historic Places, National Park Service, last updated Sept. 19, 2023, www.nps.gov/articles/the-rosenwald-schools-progressive-era-philanthropy-in-the-segregated-south-teaching-with-historic-places.

32 "Rosenwald Schools."

33 "Who Was Julius Rosenwald?" Julius Rosenwald and Rosenwald Schools National Historical Park Campaign, https://www.rosenwaldpark.org/julius-rosenwald.

34 "5,000 Schools for Black Students Rise Across the South in 'Rosenwald,'" Chicago Community Trust, Sept. 1, 2015, https://www.cct.org/stories/5000-schools-for-black-students-rise-across-the-south-in-rosenwald/.

35 Christopher Harter, "Julius Rosenwald Fund," Amistad Research Center, https://amistad-finding-aids.tulane.edu/agents/corporate_entities/448.

36 "50 Years After the Civil Rights Act, The Four Key Foundations Who Funded the Movement," Resource Generation, https://

resourcegeneration.org/50-years-after-the-civil-rights-act-the-four-key-foundations-who-funded-the-movement/.

37 "50 Years After the Civil Rights Act."

38 "50 Years After the Civil Rights Act."

39 Evan Faulkenbury, "'An Uncommon Meeting of Minds': The Council for United Civil Rights Leadership in the Black Freedom Struggle, 1963–1967," *Journal of African American History* 104, no. 3 (2019): 395, www.journals.uchicago.edu/doi/full/10.1086/704118.

40 Faulkenbury, "Uncommon Meeting of Minds," 395.

41 Tocqueville, *Democracy in America*, 245.

42 Ula Van Zyl, "Impressionism: The Worst Thing to Ever Happen to Art?" *Lighthouse Art Space* (blog), March 3, 2023, https://www.lighthouseartspace.com/blog/impressionism-the-worst-thing.

43 Tyler Cowen, *In Praise of Commercial Culture* (Cambridge, MA: Harvard University Press 1998), 116

44 "Paul Durand-Ruel," Durand-Ruel & CIE: Archives of Impressionism, http://durand-ruel.fr/en/paul-durand-ruel/.

45 "Peggy Guggenheim," Guggenheim New York, https://www.guggenheim.org/about-us/history/peggy-guggenheim.

46 "Solomon R. Guggenheim," Guggenheim New York, https://www.guggenheim.org/about-us/history/solomon-r-guggenheim.

47 James Panero, "Outsmarting Albert Barnes," Philanthropy Roundtable, last modified in Dec. 2022, https://www.philanthropyroundtable.org/magazine/outsmarting-albert-barnes/.

48 Ingrid Robeyns, *Limitarianism: The Case Against Extreme Wealth* (New York: Astra House, 2024), 47–48.

49 John Ruskin, *St. Mark's Rest: The History of Venice* (New York: John Wiley & Sons, 1877), preface, https://tile.loc.gov/storage-services/public/gdcmassbookdig/stmarksresthisto00rusk/stmarksresthisto00rusk.pdf.

50 Melinda Watt, "Nineteenth-Century European Textile Production," The Met, Oct. 1, 2004, https://www.metmuseum.org/toah/hd/txtn/hd_txtn.htm.

51 Philip Oltermann, "Slovakia Purges Heads of National Theatre and Gallery in 'Arts Crackdown,'" *The Guardian*, Aug. 10, 2024, www.theguardian.com/world/article/2024/aug/10/slovakia-purges-heads-of-national-theatre-and-gallery-in-arts-crackdown.

52 Aristotle, *Politics*, trans. Benjamin Jowett (Kitchener, Ont.: Batoche Books, 1999), 115–16.

53 Mancur Olson, *The Logic of Collective Action: Public Goods and the Theory of Groups* (Cambridge, MA: Harvard University Press, 1965).

54 Eamonn Butler, *Public Choice—A Primer*, Institute of Economic Affairs (2012): 44, 58, https://iea.org.uk/wp-content/uploads/2016/07/IEA%20Public%20Choice%20web%20complete%2029.1.12.pdf.

55 Tocqueville, *Democracy in America*, 664–65.

56 Chris Edwards, "How the Federal Government Spends $6.7 Trillion," Briefing Paper No. 174, CATO Institute, March 12, 2024, https://www.cato.org/briefing-paper/how-federal-government-spends-67-trillion.

57 Jason Fernando, "What Are Public Goods? Definition, How They Work, and Examples," Investopedia, updated May 31, 2024, https://www.investopedia.com/terms/p/public-good.asp.

58 Thom File, "Voting in America: A Look at the 2016 Presidential Election," United States Census Bureau, May 10, 2017, https://www.census.gov/newsroom/blogs/random-samplings/2017/05/voting_in_america.html.

59 Elizabeth Gravier, "The Average Net Worth of Americans by Age: See How You Rank," Oct. 8, 2024, https://www.cnbc.com/select/americans-average-net-worth-by-age/.

60 Edward Lotterman, "Farm Bills and Farmers: The Effect of Subsidies over Time," Federal Reserve Bank of Minneapolis, Dec. 1, 1996, www.minneapolisfed.org/article/1996/farm-bills-and-farmers-the-effects-of-subsidies-over-time.

61 "Medicare and Medicaid Act (1965)," Milestone Documents, National Archives, https://www.archives.gov/milestone-documents/medicare-and-medicaid-act.

62 Aamer Madhani, Collin Binkley, and Colleen Long, "Biden Says Too Many Americans Are Saddled with School Debt as He Cancels Federal Loans for 153,000," Associated Press, Feb. 21, 2024, https://apnews.com/article/biden-student-loan-forgiveness-2024-california-cc23ba93a733b583f3ee8963cdd02566.

63 Lorie Konish, "What Could Happen to Social Security Benefits in 2033 if the Program's Trust Fund Isn't Fixed," CNBC, Oct. 22, 2024.

64 John O. McGinnis, "America's Transfer State," *Law & Liberty*, May 30, 2024, https://lawliberty.org/americas-transfer-state/.

65 Budget Staff, "Working Papers: A Growing Culture of Government Dependency," House Budget Committee (2022), https://budget.house.gov/resource/budget-staff-working-papers-a-growing-culture-of-government-dependency.

66 "Long-Term Financial Implications of Current Federal Budget Policies," Budget Model, Penn Wharton, University of Pennsylvania, Dec. 19, 2022, https://budgetmodel.wharton.upenn.edu/issues/2022/12/19/long-term-implications-of-current-budget-policies.

67 Rachel Lu, "Pronatal Fiscal Reform," *Law & Liberty*, May 17, 2023, https://lawliberty.org/pronatal-fiscal-reform/.

68 John F. Kennedy, "Inaugural Address," Jan. 20, 1961, Washington, DC, John F. Kennedy Presidential Library and Museum, https://www.jfklibrary.org/asset-viewer/archives/usg-17.

69 Ted Van Green, "6 Facts About Americans' Views of Government Spending and the Deficit," Pew Research Center, May 24, 2024, https://www.pewresearch.org/short-reads/2023/05/24/6-facts-about-americans-views-of-government-spending-and-the-deficit/.

70 Richard Rubin, "Federal Debt Is Soaring. Here's Why Harris and Trump Are Not Talking About It," *Wall Street Journal*, Sept. 16, 2024, www.wsj.com/politics/policy/federal-debt-deficit-trump-harris-5a0d30d2?mod=hp_lead_pos7.

71 Erica York, "Summary of the Latest Federal Income Tax Data, 2024
    Update," Tax Foundation, March 13, 2024, https://taxfoundation.org/
    data/all/federal/latest-federal-income-tax-data-2024/#:~:text=The%20
    share%20of%20income%20taxes,policy%20during%20the%20
    coronavirus%20pandemic.

72 York, "Summary of the Latest Federal Income Tax Data."

73 Scott Hodge, "Putting a Face on America's Estate Tax Returns,"
    Nov. 7, 2022, Tax Foundation, https://taxfoundation.org/data/all/
    federal/estate-tax-returns-data/. Some might object that lower-income
    households bear heavy Social Security payroll taxes. That is true, but
    the OASDI tax is capped at the taxable maximum, "Contribution and
    Benefit Base," *Social Security Administration*, last modified October
    2024, accessed August 20, 2025, https://www.ssa.gov/oact/cola/
    cbb.html. Meanwhile, Medicare's payroll tax applies to all earnings
    and high earners pay an additional 0.9 percent on wages above
    statutory thresholds. "Topic No. 560, Additional Medicare Tax,"
    Internal Revenue Service, last revised July 8, 2025, https://www.irs.
    gov/taxtopics/tc560. More importantly, when all federal taxes are
    considered (individual income, payroll, corporate, excise, estate, and
    gift), the system remains progressive: the average federal tax rate rises
    with income, and the top 1 percent faced about a 30 percent average
    federal tax rate in 2019, with progressivity persisting in 2021. "The
    Distribution of Household Income, 2019," Congressional Budget
    Office Washington, DC, November 15, 2022, https://www.cbo.gov/
    publication/58781; Congressional Budget Office, "The Distribution of
    Household Income in 2021," *Congressional Budget Office* Washington,
    DC, September 11, 2024, https://www.cbo.gov/publication/60341.
    In addition, taxes whose incidence falls on capital further increase
    progressivity at the top: the Congressional Budget Office estimates
    75 percent of the corporate income tax to owners of capital (and 25
    percent to labor). "A Call for New Research in the Area of Taxes and
    Transfers," Congressional Budget Office, July 25, 2023, https://www.
    cbo.gov/publication/59297, and the estate tax is paid almost entirely
    by the very wealthy. "Who Pays the Estate Tax?," Urban-Brookings
    Tax Policy Center, accessed August 20, 2025, https://taxpolicycenter.
    org/briefing-book/who-pays-estate-tax#:~:text=the%20estate%20
    tax%3F,Who%20pays%20the%20estate%20tax%3F,family%20
    businesses%20pay%20the%20tax. While, of course, research on such
    issues is continuing, these features together mean that, even accounting
    for payroll taxes, higher-income households pay more not only in dollars
    but as a fraction of income.

74 "How We Work," Programs and Projects, Peter G. Peterson Foundation,
    https://www.pgpf.org/what-we-are-doing.

75 See James R. Hagerty, "Peter Peterson, Blackstone Co-Founder, Dies at
    91," *Wall Street Journal*, March 20, 2018, www.wsj.com/articles/peter-
    peterson-blackstone-co-founder-dies-at-91-1521572478.

CHAPTER 7. AMERICA'S COMMERCIAL REPUBLIC

1 Gordon Lloyd, "The Philosophical Case for the Commercial Republic," Pepperdine University School of Public Policy Working Papers, Paper 65 (2017): 2, https://digitalcommons.pepperdine.edu/cgi/viewcontent.cgi?article=1066&context=sppworkingpapers.

2 Phillip Jackson, "Doux Commerce," *Future Commerce*, Feb. 9, 2024, https://www.futurecommerce.com/the-senses/doux-commerce.

3 Joel Mokyr, "The European Enlightenment, the Industrial Revolution, and Modern Economic Growth," Max Weber Lecture, European University, March 27, 2007, 2, 26–30.

4 James Otteson, *The Essential David Hume*, Fraser Institute, 2021, chap. 5, 43, https://www.essentialscholars.org/sites/default/files/2023-01/essential-david-hume-ch5.pdf.

5 Renée Lettow Lerner, "Enlightenment Economics and the Framing of the U.S. Constitution," *Harvard Journal of Law & Public Policy* 35, no. 1 (2012): 37–39, https://journals.law.harvard.edu/jlpp/wp-content/uploads/sites/90/2013/10/35_1_37_Lerner-1.pdf.

6 Jeffrey Rosen et al., "Montesquieu and the Constitution," speech, Aug. 24, 2023, National Constitution Center, https://constitutioncenter.org/media/files/Montesquieu_and_the_Constitution_WTP_transcript.pdf.

7 Montesquieu, "Book XX of Laws in Relation to Commerce, Considered in Its Nature and Distinctions," *The Spirit of the Laws*, book 20, ContextUS, https://contextus.org/The_Spirit_of_the_Laws%2C_Book_XX_Of_Laws_in_Relation_to_Commerce%2C_Considered_in_its_Nature_and_Distinctions.1.3?lang=en.

8 Céline Spector, "Commerce," *A Montesquieu Dictionary*, https://dictionnaire-montesquieu.ens-lyon.fr/en/article/1378153189/en/#:~:text=Fleeing%20the%20evils%20of%20political,against%20the%20abuse%20of%20power.

9 Spector, "Commerce."

10 Montesquieu, "Book XX of Laws in Relation to Commerce."

11 Letter from George Washington to Joseph Reed (May 28, 1780), in vol. 2 of William B. Reed, *Life and Correspondence of Joseph Reed* (Philadelphia, PA: Lindsay and Blakiston 1847), 206, https://www.google.com/books/edition/Life_and_Correspondence_of_Joseph_Reed/Ob4zHRo2ie4C?hl=en.

12 Thomas Jefferson, "First Annual Message" (Dec. 8, 1801), in *The Writings of Thomas Jefferson*, vol. 3, ed. Andrew A. Lipscomb and Albert Ellery Bergh (Washington, DC: Thomas Jefferson Memorial Association, 1905), 327.

13 Gouverneur Morris, *To Secure the Blessings of Liberty: Selected Writings of Gouverneur Morris*, ed. and intro. J. Jackson Barlow (Indianapolis: Liberty Fund 2012), 11.

14 James Madison, "Federalist No. 10" (1787), National Constitution Center, https://constitutioncenter.org/the-constitution/historic-document-library/detail/james-madison-federalist-10-1788.

15 James Madison, "Property," in the National Gazette (March 29, 1792), reprinted in *The Mind of the Founder: Sources of the Political Thought of James Madison*, ed. Marvin Meyers, rev. ed., (Waltham, MA: Brandeis University Press, 1981), 186.

16 Madison, "Property," 186.

17 Robert A. Dahl, "James Madison: Republican or Democrat?" *Perspectives on Politics* 3, no. 3 (2005): 442–43, www.cambridge. org/core/journals/perspectives-on-politics/article/james-madison-republican-or-democrat/3AE3F5D35A515CA0DE3743C90D5A36A8.

18 James Madison, "Federalist No. 10."

19 Dani Rodrik, "When Ideas Trump Interests: Preferences, Worldviews, and Policy Innovations," *Journal of Economic Perspectives* 28, no. 1 (2014): 197, https://drodrik.scholar.harvard.edu/files/dani-rodrik/files/jep2e282e12e189.pdf.

20 John Lettieri and Kenan Fikri, "The Case for Economic Dynamism and Why It Matters for the American Worker," Economic Innovation Group, p. 7, https://eig.org/wp-content/uploads/2022/10/Case-for-Dynamism-FINAL-Web.pdf.

21 U.S. Constitution, art. 1, sec. 8, National Constitution Center, https://constitutioncenter.org/the-constitution/full-text.

22 U.S. Constitution, art. 1, sec. 8.

23 "Artl.S10.C1.6.1 Overview of Contract Clause," Constitution Annotated, https://constitution.congress.gov/browse/essay/artI-S10-C1-6-1/ALDE_00013037/.

24 "The Contract Clause: Reawakened in the Age of COVID-19," *Harvard Law Review* 136, no. 8 (2023): 2132–34, https://harvardlawreview.org/print/vol-136/the-contract-clause-reawakened-in-the-age-of-covid-19/.

25 "Money and the Constitution," American History from Revolution to Reconstruction, *University of Groningen American Studies Program*, www.let.rug.nl/usa/essays/general/a-brief-history-of-central-banking/money-and-the-constitution.php#:~:text=Section%208%20permits%20Congress%20to,only%20with%20the%20federal%20government.

26 "Money and the Constitution."

27 "Artl.S10.C2.1 Overview of Import-Export Clause," Constitution Annotated, https://constitution.congress.gov/browse/essay/artI-S10-C2-1/ALDE_00013364/.

28 Russell S. Sobel, "Entrepreneurship," *Econlib*, Library of Economics and Liberty, Liberty Fund Inc., https://www.econlib.org/library/Enc/Entrepreneurship.html.

29 William D. Nordhaus, "Schumpeterian Profits in the American Economy: Theory and Measurement." NBER Working Paper No. 10433. Cambridge, MA: National Bureau of Economic Research, 2004 (over 1948–2001 U.S. innovators captured only about 2.2 percent of the total surplus from technological advance; the rest flowed to consumers),https://www.nber.org/papers/w10433.

30 Noah Rich, "Does More Money Make You More Risky?" *Michigan*

Journal of Economics, July 11, 2022, https://sites.lsa.umich.edu/mje/2022/07/11/does-more-money-make-you-riskier/.

31 Nicole Goodkind, "The Very Rich Are Often Bad Investors. Here's Why," CNN, Sept. 25, 2023, www.cnn.com/2023/09/25/investing/premarket-stocks-trading/index.html.

32 Ernest Gellner, *Nations and Nationalism* (Ithaca, NY: Cornell University Press, 1983), 22, as quoted in Jerry Z. Muller, "The Threat of Democracy to Capitalism," *Journal of Applied Corporate Finance* 36, no. 2 (2024): 1.

33 "Gates Focuses Attention on Accessibility of Technology Products," Microsoft News, Feb. 23, 1998, https://news.microsoft.com/1998/02/23/gates-focuses-attention-on-accessibility-of-technology-products/.

34 "FAQs," Meta Investor Relations, https://investor.fb.com/resources/default.aspx.

35 Stephen Caldwell, "Sam Walton's Legacy Extends Well Beyond Walmart," Sam M. Walton College of Business, University of Arkansas, Feb. 9, 2021, https://walton.uark.edu/magazine/posts/sam-waltons-legacy-extends-well-beyond-walmart.php/; Harold Meyerson, "In Wal-Mart's Image," *American Prospect*, Aug. 14, 2009, https://prospect.org/culture/wal-mart-s-image/.

36 Tefi Alonso, "How Home Depot Changed the Home Improvement Industry," Cascade, Nov. 25, 2022, https://www.cascade.app/studies/home-depot-strategy-study.

37 Tom Eisenmann, "Why Start-ups Fail," *Harvard Business Review* (May–June 2021), https://hbr.org/2021/05/why-start-ups-fail.

38 Richard Stern, "Wealth: What It Is and How It Is Used to Drive Innovation and Create Prosperity for All," *Heritage Foundation*, July 2, 2024, https://www.heritage.org/markets-and-finance/report/wealth-what-it-and-how-it-used-drive-innovation-and-create-prosperity.

39 Rich, "Does More Money Make You More Risky?"

40 Ivelina Niftyhontas, "Journey Through Time: A Comprehensive History of Venture Capital," GoingVC, Dec. 7, 2023, www.goingvc.com/post/journey-through-time-a-comprehensive-history-of-venture-capital#:~:text=Often%20hailed%20as%20the%20%22father,but%20ARDC%20changed%20the%20game.

41 Brett Rhyne, "Bulletin on Entrepreneurship," National Bureau of Economic Research, Oct. 14, 2022, https://www.nber.org/be/20222/how-do-startup-founders-fare-venture-capitalists.

42 Rhyne, "Bulletin on Entrepreneurship."

43 "Yale's Strategy," Yale Investments Office, https://investments.yale.edu/about-the-yio.

44 Albert O. Hirschman, *The Passions and the Interests: Political Arguments for Capitalism before Its Triumph* (Princeton, NJ: Princeton University Press, 1977).

45 John Cassidy, "Piketty's Inequality Story in Six Charts," *The New Yorker*,

March 26, 2014, www.newyorker.com/news/john-cassidy/pikettys-inequality-story-in-six-charts.

46 Cassidy, "Piketty's Inequality Story."

47 N. Gregory Mankiw, "Yes, *r > g*. So What?" *American Economic Review* 105, no. 5 (2015): 43, https://scholar.harvard.edu/files/mankiw/files/yes_r_g_so_what.pdf.

48 Mankiw, "Yes, *r > g*. So What?"

49 Gerald Auten and David Splinter, "Income Inequality in the United States: Using Tax Data to Measure Long-Term Trends, Sept. 29, 2023, https://davidsplinter.com/AutenSplinter-Tax_Data_and_Inequality.pdf.

50 Auten and Splinter, "Income Inequality," 10.

51 Auten and Splinter, "Income Inequality," 1.

52 Auten and Splinter, "Income Inequality," 39.

53 Bruce D. Meyer and James X. Sullivan, "Consumption and Income Inequality in the United States since the 1960s" *Journal of Political Economy*, 131, no. 2 (2023).

54 Philip Gramm, Robert Ekelund, and John Early, *The Myth of Government Inequality: How Government Biases Policy Debate* (Lanham, MD: Rowman & Littlefield, 2022), 178.

55 David Ricardo, *On the Principles of Political Economy and Taxation*, ch. 2: "On Rent," https://www.marxists.org/reference/subject/economics/ricardo/tax/ch02.htm.

56 William McBride, "Thomas Piketty's False Depiction of Wealth in America," Tax Foundation, August 4, 2014, https://taxfoundation.org/research/all/federal/thomas-piketty-s-false-depiction-wealth-america/.

57 Edward N. Wolff and Maury Gittleman, "Inheritances and the Distribution of Wealth; or Whatever Happened to the Great Inheritance Boom?" *BLS* Working Paper 445 (Jan. 2011), https://www.bls.gov/osmr/research-papers/2011/pdf/ec110030.pdf.

58 Thomas Jefferson to Isaac McPherson, Aug. 13, 1813, in *The Writings of Thomas Jefferson*, ed. Andrew A. Lipscomb and Albert Ellery Bergh (Washington, DC: Thomas Jefferson Memorial Association of the United States, 1905), 333–35. Also available at https://press-pubs.uchicago.edu/founders/documents/a1_8_8s12.html.

59 Erik Brynjolfsson et al., "GDP-B: Accounting for the Value of New and Free Goods in the Digital Economy," National Bureau of Economics Research Working Paper 25695 (March 2019): 2, https://www.nber.org/papers/w25695.

60 Brynjolfsson et al., "GDP-B."

61 Brynjolfsson et al., "GDP-B," 47.

62 Wim Naudé and Paula Nagler, "New Technology Isn't the Cause of Inequality—It's the Solution," The Conversation, Sept. 17, 2019, https://theconversation.com/new-technology-isnt-the-cause-of-inequality-its-the-solution-123476.

63 John O. McGinnis, "Innovation and Inequality," *National Affairs*

(Winter 2013), https://www.nationalaffairs.com/publications/detail/innovation-and-inequality.

64 William J. H. Andrewes, "A Chronicle of Timekeeping," *Scientific American*, Feb. 1, 2006, https://www.scientificamerican.com/article/a-chronicle-of-timekeeping-2006-02/.

65 "5 Years Later: A Look Back at the Rise of the iPhone," Comscore, June 29, 2012, https://www.comscore.com/Insights/Blog/5-Years-Later-A-Look-Back-at-the-Rise-of-the-iPhone.

66 "Patents," World Intellectual Property Organization, https://www.wipo.int/web/patents.

67 Matt Palmquist, "In with the New Products, and the Old Ones Too," *Strategy + Business*, Oct. 30, 2014, www.strategy-business.com/blog/In-with-the-New-and-the-Old-Too.

68 Martin E. De Simone et al., "From Chalkboards to Chatbots: Transforming Learning in Nigeria, One Prompt at a Time," *World Bank Blog*, Jan. 9, 2025, https://blogs.worldbank.org/en/education/From-chalkboards-to-chatbots-Transforming-learning-in-Nigeria.

69 Google, "Online Courses with Certificates—Grow with Google," accessed August 18, 2025, https://grow.google/certificates/; Lisa Gevelber, "Google Career Certificate Graduates Reach 1 Million," *The Keyword* (Google blog), May 29, 2025, https://blog.google/outreach-initiatives/grow-with-google/google-career-certificate-graduates-reach-1-million/; Grow with Google, "Grow Your Skills & Prepare for New Jobs—Our Mission," accessed August 18, 2025, https://grow.google/our-mission/; Social Finance, "Google Career Certificates Fund," accessed August 18, 2025, https://socialfinance.org/work/google/; Madeleine Chiasson, Paige Korbakes, and Taylor Sprague, Google Career Certificates Implementation Field Guide (Boston: Jobs for the Future, August 31, 2023), https://www.jff.org/wp-content/uploads/2023/09/Google-Career-Certificates-Best-Practices-Guide-Final.pdf; North Carolina Community College System, "North Carolina Community College System Partners with Google to Offer AI and Tech Training Programs to All NC Community Colleges," news release, November 14, 2024, https://www.nccommunitycolleges.edu/news/north-carolina-community-college-system-partners-with-google-to-offer-ai-and-tech-training-programs-to-all-nc-community-colleges/.

70 Dennis Peng, "Cell Phone Cost Comparison Timeline," *Ooma Home Phone Blog*, Sept. 16, 2019, www.ooma.com/blog/home-phone/cell-phone-cost-comparison/?srsltid=AfmBOoox8G6hwz48NTT2E84Wz3FovpVyW1vHTJNXxE52vf0cT73zmGa5.

71 Thomas Gregory, "The First TV: A Complete History of Television," *History Cooperative*, Oct. 31, 2024, https://historycooperative.org/the-first-tv-a-complete-history-of-television/.

72 Jennifer Korn, "Google Will Stop Selling Glass as It Looks to Cut Costs," CNN, March 16, 2023, https://www.cnn.com/2023/03/16/tech/google-glass-gone/index.html.

73 Charlotte Alter, "The Man Who Thinks He Can Live Forever," *Time*, Sept. 23, 2024, https://time.com/6315607/bryan-johnsons-quest-for-immortality/.

74 Kaif Shaikh, "Tech Mogul's Anti-Aging Drug Fast-Forwards His Age in a Forever Young Flop," *Interesting Engineering*, Jan. 15, 2024.

75 Michael J. Sandel, *What Money Can't Buy: The Moral Limits of Markets* (New York: Farrar, Straus and Giroux, 2012), 172–76.

76 Kay S. Hymowitz, "When Everything Is Up for Sale," *Finance and Development, IMF*, Sept. 1, 2012, www.imf.org/external/pubs/ft/fandd/2012/09/pdf/bk_sandel.pdf.

77 Thomas Wells, "Why Michael Sandel Is Wrong About Markets, but Right About Capitalism," *ABC: Religion and Politics*, (Aug. 17, 2013), https://www.abc.net.au/religion/why-michael-sandel-is-wrong-about-markets-but-right-about-capita/10099664.

78 Bettina Roth et al., "Intelligence and School Grades: A Meta-Analysis," *Intelligence* 53 (Nov.–Dec. 2015): 118–37, https://www.sciencedirect.com/science/article/abs/pii/S0160289615001269.

79 Emily A. Willoughby et al., "Genetic and Environmental Contributions to IQ in Adoptive and Biological Families with 30-Year-Old Offspring," *Intelligence* 88, no. 7 (2021): 101579.

80 Ellen R. Delsio, Interview with Mariah Evans, "The More Books at Home, The Higher the Child's Education," *Education World*, www.educationworld.com/a_issues/.

81 James Andrew Lewis, "Technology + Power," Center for Strategic and International Studies, March 30, 2022, www.csis.org/analysis/technology-and-power.

82 "Press Kit: Moore's Law," Intel Newsroom, Sept. 18, 2023, www.intel.com/content/www/us/en/newsroom/resources/moores-law.html#gs.e1jwdi.

83 "Press Kit: Moore's Law."

84 "Press Kit: Moore's Law."

85 Ray Kurzweil, *The Singularity Is Near: When Humans Transcend Biology* (New York: Viking, 2005), 120.

86 Robert Bellafiore Jr., "The Anomaly of Economic Growth," *City Journal*, June 3, 2024, www.city-journal.org/article/review-of-growth-a-history-and-a-reckoning-by-daniel-susskind.

87 Adobe Acrobat Team, "Fast-Forward—Comparing a 1980s Supercomputer to the Modern Smartphone," *Adobe Blog*, Nov. 8, 2022, https://blog.adobe.com/en/publish/2022/11/08/fast-forward-comparing-1980s-supercomputer-to-modern-smartphone.

88 Kurzweil, *Singularity Is Near*, 245.

89 "Our History," Nolo, https://www.nolo.com/about/history.

90 Robert Pearl and Brian Wayling, "The Telehealth Era Is Just Beginning," *Harvard Business Review* (May–June 2022), https://hbr.org/2022/05/the-telehealth-era-is-just-beginning.

CHAPTER 8. AMERICA'S PHILANTHROPIC REPUBLIC

1 Tocqueville, *Democracy in America*, trans. Harvey Mansfield and Delba Winthrop (Chicago: University of Chicago Press, 2012), 489.

2 Daniel King and Martyn Griffin, "Nonprofits as Schools for Democracy: The Justifications for Organizational Democracy Within Nonprofit Organizations," *Nonprofit and Voluntary Sector Quarterly* 48, no. 5 (2019): 910–30, https://doi.org/10.1177/0899764019837603.

3 Tocqueville, *Democracy in America*, 496.

4 Tocqueville, *Democracy in America*, 489.

5 Tocqueville, *Democracy in America*, 490.

6 Tocqueville, *Democracy in America*, 490.

7 Tocqueville, *Democracy in America*, 492.

8 Harvey Mansfield, *Tocqueville: A Very Short Introduction* (Oxford: Oxford University Press, 2010), 81.

9 Tocqueville, *Democracy in America*, 180.

10 Tocqueville, *Democracy in America*, 491.

11 Tocqueville, *Democracy in America*, 489.

12 Nathan Dietz and Robert T. Grimm, "A Less Charitable Nation: The Decline of Volunteering and Giving in the United States," USC Conference Paper, https://cppp.usc.edu/wp-content/uploads/2019/03/Grimm-Robert-Dietz-and-Grimm_A-Less-Charitable-Nation_March-2019-USC-Conference-Paper.pdf.

13 "Who Gives Most to Charity," Philanthropy Roundtable, https://www.philanthropyroundtable.org/almanac/who-gives-most-to-charity.

14 "The Story of the Creation of the Nation's First Hospital," In the Beginning, History of Pennsylvania Hospital, Penn Medicine, https://www.uphs.upenn.edu/paharc/features/creation.html.

15 "1751–1800," Historical Timeline, History of Pennsylvania Hospital, Penn Medicine, https://www.uphs.upenn.edu/paharc/timeline/1751/.

16 "A Narrative History of Mass General," Massachusetts General Hospital, https://www.massgeneral.org/museum/history (discussing early contributions to the hospital, including those up to $20,000, or about $500,000 in today's money).

17 "History of the Museum," The Met, https://www.metmuseum.org/about-the-met/history.

18 "Race and Antebellum New York City," Examination Days, New York African Free School Collection, https://www.nyhistory.org/web/africanfreeschool/history/manumission-society.html.

19 Derrick Nunnally, Couple Gives YMCA First One Million, *Philadelphia Inquirer*, Sept. 24, 2008, Inquirer.com/philly/news/breaking/20080924_Couple_gives_Phila__YMCA_its_first__1_million_donation.html#:~:text=Phil%20and%20Barbara%20Albright%20of,president%20of%20Philadelphia-area%20YMCAs.

20 "A Past as Rich as Our Present," *The YMCA*, https://www.ymcachicago.org/ymca-of-metro-chicago-history.

21 Jason De Stefano, "A Mass Politics of Beauty: On Hull-House's 'Radical Craft,'" Cleveland Review of Books, May 22, 2025, https://

clerevie**w**ofbooks.com/a-mass-politics-of-beauty-on-hull-houses-
radical-craft/#:~:text=private%20Miss%20Kirkland%E2%80%99s%20
School%2C%20where,of%20the%20University%20of%20Illinois.

22 De Stefano, "A Mass Politics of Beauty."
23 History of the Peabody Institute, https://peabody.jhu.edu/explore-
peabody/our-history/
24 History of the Peabody Institute.
25 Sarah Hotchkiss, "The Mechanics' Institute: An Historical Oasis," Dec.
11, 2011, NPR, www.kqed.org/arts/76913/the_mechanics_institute_
an_historical_oasis.
26 Hotchkiss, "The Mechanics' Institute."
27 Robert Putnam, *Bowling Alone: The Collapse and Revival of American
Community* (New York: Simon & Schuster, 2000), 27.
28 Putnam, *Bowling Alone*, 115, 231.
29 "More Leisure Time, but Less Enjoyment?" Maryland
Population Research Center, www.popcenter.umd.edu/news/
news_1409844450968.
30 "Habitat for Humanity Launches New Construction Training Program,"
Arizona PBS, July 30, 2024, https://azpbs.org/horizon/2024/07/
habitat-for-humanitys-new-construction-training-program-aligns-with-
arizona-values/.
31 "Nature Conservancy Interpretive Nature Walks," Meetup, www.
meetup.com/nature-conservancy-interpretive-nature-walk-series/.
32 "Careers at CZI," Chan Zuckerberg Initiative, https://chanzuckerberg.
com/careers/.
33 Robin Hood Foundation, https://robinhood.org/.
34 "Meet Our Partners," Boys and Girls Clubs of America, www.bgca.org/
about-us/our-partners/.
35 "Boys & Girls Clubs of America Announces $281 Million Gift from
MacKenzie Scott" *Boys and Girls Clubs of America*, www.bgca.org/
news-stories/2022/March/boys-and-girls-clubs-of-america-announces-
281-million-dollar-gift-from-mackenzie-scott.
36 "YMCA Receives Major Donation from MacKenzie Scott," *YMCA of
the USA*, www.prnewswire.com/news-releases/ymca-receives-major-
donation-from-mackenzie-scott-301193504.html.
37 David Schizer, "Subsidizing Charitable Contributions: Incentives,
Information, and the Private Pursuit of Public Goals," *Tax Law Review*
62 (2009): 221, 243.
38 Jonathan R. Macey, "Public and Private Ordering and the Production
of Legitimate and Illegitimate Legal Rules," *Cornell Law Review* 82
(1997): 1123, 1141.
39 James Douglas, *Why Charity? The Case for a Third Sector* (Beverly Hills,
CA: Sage Publications, 1983), 133–35, 136.
40 "Who Gives Most to Charity?"
41 Hans Peter Schmitz and Elena M. McCollim, "Billionaires in
Global Philanthropy: A Decade of the Giving Pledge," *Society* 58,
no. 2 (2021): 120–30, https://pmc.ncbi.nlm.nih.gov/articles/

PMC8147574/#:~:text=Among%20the%20US%20billionaire%20 population,Giving%20Pledge%20(Wang%202020).

42 Quentin Skinner, *The Foundations of Modern Political Thought*, vol. 1: *The Renaissance* (Cambridge: Cambridge University Press, 1978), 56.

43 Tom Baker and Alistair Sisson, "'The World's Mayor'—How Michael Bloomberg Uses Philanthropy to Change the Way Cities Are Run," *Chronicle of Philanthropy*, Oct. 4, 2024, www.philanthropy.com/article/ the-worlds-mayor-how-michael-bloomberg-uses-philanthropy-to- change-the-way-cities-are-run.

44 "What Works Cities Certification," https://whatworkscities.bloomberg. org/.

45 "Mayor's Challenge," https://www.bloomberg.org/government- innovation/spurring-innovation-in-cities/mayors-challenge/.

46 Alex Rozier, "Gates Foundation Speaks Out About Seattle's 'Homeless Crisis,'" King 5 News, Feb. 2, 2016, https://www.king5.com/article/ news/local/seattle/gates-foundation-speaks-out-about-seattles- homeless-crisis/281-65536558.

47 "Coordinated Entry," Building Changes, https://buildingchanges.org/ wp-content/uploads/2021/06/2021_FHIBrief_CoordinatedEntry.pdf.

48 Christina McHugh, "Investment Matters: The Lasting Impacts of the Gates Foundation's Data Driven Culture Initiative," King County, Feb. 4, 2021, https://dchsblog.com/2021/02/10/investment-matters-the- lasting-impacts-of-the-gates-foundations-data-driven-culture-initiative/.

49 "Education," W. K. Kellogg Foundation, https://www.wkkf.org/where- we-work/michigan/battle-creek/#education.

50 Greyson Steele, "GVSU Expands Programming in Battle Creek with $10M Grant from W. K. Kellogg Foundation, "*Battle Creek Enquirer*, June 3, 2024, www.battlecreekenquirer.com/story/ news/local/2024/06/03/gvsu-to-renovate-kendall-center-expand- programming-in-battle-creek/73955725007.

51 Eliza Shapiro, "$160 Million Later, New Pool and Rink Will Replace Central Park Eyesore," *New York Times*, Oct. 9, 2024, https://www. nytimes.com/2024/10/09/nyregion/central-park-harlem-meer- center.html. This project is only one of many recent projects that the very wealthy have sponsored to benefit all New Yorkers. See Reza Chowdhury, "Public Spaces in New York Recently Built by Billionaires," https://x.com/RezaC1/status/1979344427664507270 (1.Little Island — Barry Diller & Diane von Furstenberg 2. Pier 57 Rooftop Park — Google / Larry Page & Sergey Brin 3. Domino Park — Jed Walentas / Two Trees Development 4. Hudson Yards Public Square & Vessel — Stephen Ross / Related Companies 5. High Line – Moynihan Connector — Brookfield Properties / Bruce Flatt 6. Perelman Performing Arts Center — Ronald O. Perelman + Michael Bloomberg).

52 "2024–2025 Best Global Universities Rankings," *U.S. News & World Report*, www.usnews.com/education/best-global-universities/rankings.

53 Ginia Bellafante, "Harvard's Endowment Is $53.2 Billion. What Should It Be For?," April 26, 2025, New York Times,

https://www.nytimes.com/2025/04/26/business/harvard-endowment-trump.html

54 Sarah Wood, "15 Universities with the Biggest Endowments," *U.S. News & World Report*, Oct. 2, 2023, www.usnews.com/education/best-colleges/the-short-list-college/articles/10-universities-with-the-biggest-endowments.

55 "50 Universities with the Most Nobel Prize Winners," Best Masters Programs, www.bestmastersprograms.org/most-nobel-prize-winners/.

56 See "Science in China: Soaring Dragons," *The Economist*, June 15, 2024, 67–70, www.scribd.com/document/768438062/Soaring-Dragons.

57 Alex Nester, "Meet the Man Trying to Shake Up Yale's Secretive Governing Body," *The Free Beacon*, April 12, 2021, https://freebeacon.com/campus/meet-the-man-trying-to-shake-up-yales-secretive-governing-body/.

58 Crimson News Staff, "Members of the Harvard Corporation 2022," *Harvard Crimson*, May 26, 2022, www.thecrimson.com/widget/2022/5/26/corporation-members/.

59 Miles J. Herszenhorn and Claire Yuan, "Harvard Corporation Members Donated Heavily to Democrats Ahead of 2022 Midterm Elections," *Harvard Crimson*, Feb. 2, 2023, www.thecrimson.com/article/2023/2/2/harvard-corporation-democrat-donations/.

60 David Gura, "Combative Billionaire Bill Ackman Uses Bare-Knuckle Boardroom Tactics in a Wider War," NPR, Jan. 24, 2024, www.npr.org/2024/01/24/1225216895/bill-ackman-wall-street-harvard-dei-plagiarism-penn-college-free-speech.

61 Aaron Sibarium, "Former Penn President Signed Off on Sanctions for Speech of Controversial Conservative Prof. She Let an Anti-Semitic Literary Festival Proceed Under the Banner of Free Expression," *The Free Beacon*, Feb. 26, 2024, https://freebeacon.com/campus/former-penn-president-signed-off-on-sanctions-for-speech-of-controversial-conservative-prof-she-let-an-anti-semitic-literary-festival-proceed-under-the-banner-of-free-expression/.

62 Stephanie Saul et al., "Penn's Leadership Resigns amid Controversies over Antisemitism," *New York Times*, Dec. 9, 2023, www.nytimes.com/2023/12/09/us/university-of-pennsylvania-president-resigns.html.

63 Juliet Chung, "Harvard Stood Up to Trump. Now It Wants Donors to Help." *Wall Street Journal*, April 18, 2025, www.wsj.com/us-news/education/harvard-donations-trump-federal-funding-freeze-cf3dd82a. There are other examples of the rich providing funds for entities targeted by the Trump administration. After federal cuts to public broadcasting, the Knight Foundation and other major philanthropies backed by wealthy donors are racing to assemble about $50 million in bridge funding to stabilize vulnerable PBS and NPR member stations. Benjamin Mullin, "The Race to Rescue PBS and NPR Stations," *New York Times*, August 19, 2025, https://www.nytimes.com/2025/08/19/business/the-race-to-rescue-pbs-and-npr-stations.

html

64 William D. Cohan, "How Loud Billionaires Convert Their Wealth into Power, *New York Times*, Feb. 5, 2024, www.nytimes.com/2024/02/05/opinion/ackman-billionaires-musk-trump-social-media-x.html.

65 Amanda B. Moniz, "The Storied History of Giving in America," *Smithsonian Magazine*, Nov. 23, 2020, www.smithsonianmag.com/smithsonian-institution/storied-nuanced-history-giving-180976363/.

66 Margot L. Crandall-Hollick, "The Charitable Deduction for Individuals: A Brief Legislative History," Congressional Research Service, June 26, 2020, https://crsreports.congress.gov/product/pdf/R/R46178.

67 Eric J. Belasco et al., "Whither Agricultural Policy in 2021: Agricultural Policy in Disarray: Reforming the Farm Bill," American Enterprise Institute, Feb. 2021, www.aei.org/wp-content/uploads/2021/01/Whither-Agricultural-Policy-in-2021-and-Beyond.pdf?x91208.

68 Loren Yager and Rachel Schmidt, "The Advanced Technology Program: A Case Study in Federal Technology," American Enterprise Institute, 1997, www.aei.org/wp-content/uploads/2014/06/-the-advanced-technology-program-a-case-study-in-federal-technology-policy_154142517425.pdf.

69 Astead W. Herndon, "George Soros's Foundation Pours $220 Million into Racial Equality Push," *New York Times*, July 13, 2020, www.nytimes.com/2020/07/13/us/politics/george-soros-racial-justice-organizations.html.

70 "Challenging Inequality," Ford Foundation, https://www.fordfoundation.org/work/challenging-inequality/.

CHAPTER 9. THE RICH IN LIBERAL AND ILLIBERAL DEMOCRACY

1 Nicholas Capaldi, *John Stuart Mill: A Biography* (Cambridge: Cambridge University Press, 2004), 267.

2 Capaldi, *John Stuart Mill*, 267.

3 Capaldi, *John Stuart Mill*, 267.

4 Capaldi, *John Stuart Mill*, 267.

5 Capaldi, *John Stuart Mill*, 267.

6 Ingrid Robeyns, *Limitarianism: The Case Against Extreme Wealth* (New York: Astra House, 2024), 5.

7 John Gillespie Magee Jr., "High Flight," Poetry Foundation, https://www.poetryfoundation.org/poems/157986/high-flight-627d3cfb1e9b7.

8 "Impact Report 2022," Tesla, https://www.tesla.com/ns_videos/2022-tesla-impact-report-highlights.pdf.

9 "Impact Report 2022."

10 Miriam Ahmed, "Top Ten Leading Carbon Capture Companies," *Energy Digital*, February 23, 2023, https://energydigital.com/top10/top-10-leading-carbon-capture-companies.

11 Jeff Kart, "Novoloop Startup That Converts Plastic Waste into

Performance Products Raises $11 Million in Series A," *Forbes*, Feb. 16, 2022, www.forbes.com/sites/jeffkart/2022/02/15/novoloop-startup-that-converts-plastic-waste-into-performance-products-raises-11-million-in-series-a/.

12 Andrew Lee, "Green Battery Backed by Billionaires Gates, Bezos and Branson Plans Factory to 'Reshape Energy System,'" *Recharge News*, Dec. 23, 2022, www.rechargenews.com/energy-transition/green-battery-backed-by-billionaires-gates-bezos-and-branson-plans-factory-to-reshape-energy-system/2-1-1379772?ref=upstract.com&zephr_sso_ott=0hSQZK.

13 Susan Rubin Suleiman, "Anti-Democratic Politics in Hungary: Viktor Orban and 'Illiberal Democracy,'" Scowcroft Institute of International Affairs, https://bush.tamu.edu/wp-content/uploads/2021/07/Suleiman-Paper-No.-20.pdf.

14 Mark F. Plattner, "Illiberal Democracy and the Struggle on the Right," *Journal of Democracy* 30, no. 1 (2019): 5–19, https://www.journalofdemocracy.org/articles/illiberal-democracy-and-the-struggle-on-the-right/.

15 Rob Henderson, "'Luxury Beliefs' That Only the Privileged Can Afford," *Wall Street Journal*, Feb. 9, 2024, www.wsj.com/us-news/education/luxury-beliefs-that-only-the-privileged-can-afford-7f6b8a16.

16 Pierre Retat, "Luxury," trans. Philip Stewart, in *A Montesquieu Dictionary* [online], Sept. 2013, https://dictionnaire-montesquieu.ens-lyon.fr/en/article/1376473009/en/.

17   Arno J. Meyer, *The Persistence of the Old Regime: Europe to the Great War* (New York: Pantheon, 1981).

18 Perez Zagorin, "The Court and the Country: A Note on Political Terminology in the Earlier Seventeenth Century," *English Historical Review* 77, no. 303 (1962): 306–11.

19 Patrick J. Deneen, "Aristopopulism: A Political Proposal for America," Institute for Human Ecology, March 20, 2019, https://www.youtube.com/watch?v=o_ozFy_dNLc.

20 Michael Broers, *Europe After Napoleon, Revolution, Reaction, and Romanticism, 1814–1848* (Manchester: Manchester University Press, 1996), 57.

21 Peter Schrag, *The Decline of the Wasp* (New York: Simon & Schuster, 1971).

22 Claire Giangravé, "*U.S. Catholic Bishops Report to the Vatican Shows a Church Split by Politics*, Sept. 23, 2022, Religion News Service, https://religionnews.com/2022/09/23/u-s-catholic-bishops-report-to-the-vatican-shows-a-church-split-by-politics/.

23 Kate Taylor, "The Domino's Pizza Founder Created a Catholic 'Paradise' Town with No Birth Control or Pornography," *Business Insider*, Jan. 11, 2016, www.businessinsider.com/dominos-founders-catholic-paradise-2016-1.

24 Jason Wilson, "The Far-Right Financier Giving Millions to the Republican Party to Fight 'Woke Communists,'" Aug. 4, 2023, *The*

Guardian, www.theguardian.com/us-news/2023/aug/04/far-right-republican-donor-woke-thomas-klingenstein.

25 See chapter 3.

26 Oren Cass, "Why Trump Is Right About Tariffs," *Wall Street Journal*, Oct. 27, 2023, https://www.wsj.com/economy/trade/why-trump-is-right-about-tariffs-3cad4097.

27 Shawn Hubler et al., "California Bans Legacy Preferences at Private Universities," *New York Times*, Sept. 30, 2024, www.nytimes.com/2024/09/30/us/california-bans-legacy-preferences-private-universities.

28 Laura Spitalniak, "A Look at Five States Weighing Legacy Admissions Bans," March 28, 2024, *Higher Ed Dive*, www.highereddive.com/news/5-states-weigh-legacy-admissions-bans/711428/.

CHAPTER 10. THE RICH AND THE FUTURE

1 See Florin Diacu, *Megadisasters: The Science of Predicting the Next Catastrophe* (Princeton, NJ: Princeton University Press, 2010).

2 See Bill Joy, "Why the Future Doesn't Need Us," *Wired*, Apr. 1, 2000, https://www.wired.com/2000/04/joy-2/.

3 Robert Friedel, *A Culture of Improvement: Technology and the Western Millennium* (Cambridge, MA: MIT Press, 2007), 85, 113, 131, 374.

4 Nick Robins-Early, "AI's 'Oppenheimer Moment': Autonomous Weapons Enter the Battlefield," *The Guardian*, July 14, 2024, /www.theguardian.com/technology/article/2024/jul/14/ais-oppenheimer-moment-autonomous-weapons-enter-the-battlefield.

5 Arash Keshavarzi Arshadi et al., "Artificial Intelligence for COVID-19 Drug Discovery and Development," *Frontiers in Artificial Intelligence*, Sec. Medicine and Public Health, vol. 3 (2020), https://doi.org/10.3389/frai.2020.00065; Joel Kowalewski et al., "Predicting Novel Drugs for SARS-CoV-2 Using Machine Learning from a >10 Million Chemical Space," *Heliyon* 6, no. 8 (2020): e04369.

6 Robert Frank, "Jeff Bezos' Family Office Is Making Big Investments in AI," CNBC, updated Dec. 2, 2024. (Jeff Bezos has invested in Perplexity, a new kind of smart search engine.)

7 Sam Biddle, "How Peter Thiel's Palantir Helped the NSA Spy on the Whole World," *The Intercept*, Feb. 22, 2017, https://theintercept.com/2017/02/22/how-peter-thiels-palantir-helped-the-nsa-spy-on-the-whole-world/.

8 Shweta Surender, "AI in Military Drones: Game-Changing Capabilities," MarketsandMarkets, Sept. 24, 2024, www.marketsandmarkets.com/blog/AD/ai-in-military-drones-game-changing-capabilities.

9 Gil Press, "Detecting Deepfakes: Fighting AI with AI," *Forbes*, Aug. 6, 2024, www.forbes.com/sites/gilpress/2024/08/06/detecting-deepfakes-fighting-ai-with-ai/.

10 Thomas H. Costello et al., "Durably Reducing Conspiracy Beliefs Through Dialogues with AI," last edited July 18, 2024, PsyArXiv Preprints, https://osf.io/preprints/psyarxiv/xcwdn.

11 Jay P. Kesan and Rajiv C. Shah, "Shaping Code," *Harvard Journal of Law and Technology* 18 (2005): 319, 334.

12 "UC Berkeley—Center for Human-Compatible Artificial Intelligence (2021)," Open Philanthropy, www.openphilanthropy.org/grants/uc-berkeley-center-for-human-compatible-artificial-intelligence-2021/.

13 Sigal Samuel, "Elon Musk Wants to Merge Humans with AI. How Many Brains Will Be Damaged Along the Way?" *Vox*, March 21, 2024, www.vox.com/future-perfect/23899981/elon-musk-ai-neuralink-brain-computer-interface.

INDEX